Bodily Regimes

Bodily Regimes

Italian Advertising under Fascism

Karen Pinkus

 University of Minnesota Press
Minneapolis
London

Published by the University of Minnesota Press
111 Third Avenue South, Suite 290, Minneapolis, MN 55401-2520
Printed in the United States of America on acid-free paper

Library of Congress Cataloging-in-Publication Data
Pinkus, Karen.
    Bodily regimes : Italian advertising under fascism / Karen Pinkus.
        p.   cm.
    Includes bibliographical references and index.
    ISBN 0-8166-2562-X. — ISBN 0-8166-2563-8 (pbk.)
    1. Advertising—Italy—History.   2. Propaganda—Italy—History.
    3. Human figure in art.   4. Commercial art—Italy—History.
    5. Fascism and art—Italy—History.   I. Title.
    HF5813.I8P56   1995
    659.1—dc20   94-37311

For Bob

Contents

Illustrations

A Note on Pictorial Sources

Most of the images reproduced in this text derive either from posters or from magazine advertisements. Commonly a firm might sponsor a campaign in which the same image was reproduced in large format as a color lithograph to be hung in urban public spaces, and also in a small format, sometimes in black and white in magazines or newspapers. The point is that in one form or another, the vast majority of these images were well-diffused in the public eye, even if specific data about the places of publication or numbers of editions printed is not available.

Given the primarily theoretical focus of this book, the author and editors decided to print the images in black and white. Nevertheless, advertising posters from the Italian 1930s were often rendered in extremely bold tones and striking contrasts, with intense visual effect. Readers who are unfamiliar with the images here might wish to consult some of the following sources where many of the images from the fascist period can be found in color: Giuseppe Priarone, *Grafica pubblicitaria in Italia negli anni trenta* (Florence: Cantini, 1989); Steven Heller and Louise Fili, *Italian Art Deco* (San Francisco: Chronicle Books, 1993); Giovanni Fanelli and Ezio Godoli, *Il futurismo e la grafica* (Milan: Edizioni Comunità, 1983); Pontus Hulton, *Futurism and Futurisms* (New York: Abbeville Press, 1986); and the exhibition catalog *Annitrenta: Arte e cultura in Italia* (Milan: Mazzotta, 1982).

Acknowledgments

I am very grateful to the libraries and collections that have allowed me to reproduce these images and to study a much greater number of them. In particular, I acknowledge the New York Public Library; the Special Collections Department of Northwestern University; the Museum of Modern Art, New York; the Raccolta Salce of the Museo Civico, Treviso; the Biblioteca della Storia del Tessuto e dell'Arte Contemporanea, Venice; the Biblioteca Nazionale Braidense, Milan; the Raccolta Stampa Bertarelli, Milan; the Archivio della Triennale, Milan; the Centro Documentazione della Fiat, Turin; the Archivio del Novecento, Rovereto; the Centro Minguzzi at the Roncati Clinic, Bologna; the Centro di Documentazione delle Donne, Bologna.

The research for this book was greatly facilitated by a generous grant from the Getty Foundation for Art History and the Humanities. Northwestern University provided funds for the collection and reproduction of images. I am also indebted to a great number of friends and colleagues who have supported this project. In Italy, Antonio Niero has been a constant source of encouragement and information. Caterina Spada and Maurizio Giuffredi granted me access to family "archives" and inspired me through their intellectual perseverance in the face of a thousand obstacles. In the United States, Russell Maylone, Luigi Ballerini, Teodolina Barolini, Mary Ann Caws, and Albert Ascoli supported my early efforts. Holly Clayson, Mimi White, and all the participants in the Northwestern Cultural Studies Work Group (1991–92) gave me a rigorous intellectual context for my "iconography" of fascist bodies. Vincent Crapanzano has, as always, provided uncanny readings and references. I am particularly grateful to Michael Hardt for his extremely attentive reading of the manuscript, and to Biodun Iginla of the University of Minnesota Press for all of his support. Of my many friends who have directly or indirectly contributed to this project, I would especially like to acknowledge Ann Simmons, Scott Durham, Timothy Murray, Paul Michelman, Sharon Achinstein, Hilary Barta, Maria Sepa, David Auerbach, Bernie Yenelovis, and Richard Block. Many thanks to my family.

1 / The Body and the Market

In writing this book I have dug into the dark reaches of Italian memory and sifted through the forgotten icons of a generation that now passes itself off as dead. I present fascist print ephemera, wrenched from its more familiar context in design history, displaced into the frame of a critique that spans a variety of disciplines including psychoanalysis, anthropology, feminism, art history, semiotics, and Marxism. Popular imagery that survived from the *ventennio* was pushed into the collective unconscious by both the Right and the Left in Italy. The very act of retrieving these objects is inherently a political one, prior to any particular commentary one might wish to make. But even more radical than the return to the repressed of fascist artifacts is the notion I sustain that advertising images—in particular, images of the body—are not somehow symbols of an aberrant, monstrous oppression, but form a ground for the present Italian state and its economy. (Italy has the fifth largest economy in the world at the time of this writing, in terms of per capita income and gross national product.)

Having stated what I perceive as the larger implication of this study for late capitalism in Italy, I have *not* chosen to follow the trajectory of iconographic elements from their origins under the regime up to the present. Instead, this book remains faithful to a historical specificity. My title immediately brings these advertising images of the body into proximity with fascist

1

ideology, and throughout this chapter in particular I explore the significance of the regime as a critical contextual moment. More specifically, the vast majority of the advertisements I have chosen to examine date from the 1930s. They represent mature fascist market conditions *after* the establishment of Mussolini's government in 1922, but *before* the beginning of World War II.

At various points in this narrative, I also discuss propaganda images created specifically by the state for a particular "target" of consumers. In spite of a clarity of direction exhibited by these images, their relation to capital remains highly complex. It would be wrong to suggest that all fascist language represents a seamless coincidence of the state and capitalism. Corporatist organization, developed as an antidote to liberal individualism, unionism, and other forms of worker activism, would pass itself off as a perfectly ordered, monolithic block. Indeed, the corporations (that is, the various occupational groups under the fascist system) were often represented in visual language as a family tree, a structure whose logic of descent or affiliation is strictly dictated by inextricable (blood) ties. This ordered "family" of professions grew out of syndicalist and nationalist ideals, and posited itself in sharp contrast to the illegitimate foundlings under the liberal system. However, the contradictions between the order of corporatist ideality and the lived practices of persons emerge precisely in images of the body, in the visual dialogue between "pure" propaganda and the homunculi of "pure" capitalism.

This chapter commences with a discussion of the body in its relation to conscious strategies of the advertising industry, as well as to a (political) unconscious. The body has become a legitimate and important field of study within the larger discipline of cultural studies. The foregrounding of the body often is meant as a subversive or radical gesture, a way of turning attention away from institutions (ideology in the sense of false consciousness) and toward the everyday lived reality of individuals (ideology in an Althusserian sense, for example). In my discussion, however, I begin with an attempt to respect the position of the body in even the most reactionary writings of the regime, while I also recognize the ways in which representation slips away from the grasp of state apparatuses. In essence, then, my writing follows a passage from the greatest degree of control toward the hallucinatory fragmentation of the body, broken apart and disavowing its own corporeality.

I begin a specific iconographic investigation in chapter 2 with the non-Italian body, the body of the racial other, as it evolves in popular culture throughout the decade, culminating in the declaration of the New Roman Empire in East Africa. The centrality of the black body in the cultural imagination cannot be overemphasized, although it is an element of Italian history that has remained deeply buried. The sense of a national Italian (and specifically Aryan) identity that developed during fascism also permeates and is conditioned by the market itself. Through the relation with blackness, the Italian public comes to define its own productive and consumptive goals. The Ethiopian War had such a profound impact on the autarchic objectives of *all* advertising that the brief period of colonialism still colors the rhetoric of public persuasion in Italy today.

From this intense formation of nationality through the other, I turn in chapter 3 to representations of producing and consuming bodies on Italian soil. The question of the potential representability of labor itself in the advertisement of various goods and services was of the utmost urgency for the regime in its attempt to deny class difference. Chapter 4 moves from concrete images of work or consumption to more metaphoric considerations of "body armor." While the regime and its various allied institutions impose forms of control on the body, particularly with regard to gender and sexuality, the images in this section represent strategies of self-containment and protection against *all* forms of desire. Body armor allows the subject to exist under conditions of extreme control by blocking the flow of desire both from the outside and from the inside.

Finally, chapter 5 addresses what I have chosen to classify as the "disappearing body," images of partial effacement or eclipse. The accompanying discourses concerning toxicity, annihilation, and negation belie a reading of the silhouetted shape as merely a "beautiful" design solution. These bodies do not all develop the hard shell that might allow them to persist as perfect fascist subjects; instead they inhabit a kind of neither-norness, a realm of disavowal.

The body *should* return to all of its robust materiality, according to a scheme that views fascism as a rupture in the otherwise uninterrupted march toward a democratic state. But my narrative ends before the explosive catharsis of the war, and long before the economic "boom," at a time when yet unrealized fantasies of radiation and annihilation permeate the imagination at a subterranean level. Indeed, I do nothing in this book to return the body to some position of normalcy; I deliberately leave it suspended in a pathetic state of half-being.

There are, of course, alternative histories. One example might be the ludic scene-shifting of Maurizio Nichetti's film *The Icicle Thief (Ladri di saponette)*. A black-and-white neorealist figure emerges into the full-color ethos of a detergent commercial; a blond "northern" model arrives back in time with an overflowing shopping cart. In this narrative, bodies materialize and dematerialize between two different markets, and motion is made possible precisely through the technological capacities of film and video recording. But the paper cutouts of the 1930s, the little puppets and dolls, the frozen print characters of the fascist market, do not enjoy the playful kinesis of television commercials; they can only stare blankly toward the future, as in Benjamin's interpretation of Klee's Angel. The images of fascist advertising are thus not "dead," but are existing in a state of frozen animation. As long as Western culture exchanges and values these printed ephemera as "historical artifacts" or "objects of collectionism," they will never fully awaken. Whether or not the reanimation of the figures produced under fascism is to be desired, it seems important to unlock the door and leave a passage open, in both directions.

Is Advertising a Humanism?

The body, advertising, and fascism: what are the terms that tie these three elements together?

When I first began to look at images from the 1930s (posters, points-of-sale, *dépliants,* postcards), I could not help but be attracted by what I perceived as their iconic simplicity; their clarity of line and shape; and the perfect equation between text, image, and product. Many of these advertisements seem to exemplify the classical ideals of brevity and harmony codified in Renaissance and baroque emblem theory;[1] yet their signifying power might be seen as greater than early humanist forms, because instead of limiting themselves to an elite circle of readers by veiling knowledge, these ads clearly celebrate the creation of a new, mass audience in Italy. The aesthetic value of such images, for me, lies in the degree to which they are embedded in a consumer market that was only becoming modernized during the early years of fascist control. I understand these images to be "beautiful" solutions to problems in mass communication in the sense that mathematical equations may be construed as aesthetic for their simplicity and elegance. The inevitable question of how to reconcile this admiration for formal and stylistic force with the sheer abjectness of the content of fascist advertisements has been raised over and over during the course of this study. The answer remains unresolved.

This project, then, attempts neither a strict critique of fascist economic policies and markets, nor an objective history of design styles, but a survey of corporeal forms suspended somewhere between these two fields. Although many of the artists whose work appears in the following pages did identify themselves with a particular style within the broad cross-currents of modernism, I am less interested here in tracing conscious affiliations than in reading something like a political unconscious of images that I seek primarily through iconography.[2] The narrative of this unconscious, to the degree that it reveals itself through the repetition of motifs, and through visual forms of parapraxis in popular culture, appears decidedly heterogeneous. There is no single unconscious of fascism, nor do all the signifiers that reveal themselves suggest absolute resistance. In this sense, my own narrative reflects broadly on various forms of adaptation to and against the lived realities of the regime.

Such fragmentation might seem antithetical to the canonical art historical narratives of iconography, a method normally applied to oil paintings of the early modern period. Conventional art history tends to privilege imagery and its organization over the artist's own psychological biography (often simply because so little information survives from periods predating modernity, not because of an inherent lack of interest in knowing the artistic subject in relation to his or her work).[3] As refined by Erwin Panofsky and the Warburg school, iconography also implicitly emphasizes certain styles of depiction that combine pictorial realism and (Renaissance) geometrical perspective with the presence of objects that one senses are "charged" with a symbolic dimension. In his later works, Panofsky elaborated a tripartite scheme of interpretation for artworks that begins with a preiconographic or "factual" stage; proceeds to an iconographic or "conventional" stage (in which social codes and gesture begin to play a role); and ends with the "iconological," where the specificity of meaning of the image is granted a "full" context. Although Panofsky described the hermeneutic relation among these three stages as circular, it is clear that an iconological reading of a visual text implies a deep structure of meaning and requires a great degree of erudition on the part of the viewer. At each stage of the interpretive process, the viewer confronts the same object, but manages to see progressively more. In the case of the informed viewer, one wonders how he or she actually manages to perform the preliminary or a priori stages of the operation, since what we are talking about is clearly a case of a false naïveté, of *not* seeing certain symbolic elements or attributes. The circle would seem to short-circuit, to rush precipitously toward the iconological phase, which then becomes overdetermined.

At Panofsky's final, iconological level a text becomes endowed with a possible "unconscious," not understood in a specifically Freudian sense, but implying a spectrum of meanings "beyond what the creator may have intended." The examples Panofsky used in his methodological essay (the introduction to his *Studies in Iconology*) focus on Leonardo's *Last Supper,* and the level of "deep" meaning is inherently linked with a desire to know the biographical subject who has created the work. Panofsky's humanism permeates his choice of objects and, in a tautology that still is being unraveled today, the method itself. Implicit in Panofsky's iconology is the excessive attention given to content and the academic corpus of textual authorities that elevate the painting from a handcrafted or artisanal object:

> This *circulus methodicus* [of the three levels] applies, of course, not only to the relationship between the interpretation of *motifs* and the history of *style,* but also to the relationship between the interpretation of *images, stories,* and *allegories* and the history of *types,* and to the relationship between the interpretations of *intrinsic meanings* and the history of *cultural symptoms* in general.[4]

The general "acculturation" of the discipline of art history is specifically bound up, in Panofsky's essay, with the culture of Renaissance humanism and with the discipline's own implicit hierarchy of genres that placed history painting at the highest rank. The question of whether iconology can have any interest for works of mass culture is particularly encouraging because it opens up the possibility for a discussion of "popular" images at the highest level of intellectual privilege, placing them in a methodological frame that primarily has been reserved for "humanist" texts. The ironic replacement of the heroic figures of the classical *istoria* with the cartoonlike puppets of modern mass culture in their capacity as mythmakers opens a passage to the larger narratives of the political unconscious that constitute market culture.

In any case, this is clearly not the place to tackle broader issues of art historical methods of the twentieth century. It seems important, however, to raise the terms of iconography and iconology in order to ask about their potential applicability to modern design. More traditional procedures of art history shift focus away from style, form, or abstraction toward iconicity understood as a specific vocabulary drawn upon by artists such that the particular choices (the visual *parole*) are made significant through recourse to the entire *langue.* I often locate meaning in the *repetition* of motifs, in the classification of bodies. If, as Panofsky claimed, iconography and iconology together constitute a method of research and not a judgment of taste, why not apply them to a study of the figures of advertising — figures imposed on the viewer for specific and "rational" purposes, but often generating meanings "beyond the intention of their creators"? In a sense, the fear of the slippage or irretrievability of meaning underlies both the optimistic program of Panofsky's later work and the bold front of logical positivism that constitutes the discourse of advertising. The human body is idealized, in both areas of research, as a kind of comforting, knowable conveyor of signs, a semaphore of unambiguous gestures. Such an approach cannot be sustained, but it might be an appropriate starting point of a discussion of the reception of images.

Within the context of modernism itself, moreover, there were designers who believed in the utopia of a universal language of symbols that would specifically contain meaning within the bounds of intentionality. I am thinking of individuals such as Otto Neurath, who developed the visual and statistical language of "isotype" during the 1920s. The signifying components of this language — the signs — are simple, black-and-white, greatly reduced icons, but the pretense to universality can be sustained only within limits. Design scholar Ellen Lupton writes of Neurath's rejection of Saussurean linguistics that "the implicit, *rhetorical* function of reduction is to suggest that the image has a natural, scientific relationship to its object, as if it were a natural, necessary essence rather than a culturally learned sign."[5] The extremism of this vision does not stand up against the complex system of representation governed by the market, but there is nevertheless an undeniable stylistic link between isotype and some of the quasi-semaphoric bodily gestures that I present throughout this book.

Modernist thinking about the advertising image often has returned to considerations of the "emblematic" function of visual symbols through Benjamin's influential redemption of allegory. The structural resemblance between advertisement and emblem (both rely on the combination of *inscriptio, pictura,* and *subscriptio*) is perhaps less important than the arbitrariness of meaning produced in both forms.[6] Benjamin compares the symbolic dimension of attributes in the seventeenth-century baroque emblem to the price inscribed on the commodity. He responds to Marx's statement that although the commodity seems like a trivial thing, it is actually bewildering and full of metaphysical subtleties:

> The "metaphysical subtleties" in which, according to Marx, [the commodities] indulge, are above all those of fixing their price. How the price of the commodity is arrived at can never be totally foreseen, not in the course of its production, nor later when it finds itself in the market. But just this is what happens with the

object in its allegorical existence. The meaning which the melancholy of the allegoricist consigns to it is not one that was expected. But once it contains such meaning, then the latter can at
any time be removed in favor of any other. The fashions of meanings [in baroque allegory] changed almost as rapidly as the price
of commodities change. The meaning of commodity is indeed:
Price; as commodity it has no other. Thus the allegoricist with
the commodity is in his element.[7]

While forms remain fixed, or "petrified" in the emblem, their content is
subjugated to the will of the melancholic who cathects the fragment with
meanings. For Benjamin, therefore, the forms of modernity are tired, recycled, and only become charged with difference and novelty according to
changes in the market. Just as Renaissance oil painting cannot be reduced
to the poses and emblematic attributes of the human subjects represented,
advertising images are not simply rendered comprehensible through reference to a hagiographical handbook of body types. My readings are, nevertheless, often characterized by a tension between a stylistic coherence that
points toward or suggests the utopia of a universal linguistic system, and
the contradictory, disjointed quality both of the mass cultural context and
of the commodity with its fluctuating status of "meaning."

As for high art in the early modern period, in the modern marketplace
commercial art should be studied in relation to commissions (following Fortunato Depero's comparison of the great humanist patrons with the cap-
tains of modern industry).[8] Documentation about a given commission (an
iconological program) or ad campaign cannot be confused with reception
itself—this would result in an intentional fallacy where visual images serve
as an ideal or unmediated translation of words. But it would seem irrespon-
sible not to utilize the available documents of corporate culture in a search
for what "lies behind" images; especially because, compared with the inter
hominem, courtly world of High Renaissance commissions, the culture of
the modern office exhibits an extreme obsession with contracts, the "proof"
of transactions and agreements made between factions. Meaning seems to
derive, then, from a combination of attention to the repetition of certain
motifs or topoi, and reflections on the way images may have been received
by the viewing public. It is possible that some of the primary documentation—the iconographic programs, if we like—of a campaign strategy will
serve in our discussion of reception, but not always with the bold positivism that characterizes the language of advertising psychology. So, another
way to think about the problem is to distinguish between this psychology

and a reading of images informed by psychoanalysis; the latter approach not only recognizes the existence of an unconscious of reading, but also seeks out the gaps and disjunctures between presentation and reception.

If the aim of advertising, at least in theoretical terms, is to achieve identification, then it is equally clear that the *theory of advertising* from the 1930s must utterly deny psychoanalysis. The paranoid language of Bragaglia in his well-known article in *Critica fascista* sums up the problem. Discussing Freud's attribution of polymorphous perversion and infantile sexuality to *all* children, Bragaglia counters: "I do not identify myself in that. When I was a boy, as I remember well, I set traps for the girls of my own age... [these are] healthy instincts."[9] As will become evident throughout this book, the widespread cultural rejection of psychoanalysis is a key factor in understanding both the market and the place of the body in the market during fascism. What most disturbed the public (many of whom never read Freud and received their information through highly reductive versions of his writings or through secondhand accounts) was the "deterministic nucleus" perceived to be at the center of psychoanalysis.[10] Freudian doctrine not only violates the most personal and subjective knowledge possible for a fascist, it also leads logically to the conclusion that any given ad campaign can function only through a kind of insidious determinacy or subliminal force. Since the *science* of advertising was based on rational models of (conscious) behavior, it could not possibly find a place for the unconscious. What was at stake in this rejection was not simply a cultural mistrust of therapy, but a fundamental *episteme* that saw the market and the individual bound up in a perfectly rational relation.

The fascist demands a rational campaign, and generally will not be persuaded by anything that "plays" in any way, or involves a parapraxis that seems to "slip from his control." "Not everyone likes puns, double entendres, kidding around, or caricature," warned an article from *L'ufficio moderno*, the authoritative monthly journal of commercial interests and advertising. "We Italians are not humorists.... the humoristic ad, that is, an ad that makes use of a humoristic text, is not effective... all products lend themselves to humor, but the act of acquisition, especially if it is entrusted to women, is such a serious thing that it does not allow for 'lexicological entertainment.'"[11] A certain form of humor does, however, enter the vocabulary of advertising during the 1930s. As I will suggest, particularly in chapter 2, advertising humor is a discourse whose parameters are determined by a self-limited group of (male) subjects; its logic does not extend beyond the fundamental thrust of the marketplace, as a quantifiable act that is reducible to the exchange of capital. All products *lend* themselves to humor, as stated in the article, but a loan is only a temporary measure that ultimately is bound to the finality of the *sale*.

Body and Psychology

The science of "publicity" (indistinguishable in the Italian from *pubblicità,* the term for advertising) presupposes a fundamental hostility on the part of the public toward text and image, which have begun to invade modern life.[12] If publicity assaults the subject, it is only logical that the subject will develop defenses, barriers, against this onslaught, this overabundance. In Italy, various "psychologies," or strategies, of assault were taken directly from American, German, and sometimes French writings on the subject, and so the whole dynamic of the "struggle for man's attention" must also be understood within a national psychology of inferiority; the struggle is not only against the defenses of individual consumers, but also against the "backwardness" of the entire body politic.[13] The terms of this struggle, however, do not pertain to the conscious and unconscious mind, but rather concern two areas of the conscious mind: the objective and the subjective, this latter being the seat of "private" sentiments that involve the subject (the consumer) as an individual who must be moved to exhibit some *vis pubblicitaria.*

Laboratories were set up in Milan and Turin to measure the will and defenses of subjects "assaulted" by publicity images, quantifiable in physiological responses such as breathing and heartbeat. An average "attentional reaction" was calculated by one theorist as a quotient of 1.42. In the lab, a successful poster for "Anti-aerial propaganda" was bombarded on a group and elicited an *individual* attentional reaction of 1.65. This number was multiplied by the calibrated attentional coefficient of the subject (α), arrived at by determining the relation between the median attentional reaction and the individual reaction, finally yielding the following equation:[14]

$$1.65 \times \alpha = 1.65 \times 1.08 = 1.775$$

Not all writers on the subject are quite so precise in their methods, but the positivist literature generally exhibits the following characteristics: (1) the sense that advertising must seek to infiltrate the subject, who is naturally inclined to defend against it, and (2) the importation of numbers and methods from foreign and "more advanced" sources. The first problem is often approached by placing particularly large posters at strategic urban locations—

along well-traveled train lines, or in trams where one has no choice but to focus on the ad if one wishes to avoid making eye contact with fellow passengers.[15] The second characteristic is a problem that reaches to the core of fascism itself, and that I address with particular attention in a discussion of autarchic production and consumption in chapter 3. A certain humanizing language that is associated with a variety of different political positions will seek to "protect" the hapless consumer from the assault of big business and its interests, but, as I will continually suggest, this very language is appropriated by and subsumed into various institutions of the regime hierarchy. Ultimately, advertising makes itself over into a humanism, inasmuch as it takes humankind (and the human body) as its focus; but it remains a mystified and repressive institution inasmuch as humanism is, precisely, an ideology.[16]

"The purpose of the advertisement," Benjamin wrote, "is to blur over the commodity character of things. Allegory struggles against this deceptive transfiguring of the commodity world by disfiguring it. The commodity tries to look itself in the face."[17] The importance of Benjamin's opposition of advertisement and allegory is that, while the language (both visual and discursive) of advertising tries to humanize products to dissimulate their real commodity nature, the (Marxist) critic tries to smash apart the "given order" of history. For Benjamin, the typical ad exemplifies a seamlessness that tries to pass itself off as coherent, transhistorical, and "mythic," while a fragmentary, allegorical form like the collage radically blasts apart myth, revealing it for the commodity sham it is. This kind of thinking, of course, lies at the basis of a significant body of modern and postmodern art that cuts apart advertising and makes it into collage, but my own work leads me to suggest that the putative soft evasiveness of the ad does not always function as myth. I see certain contradictions at work in the ad, even before it has met its match in allegory, and these result, in part, from built-in defense mechanisms of the market against its own power.

One of the least polemical aspects of the psychology of advertising promotes the use of the human figure as a means of achieving instant identification on the part of a viewer. In fact, "identification" used in this context does not belong to any science, but to part of the commonsense logic of a less developed, more ad hominem kind of exchange associated with the pre-Taylorized, preindustrial market. Ironically, identification as "return" to an earlier innocence masks the inevitability of the dominance of the brand name in the cycle of production, distribution, and consumption. "Backward" Italy could no longer afford to languish in the turn-of-the-century ethos of the independent wholesaler and his gentlemanly agreements with the retailer, who, in turn, made personal contacts in his own restricted community of consumers. The new, fascist slogan of production (which had already been assimilated by the American market for decades) was "From the factory to the consumer!" What begins to happen during the 1930s is the appropriation of this "personal" logic and its refashioning into a form of highly manipulated nostalgia within the brand name; this will be part of an ongoing argument throughout this book. I will return, at various points, to a consideration of the ways in which both physiognomy and gesture or body position are subjected to forms of distortion and condensation, as if they had been worked over in a dream. My invocation of these key Freudian terms here is not simply gratuitous, since, as I will argue, the body in fascism seems to express its own unconscious. Within the discourse of advertising itself, these distortions serve a purely practical end: the body calls attention to a given advertisement and serves to comfort a viewer, almost as a consolation prize for subjection to the impersonal, mass-produced, brand-name commodity good. But, as an article in *L'ufficio moderno* warns, it is not enough to pose a model and represent his or her physiognomy with mimetic conventions, since "the soul is not in the eyes, as was believed in the era of Maupassant. The gaze — languid, long, nostalgic, alive, cunning, clever, impertinent — cannot really be rendered in a photograph destined for a newspaper, which necessitates grainy prints."[18] So instead, the body must be posed in a simple gesture and placed in a suggestive environment so that its message will not become confused. Other articles recommend reducing the number of figures used in a given ad, and as the decade progresses ads will make less and less frequent use of fourth-wall narrative conventions (staged plays), shifting the focus to a kind of single body-semaphore mode of signification. As the mannequin gains increasing popularity in store windows, the use of stylized human forms of two-dimensional representations makes a strong visual link between the product in printed media and the product displayed at the point of sale.[19]

The mannequin is a kind of inexhaustible, animated salesman. Consumers — particularly women who were often responsible for making daily rounds to small specialty shops in both urban and semirural centers — clung to an older way of "personalized" salesmanship, and theorists of publicity attempted to incorporate this sociological fact into their campaigns for large retail chains or nationally distributed brands. In situations of consumption where the local salesman cannot be present to "hypnotize" the consumer, he can create a homunculus, a "little man," a "character" who will "act in his name."[20] Examples of this *lieu-tenant* salesman would include the Bibendum

1. "Bibendum," Michelin's tire man, 1910.

tire man of Michelin (figure 1), the Pierrot of Termogène, and various other sprites and fairies. Many of these figures date from the mid–nineteenth century, but their ranks swell with the creation of modern markets. The industry calls these "character types" and suggests they are essential in creating, precisely, a "character" for a given firm. The difficult task of market

"suggestion" can be undertaken by this sympathetic puppet who also acts
as a spokesperson for the company and solicits the trust of a faithful public.
Bibendum, for example, often was "played" by real actors dressed up in
rubber suits. He made various public appearances on behalf of the Michelin family. As such, he entered the mass visual vocabulary of popular culture in a context that seems divorced from strategies of selling or promotion. His white body, as I suggest in chapter 3, not only stands in for, but
actually eclipses, the corporate strategy that created him. Puffed up with this
public desire for cartoon "characters," Bibendum hides the men in suits
who pull his strings.

Ironically, the vogue for the store mannequin results from a vulgariza-
tion of the metaphysical painting of De Chirico and Carrà in the late teens.[21]
If the wartime experiments of these painters played with the representability of Nietzschean values and figured nonsense or alienation in the faceless
draper's model, then the appropriation of their style by store owners and
capitalists seems to add yet another degree of estrangement to the picture.
The irony of the mannequin's appropriation did not escape the 1930s social columnist Irene Brin, who remarked that the "false" and "stylized"
quality of these "models" posed in the windows of urban centers quickly
influenced fashion itself. Whereas the "mannequin" style of dress was comprehensible in a sophisticated couture context, it was reduced to a form of
pure alienation when diffused beyond the initial circles:

> The fall of these romantic toys was rapid, since the provincial, but
> proud window dressers, the poor, but *arriviste* interior decorators,
> swiftly copied the big department store exhibitions, the suggestions
> of Salvador Dalí and Cholly Knickerbocker for shops in Rouen or
> Caltanissetta, and very soon we saw the sisters of Cynthia [an Amer-
> ican mannequin whose "life" was photographed for magazines],
> bloodless, melancholy and secretive, against a background of snakes
> and marble fragments, offering economical rayon socks hung from
> their pinkies.[22]

In Italy the word "mannequin" is used also to designate live (runway) models, hence the further confusion between the stiff and bizarre theatricality
of the animate and inanimate. Store and runway models were expected to
impersonate a type: "the evening girl," "the morning girl," "the sporty
girl," "the strong-willed woman," "the enchanting lady of a certain age."
For Brin, then, the rigidity of social types and the limited options open to
females were perfectly crystallized in this cultural icon borrowed from the

avant-garde and retooled for admission to bourgeois consumerism. The life cycle of "Cynthia," from morning to night, from spring through winter, played out in a series of costume changes and posed tableaux, truly parallels the introduction of the city snob, with her nose permanently pointed upward, into the world of the provincial petty bourgeoisie. Moreover, the style of mannequin-inspired fashion was understood by Benjamin as a form of fetishization of the body, essentially akin to its death in allegory: "The modern woman who allies herself with fashion's newness in a struggle against natural decay represses her own productive power, mimics the mannequin, and enters history as a dead object, a 'gaily decked-out corpse.' "[23] The woman who "dies" in order to become allegory is figured in the modern prostitute, who makes her body into a commodity that can be bought and sold on the street. What we often call the "whorishness" of fashion followers and the sexualization of the body through clothes is, for Benjamin, more than just a figure of speech; it is the mechanism of commodification itself in action.

I see a strict relation between the development of the market as populated by these animated homunculi and the style of visual persuasion itself. As the market becomes modernized under fascism, the product itself gains power and prestige over the means of production. In this process, the human subject is gradually elided, mechanized, or annihilated by a violent representational act. Modernized industry calls for new means of presentation that are nonmimetic:

> The modern mannequin, because it does not strive for photographic realism, has unlimited possibilities.... What is the advantage of modern mannequins over the others? To merely suggest the appearance of a human subject in order to leave the merchandise with all of its beauty. The old mannequin wanted *its* beauty — can we say so? — to be associated with that of the material; the modern mannequin lacks this pretense; it leaves the objects to express all of their value; it is less pompous and it doesn't impose itself. In this way it is a positive thing that we have arrived at reducing it to its simplest expression. At times it is nothing more than a support, a silhouette, a thread.[24]

There is something very paranoid about this discourse of the animated mannequin during the 1930s. The market remains a site for struggle between the inherently conservative will of the consumer and the "progressive" will of the producer. A whole population of "little men" occupy the battlefield and vie for public attention. The human body ceases to exist as a way of displaying merchandise; rather, the merchandise itself—the object of publicity—takes on the form of the body and becomes subject.

In a Marxist critique of the marketplace, it is precisely the salesclerk as "character type" that most insidiously serves to push what Wolfgang Haug terms the "cash-commodity nexus" to the margins.[25] The salesclerk always wears a mask of servility that is ultimately fetishistic inasmuch as it stands in for genuine (human) expression. Moreover, while the salesclerk assumes gestures of servility and self-effacement toward the buyer, the mask worn in the act of exchange inherently imitates a dying nobility. In the encounter between the buyer and seller, there is such a confusion of class, such a "constant chatter" (as Marx wrote in the *Grundrisse*), that the buyer cannot help but let class consciousness slip away.[26] Of course, this level of ideology remains unexpressed in the discourse of advertising, which instead concentrates on generating pleasant emotions and associations for specific products.

In Corpore Ducis

Fascism brilliantly exploited the inextricable, reciprocal exchange that pertains in any state formation between the body politic and the formation of the individual body. Mussolini's own body occupied a significant place in the iconography of fascism: he never tired of seeing it displayed, and he treated it as a detached object that could be manipulated and that also corresponded to seemingly "natural" or logical iconic classifications like the various mannequin "types" mentioned earlier—"the Duce on horseback," "the bare-chested skiing Duce," "the Duce with his lovers," and so on.[27] The ability of the leader to see his own body from the external position of the viewing subject is crucial to the construction of the despot in an extremely provocative recent study, *First and Last Emperors,* by Kenneth Dean and Brian Massumi:

> The body of the leader undergoes a process of infinitization, as if stricken by a compulsion to become coextensive with quasi-corporeal space.... It can see as "one" would see it, occupying every pronoun position simultaneously. It can stand on every pedestal and don every flag. It is exemplary. It is fractured.[28]

In the case of Mussolini, however, one must be careful to understand fragmentation as multiplication rather than as dismemberment or castration. Myths and anecdotes about Mussolini's hygienic habits, his bearing and stamina, and his sexual exploits were reported routinely and formed part of a national visual vocabulary. The body of Il Duce left "afterimages" of itself in the wake of its constant motion around the nation. But this motion is not the same as a Deleuzian "nomadism," the opposite extreme of the fascist state. Rather, to be more precise, images of Mussolini flash (like the bulbs of photojournalists) constantly in the daily papers, and these hyperkinetic "appearances" actually negate bodily motion or presence.

Ironically, then, if there is a universal visual language in Italy, it is performative rather than mimetic, like that exercised by Elias Canetti's "paranoid ruler":

> If the sultan happens to fall off his horse while riding, all his followers must do likewise.... At the court of Uganda, if the king laughed, everyone laughed; if he sneezed, everyone sneezed.... In China, as was reported by a French missionary, "when the emperor laughs the mandarins in attendance laugh too; when he stops laughing, they stop. When he is sad their faces fall. One would think that their faces were on springs which the emperor could touch and set in motion at his pleasure." ... This taking the king as model is universal.... Sometimes it goes further and people regard his every movement and utterance as a *command*: for him to sneeze means, "Sneeze!"; for him to fall off his horse means "Fall off your horses!"[29]

In this sense, it is not only language, but the body itself that enacts a performative utterance. The repetition of a "Duce-like" pose, transferred from the field of propaganda to advertising, would have the unstated effect of patronage. Mussolini, we might say, had the power to act as the ultimate "celebrity endorsement" for an unlimited number of products on the open market, just as he implicitly did for both production and consumption in a general sense whenever he promoted autarchy.

Compared with consumption, however, the promotion of production was decidedly less dangerous because of its intrinsic generic quality. The Duce had himself photographed driving tractors and turning the cranks of factory machinery. Such poses remained acceptable as long as Italy itself could be characterized as a single productive entity. But when the Duce visited the Perugina chocolate plant in 1923 (as a consumer) and declared, "I say, and I authorize you to repeat it: your chocolate is really exquisite!" his words become reified and circulated as the endorsement of a particular brand name. Eventually, Mussolini's officers forced Perugina to withdraw the slogan from its advertising campaigns; the ruler's thaumaturgical touch was in direct conflict with the mechanisms of market-driven competition.[30]

In his many poses, Mussolini provided a basis for the performative acts of an ideal fascist citizen. He also appropriated monarchical stances as part of his long-standing campaign to replace the king. In other words, the body of the Duce managed to slip between its positions as the single figurehead of the state and as the every body of daily life under the fascist regime. Neither the "king" nor the "subject" represents a true body; both are simulacra, endlessly reproduced in a chain of ever-lessening fidelity to some "original" whose very status has been occluded in the process.

The Figurine

During the 1930s, Perugina-Buitoni launched a publicity campaign to raise consumer interest in chocolates, traditionally considered luxury goods. The decade was a difficult one for the sweets industry because of a number of economic factors, including the revaluation of the lira, and the higher import taxes placed on raw materials such as sugar. Perugina sponsored a radio program on the adventures of the "Four Musketeers," and consumers began to find cheap figurines of the various characters in packages of their chocolates.[31] Through a mechanism of identification, Perugina-Buitoni hoped to break apart the "front of indifference" that the consumer had developed toward their products.[32] The figurine campaign, one of the most famous in the history of Italian mass culture, turned out to be immensely popular with both children and adults, and it reflected a mania for collecting that can only be termed fetishistic. At one point during the campaign, an entire set of figurines or proof-of-purchase stamps could be redeemed for a Fiat Balilla and other, less substantial, commodity items (including more chocolate). The figurines — sympathetic, humanoid toys whose value in the adult market was limited — suddenly took on the exchange value of capital (the Balilla was the bourgeois, fascist dream-good). The only obstacle to the "game" was that one needed a complete set of the dolls, not just a certain number of any of them, which could have been acquired by investing in a certain number of chocolate packages. Some of the dolls were extremely common; others were quite rare. Collectors began to publish tables documenting the odds of finding a particular doll. At that point, the dolls ceased to have any value related to their form (musketeers in an adventure drama) or to the product itself, and became *mere* chits in a figurine stock market, traded nationally through figurine newspapers. Dolls were counterfeited, stolen, trafficked; other figurine contests multiplied across the country; winners were discussed in the papers like national heroes. All of the most squalid elements present in any stock market surfaced here, seeming to replace an "innocent" children's game. In 1938, the Ministry of Finance issued a decree prohibiting such contests except within very strictly controlled parameters. Once again, the discourse used by the legislature was humanizing: figurine contests hurt the ingenuous participants and distracted the hardworking fascist from the true value of labor itself. The "traditional" and "artisanal" nature of chocolates and other confections had been "lost" in the process; what had been developed initially as a stimulus to consumption was transformed, in rhetoric, into pure waste. In fact, the real impetus behind the decree may have been the threat that such contests, in which capital was circulated primarily between consumers, posed to the (wasteful) hegemony of the state lotteries.[33]

Many aspects of the Perugina campaign are fascinating from the point of view of the psychology of the market, but one aspect in particular bears on a discussion of the body. The figurine campaign literally saw the disembodiment of the product itself. Like a Benjaminian allegory, the collectionist frenzy blasted apart the serene world of toy homunculi and revealed commodity consumption in all its nudity. In essence, what concerned the regime was not immoderate acts of consumption of chocolate (any commodity, as I will suggest in chapter 3, could be accommodated to the national diet of autarchy), but the fact that the speculation involved perfectly mimicked that of the stock market itself. The chocolate *brokers* had traded away the humanizing veneer of the little dolls for the reality of capital accumulation; they had stripped the humanism from advertising.

Some Considerations of Style

Many of the images included in this study can be allied with one of a number of identifiable visual styles, including neofuturism, neocubism, rationalism, Bauhaus, and *novecentismo*—the Romanized, heroic, massive bodies and buildings that bore Mussolini's official stamp of approval. The question of a *single* visual style proper to fascism has been widely debated in a variety of contexts.[34] In tracing a trajectory between the inaugurating moment of the futurist movement, and the neofuturist or "second-wave futurist" publicity culture of the thirties, a key moment seems to lie in the 1915 manifesto signed by Balla and Depero (but cowritten with Prampolini) titled "The Futurist Reconstruction of the Universe."[35] This work documents a moment during the interventionist phase (just before Italy's entry into the war) when a new, more plastic, and volumetric visual style was emerging, not in the movement's original center of Milan, but in Rome. Unlike the kind of prose Marinetti and the signers of the first manifestos were producing in a polemicist context, the "Reconstruction" manifesto is decidedly more introverted, and it seeks to create a new aesthetic lexicon with terms like "plastic complex" (this referred to kinetic sculpture), the "artificial-living-being," the "futurist toy," the "infinite-systematic-discovery-invention," the "transformable outfit," and the "phono-motoplastic réclame," which was to be Depero's main contribution to the movement during the 1920s. Both Depero and Balla were interested in experimenting with the subjective impression of light. The resulting forms reached increasing levels of abstraction, while maintaining a reference to material objects through their titles.

In the futuro-fascist transformation, the body emerges from the chaos of urban life, its physiognomy pared down to a few geometrical planes. According to Marinetti, when Mussolini visited the Palazzo Chigi and saw Thayath's sculpture of his head reduced to the outline of a giant helmet, he stated: "Yes, I like it! It's me! It's how I feel! It's how I see myself!" And Marinetti proudly declared the futurists the only artists capable of translating the figure of the Duce into a "harmonious plastic beauty" because "with his celebrated inexhaustible dynamism linked to his political Genius and his corporeal vigor ready to act in a hundred different ways and a hundred different directions for greatness and prestige, the Dominator of the Empire created by him, the DUCE thus discourages any attempt at a static, realistic portrait of himself."[36] Mussolini's extemporaneous declaration of an aesthetic program suggests something that many scholars of fascism suspect intuitively, namely, that the question of style in the regime was to a degree being "made up as they went along," spurred by subjective responses of familiarity or identification rather than based on firmly established and tried tenets.[37]

It is essential to stress here that the plastic language of Depero is not the only option in response to developments and transformations from the teens to the thirties. In Milan in the early 1930s, to give just one example, a group of futurists including Mario Sironi and Carlo Carrà signed a manifesto of "mural painting" in which they identified their work specifically with a State Art for Fascism.[38] This manifesto is extremely important for a number of reasons: first, it posits the social function of art in the fascist state as a collective burden, presupposing the obsolescence of art for art's sake. Of course, in Peter Bürger's notion of the avant-garde, it was precisely the bourgeois status of "art as autonomous art" that futurism (also a group undertaking) managed to emphasize and so problematize forever. But the claim in the mural manifesto to "overturn" a private, self-indulgent aesthetics demonstrates the obsolescence of futurism itself by this point, and the rapid acceleration of the process of cultural acceptance and bourgeoisification that quickly appropriates any avant-garde activity into the stylistic norm of a culture. These artists were already impatiently seeking something novel, and they found it in the large-scale (political) mural. They recognized that "the educational function of painting is chiefly a matter of style" as opposed to any overt propagandistic content, and they could only arrive at such a conclusion after having lived through the multiple styles of futurism itself. While Depero maintained a certain identity within the market, these artists agreed to relinquish individual prestige to a nebulous "higher moral goal" dictated by the regime. Like Balla and Depero, mural artists did not utterly reject the past, but sought to replicate the great strengths of a national tradition in frescoes and wall painting: the humble style of Giotto, a referent that the early Marinetti would have found repugnant. Work in this vein would include many large, masculine madonnas, typical of the new maternity promoted by the regime; softened lines; docile and obedient peasants; earth tones; calculated sobriety. While the mural group moved toward a reaffirmation of the styles of the past, and a revival of older notions of patronage and craftsmanship characteristic of the Renaissance, Depero chose the path of "publicity art" in a mediating relation with the mechanisms of the market economy, also invoking Renaissance patronage models. The difference is that the muralists again blurred the boundaries between the autonomy of art and its social, materialist position, while Depero celebrated the inextricability of art from an autarchic, national, capitalist economy, as he filled his creations with all the joy that such a liberating (for him!) admission might allow.

Depero figures in a group of prominent artists who reveled in their new public commissions. The chance to recycle stylized body types for the promotion of a theoretically infinite number of products meant that the artist became a *Geppetto* figure, pulling the strings of an arsenal of puppets. One of Depero's most beloved puppets was the black body, and in the next chapter I discuss how futurist blackness fits into a variety of different narrative situations. In general, Depero probably would have considered his puppets as stock characters, like Pinocchio—an essentially "good" boy who lacked only a father to provide a name and a law.

2 / Selling the Black Body: Advertising and the African Campaigns

Colonial Innocence?

> We must work to create a colonial consciousness or will. It is point-
> less for us politicians to bring the Italian colonial problem to the
> stages of international congresses without public support.

The colonial minister Alessandro Lessona spoke these words in 1933
in one of his discourses before the Fascist Party.[1] The implication that before the fascist intervention in Ethiopia the populace experienced a distinct
lack of "interest" in colonial expansion has exerted a disproportionate influence on scholarship treating the subject.[2] True, in the years following
the unification of Italy, the Right was much too occupied with domestic
questions to form a block of "interest" in African questions. In fact, the eastern confines of the Italian state remained highly unstable, and it was here
that the libidinal impulses of military and political mobilization were focused. During the nineteenth century, a handful of enterprising individuals
and missionaries found the pull of Africa irresistible. Their stories seem to
lie outside of a cultural critique of national imperial force, on the margins
of modernization in Italy. Nevertheless, Italy has never really faced up to its
colonialist past or attempted cathartic gestures of apology. One reason for
this is the perception, especially after World War II, that the state apparatus

entered the sphere of action only after the "serious" colonialists — primarily France and England — had already transformed the land and reaped its dividends. In essence, a distortion of memory that manages to displace responsibility for imperialism from public consensus to an abstraction of the general "backwardness" of Italy has allowed the nation to repress a highly involved cultural history of imperial relations.

Gramsci also saw Italy's colonialist adventure in the light of its inferiority complex on the international scene (the same complex that permeates Italy's slow modernization of its advertising industry). He understood that this "complex" had ramifications for the society at all levels, from the generals who plotted land, air, and sea attacks, to the worker in a northern Italian weapons factory. But the same broad public that would like to forget this sort of global complicity also rationalizes its presence in Africa through the assignment of weak ego formation to a small number of individuals highly obsessed with asserting and maintaining their sense of power against other European nations. So the Italian Empire tends to emerge from various histories as a sort of good-natured, almost pathetic occupation of unfertile lands, a last-minute attempt on the part of *Italietta* to catch up to its neighbors. Culpability is blurred since little planning was given to the economic consequences of capturing a relatively unproductive desert state in East Africa, which, after all, was essentially "the only land available" by the time Mussolini resolved to engage in a total war. The three vowels AOI (Africa orientale italiana), printed in official documents and inscribed on public buildings, sound more like the letters of a fraternity or secret society than the proud designation of a modern dominion. Like so many of the imposing legacies of fascism, this abbreviation helps to mystify the lived reality of the colonial encounter. One feels the urgency of a project that seeks not merely to demystify, but also to penetrate into, the literal black-and-white of the colonial moment.

The myth of general cultural indifference has persisted over time, and has distorted the very historiography of Italian colonialism that would write imperialism as the exclusive experience of individual men (who would be great men). In part, as Gramsci suggested, an initial lack of "interest" through the 1920s can be attributed to the relatively late establishment of nationhood in Italy, and the retarded development of anything like a national consciousness compared with other European colonizers.[3] Then, because many of the legislative acts of racial discrimination in Italy were in essence dictated by Hitler in the late 1930s, it is often supposed that Italians avoided a period of homegrown cultural abjection of the other. But neither the relative "tardiness" of Italian entry into the field of European nationalism nor the relatively porous institutional structures of the Italian Fascist Party necessarily deflates the importance of blackness in broader cultural terms.

Images of the black body support the notion that the imperial moment was central to the shaping of the national conscience for an entire generation of Italians. And although this generation may have passed the episode off to posterity as just another example of congenial *dolce far niente,* the proximity of Italian and African bodies seems to have deeply buried repercussions for questions of an Italian body politic — questions that are emerging with particular intensity in current political life.[4] A key consideration in the historiography revolves around the accountability of individual (male) actants whose particular class affiliations, gender, and relations with industrial capital make them legible, knowable "protagonists." But there is something quite unsatisfactory in the tendency to exchange the well-researched psychobiographies of fascists (or, for earlier forms of colonialism, protofascists) for history. This project, then, attempts to recuperate a level of broad cultural consensus — "interest" in the psychoanalytic sense of this term.[5] In the general economy of a society, it is understood that "interest," or energy, cannot really be "aroused" ab nihilo by the speeches of politicians like Lessona, but is only displaced, decathected from one area to another. In this sense, the pretense to use propagandistic images to "change people's minds" is not necessarily wrong or misguided; what the fascist propaganda campaigns do not consciously articulate, however, is the fundamental concept that in the process of "change," certain categories and fantasies are dragged along from one space to another. If white men suddenly become "interested" in black women, they do not just as suddenly shed structural, organizing categories (monogamy, virginity, reproduction) through which they live out sexuality (with white women). To some degree, however, the regime governed through the illusion of an instant, unproblematic reception of its messages. In the struggle to create a "colonial will" in a putatively nonracist (or better, a diffident) society, the regime waged its most massive official propaganda campaign based on several familiar themes: the economic benefits of territorial expansion in Africa (and later, when sanctions were imposed by the League of Nations, economic autarchy); cultivation of raw materials necessary for Italian industry; national prestige; and demography (Italians in search of work would move to AOI rather than emigrating elsewhere). The unemployment problem in Italy would be solved, and the Italian, "Aryan" race would continue to thrive and grow. The optimism of the colonialist vision of the future depended precisely on the ability of the Italian race to subjugate another.

Print advertisements and posters, colonial markets, booths of "colonialist equipment" at the Triennial exhibitions (nationalistic celebrations of design
held at three-year intervals during the regime), informational brochures,
films, and so on all helped to arouse "interest" in the very concept of an
Italian African state. Simultaneously, industry cooperated with images of
the black body that were diffused in the banality of general culture — plas-
tered on billboards, boxes, confections, and magazine covers, and offered up
to the eye in the context of everyday life, associated with consumer products. These products might be strictly colonialist: furs, coffee, chocolate, and
bananas (a taste for which had to be assiduously cultivated in the Italian
public); or related in a general way to the colonizing enterprise: tents, raincoats, all-terrain trucks, cruises. Blackness was associated also with specifically European goods and services: Agfa film, Shell motor oil, local savings
banks, and insurance companies. But perhaps the notion of *association* is not
entirely accurate. Many of the advertisements for the first category of
goods, the "fruits" of colonization, go far beyond a proximity of the product with blackness; they make an utter identification. A banana grows as a
tassel from the fez of a Somali black head. A black head is formed by, its
very shaped defined by, the bananas that surround it, constituting nothing
less than the entire ethos from which blackness emerges. "I am coffee" is
the utterance offered by a black head in a popular advertisement (figure 2)
by Gino Boccasile (a prominent illustrator and graphic artist, famous for his
propaganda campaigns for the regime, with a refined obsession for selling
the black body). On closer inspection, we find that this head, peering over
the edge of a white china cup, is actually an enlarged coffee bean. In many
similar ads, there is no spatial or temporal distance between blackness and
the products that its very subjection may yield for an Italian public on the
brink of being conscious of blackness. Boccasile exploits brilliantly the
novelty of black and white proximity in his iconic conflation of the product and the laborer. But if this trick is done outside of the context of official racial information, it actually marks a very significant moment in the
history of cultural persuasion in Italy. The black bean-head represents the
selling of racial identity along with the brand name of a product as one in-
separable event in the development of the modern Italian consumer.

Prefascist Concepts of Blackness

Before the 1930s, color simply was not a significant cultural category for
the Italian public. As the critic Richard Dyer has eloquently remarked,

2. "I am coffee." Gino Boccasile's coffee bean-head. (Salce Collection, 3096.)

within the general realm of representation, white does not mean anything in particular. White is "normal," whereas black is always marked as "colored."[6] The marking of blackness, then, may well be viewed as a secondary pleasure source deriving from but leaning upon the marketing of a product. This process of drawing boundaries, of creating a sense of alterity, strongly contributes to much of the advertising I have considered. Of course, one finds many more images of the black body during the late thirties than at any other time, but to suggest that blackness springs fully grown into the consciousness of the Italian public is to ignore a long and complex iconography that dates back at least to romantic notions of savagery; to nineteenth-century sexology; and to a whole range of allied discourses. During the various military and economic maneuvers linking Italy with East Africa in the late nineteenth century, a number of organizations such as the Italian Geographical Society published descriptions of the natives.[7] At times, written descriptions were supplanted by sketches based on a standard iconography of types (the tribal warrior, the sensuous black whore, and so on). Public sentiment remained primarily anticolonialist during the period between the unification of Italy and the fall of the liberal state, but it was only with the massive Italian defeat at Adua in 1896 that any kind of mass mobilization took place. Before Adua, in any case, blackness was predominantly figured in the "benign savage," who was known through a type of escapist or adventurer periodical addressed to the provincial petty bourgeois (male) reader. This genre of fiction, full of grossly exaggerated heroism and fantasies of territorial conquest, helped to ease the boredom of everyday life for compatriots at home. The clear association of Africa with escape, energy, power, mobilization, and then with fascistization, is made in a variety of mass cultural media. During this period blackness is purely other, and so distant as to be painted in indistinct, soft watercolor tones. A style identified with the calm, benign native continues through the 1930s (figure 3). This cover of *Le vie d'Italia,* the official periodical of the Touring Club Italiano (taken over during the 1930s by the fascist travel entity), resembles a generic prefascist depiction of the black body. Blackness does not stand out in this image; it is simply part of the muted landscape. This cover does not take color as axiomatic of anything in particular, as opposed to Boccasile's bean-head, for example, where the black being is absolutely self-conscious of its exhibition before a white eye.

Of course, to suggest that the Touring Club watercolor image lacks self-consciousness is really an illusion. In Dyer's terms, blackness can be known only in relation to a universal subjectivity or nonmeaning of whiteness in the

LE VIE D'ITALIA

RIVISTA MENSILE DEL TOURING CLUB ITALIANO

ANNO XLII - NUMERO 3   MARZO 1936 - XIV E. F.

3. "Normalized" blackness from *Le vie d'Italia*, March 1936, no. 3.

racially homogeneous culture of the Italian peninsula. In a more historical sense, however, it may be fair to say that blackness did not become a repository for any *particular* fantasies or cultural positions in Italy until the Libyan conquest of 1911. To put it another way, the establishment of an Italian presence in Africa did add a geographical specificity to cultural concepts of blackness. By contrast, for the French during the nineteenth century, blackness was clearly associated with "the Islands."[8] Italy's peculiar indolence in solidifying the borders that would serve to frame the black but that also would expand and turn slowly green (the color of agricultural reclamation, as well as of unified Italy) is key. In fact, one of the first things the fascists did after the declaration of the new Roman Empire in 1936 was to reprint their maps and amend the contours of green, from Libya, down to Somalia. To possess an island is one thing: its silhouette becomes an emblem, familiar to every schoolchild; its place in the sea can easily be indicated. But a vague notion of spreading across Africa (and then, where to begin?) implied a very different approach to spatializing, and so temporalizing, conquest. The space of Italy's Africa was to be determined, primarily, by default by the areas already cut out and assigned to the other colonizers.

In addition, while France and other nations lived a period of institutional slavery that would remain emblazoned in their collective memory, as a nation Italy did not experience any mass importation of black labor into its own borders. The relation between a concept of a space and the bodies that either inhabit it or move from it into the zone a culture one construes as properly its own is at the core of how the black body is read in a given context. For Italy, it was the encounter on "black" or native soil that would shape notions of the body as a producer. For example, an 1890 advertisement for Caffè Franck, a coffee supplement, a powdered substance that could be added to pure coffee to round it out, contains no blackness (figure 4). At the turn of the century, coffee beans were still rather scarce in Europe. To keep the price of coffee down and to make it affordable to a larger percentage of the population as part of a daily ritual, various companies marketed additives, or "surrogates."[9] The advertising strategy in such cases was often first to promote the product as a form of coffee (to make a positive association with the "real" thing—*il vero caffè*), and then to focus on coffee itself as intrinsic to the fabric of European culture, while also preserving a slight tinge of exoticism. The Caffè Franck advertisement is set in the interior of a grocery in Italy. A well-dressed woman with a cane sits on a chair, waiting her turn, while engaging in animated conversation with a pleasant young man. Another woman, in short sleeves, presumably a domestic, peers

4. Caffè Franck coffee supplement. (Courtesy of Bertarelli Collection, Milan.)

into her basket, inspecting a package. Behind the counter, the proprietor takes orders, weighing various spices that he removes from wooden drawers marked with exotic tags: saffron, nutmeg, anise, and so on. On the floor are burlap sacks of coffee beans to be bought in bulk and then ground at home in mills like the one in the Franck logo. The store, itself adorned with signs promoting Caffè Franck, is clean and orderly, and although the word "colonialist" does appear on the border of the advertisement, it does not at this time bear any particular geographical connotation, nor does it convey an aura of blackness. In Italy a "colony" could be an island or a small state under Italian dominion, but it could also refer to an institution like a summer camp where working-class or petty bourgeois families might go for a week of relaxation.[10] The product designation, "caffè," is obviously an Italian word, a national product to be sold in friendly local shops like the one pictured in the advertisement. The brand name, however, sounds like a German proper name for a family of "Frankish" origins, and so the product itself is not sold in relation to any notions of Italian national identity, as will be the case during the 1920s and 1930s. Instead, the ad may appeal to a petty bourgeois identification of the "north" (France and Germany) as the center of café-leisure culture. Through a combination of word and image, focus is clearly drawn away from the "southern question," that is, a general question about the exportation of goods from the colonies. The ad does not attempt to dissimulate the trans-Europeanism of the production and distribution of certain goods. In short, this advertisement is a pretty postcard, a diorama from daily life in Italy — not Italy as autarchic producer and imperialist conqueror, but just one among the European nations in their postunification period.

Nevertheless, behind this bourgeois commercial interior lies a tacit desperation about the very lack of blackness, a growing sense of panic in Italy about the possibility of taking part of Africa. "*L'Africa vi sfugge*" — "Africa is slipping away!" — was the familiar slogan, uttered by the expansionist minister Mancini on behalf of the adventurers who struggled to procure commodity goods such as coffee. The slogan began to circulate among the antiparliamentarian forces, the same stratum of Italian society that was growing impatient with the bourgeois scenes of exchange like the one pictured in the Caffè Franck advertisement. The fact that this is an ad for a coffee *surrogate* makes this argument about missed opportunism all the more plausible, since the product itself is only a stand-in for the legitimate "fruits" of imperialism. It is possible to read in this seemingly placid image the seeds of a restless revolutionary spirit, the stirrings of the fascist impulse to conquer East Africa.

Fascist Black Bodies

Mussolini's decision to invade Ethiopia, taken in the course of 1934 and 1935, derived its compulsion from a growing cultural frustration with the complacency, the resignation I have located in the representation of the bourgeois spice market. In his famous memo of 1934, Mussolini summed up his new policy:

> The problem of Italian-Abyssinian relations has changed lately: from a diplomatic problem to a problem of force; a "historical" problem that we must resolve with the only means available for the resolution of such problems: with the use of arms. Taking previous events into account, we must draw the only logical conclusion: time is against us. The more we delay in liquidating the problem the more difficult will be the task and the greater the sacrifices. . . . Once we have agreed on this war, our objective can only be the destruction of the Abyssinian armed forces and the total conquest of Ethiopia. The empire cannot be made otherwise.[11]

There is something absolutely binding about Mussolini's rhetoric here, and it represents an utter turnaround from earlier Italian colonialist discourse. Then, in May of 1936, the country would suddenly experience the shock of victory after years of shame associated particularly with the massacre of Adua in the late nineteenth century. As an empire, Italy no longer could afford to arouse general "interest" in racism; it had to sustain the firmest principles of separation and difference.

"The purely European physical and psychological characteristics of Italians must not be altered in any way," read the final decree of the racist "scientists," published in 1938. "Union is admissible only within the group of European races, in which case we should not speak of true and proper hybridism, given that these races belong to a common body and differ only with regard to certain features, while on the whole they are heterogenous. The purely European character of Italians would be altered by cross-breeding with any Extra-European race at all."[12] Indeed, that same year, the Fascist Great Council outlawed marriage between Italians and non-Aryans. The official publication, "Party and Empire," also issued in 1938, states with absolute unambiguity that miscegenation should not be considered a threat of the past: "Italy cannot consider itself arrived. . . . He who hesitates is lost."[13] But if the racial question is defined in clear terms, issues of sexual desire remain unresolved. In 1937, Mussolini signed a law prohibiting "madamism," that is, any paraconjugal relation between Italians and natives. At the same time, however, Italian-run brothels continued to enjoy a brisk business in Africa.

Blackness flooded the Italian market after the unexpectedly one-sided battles. Most foreign analysts had predicted an arduous and lengthy campaign. In fact, the actual period between the first offensives (the war was never officially declared, demonstrating Italy's utter disrespect for the Ethiopians) and the victorious raising of the Italian flag over Addis Ababa was remarkably short, thanks primarily to the effluvium of chemical warfare. But once the capital city was occupied, the Italian generals suddenly had to contend with the very significance of success, with the question of what it might mean to be a victor in an imperial war. Italian cultural and political institutions had to realign a position toward blackness in its subordinate, subjected state. The propaganda machine of Mussolini had simply not prepared them for utter domination.

How, then, did the "consciousness-raising" campaign begin, and from what sources did it draw its iconography?

Marinetti's Mafarka: A Paradigm

In 1909, two years before Italy's Libyan campaign was initiated, Marinetti published *Mafarka le futuriste, roman africain* in Paris. Taken in the context of the avant-garde novel, this work treats a number of conventional themes: the exaltation of war against decadent licentiousness, of the male against the female, of rigidity against flow. It exploits what Fanon termed a "Manichean delusionism" characteristic of the colonial encounter, an epistemology of strict binarisms whose content may shift from one narrative segment to the next with little significance for the ultimate "pleasures" of the text.[14] These textual pleasures reside primarily in the force with which boundaries are drawn and in the extreme tension of the bodies that always threaten to burst forth from some comforting classification. The main polar categories underlying *Mafarka*—European bourgeoisie/subjugated natives, light-skinned Arabs/dark-skinned Africans, male/female, active/passive—are thrust upon the reader with such insistence that they make the novel inconceivable *except as a historical document of the avant-garde*. In other words, the power to shock the bourgeois reader is a foregone conclusion, permeating every line of the novel at the macro- and microlevels of the text.

In 1910, when the work was translated into Italian (without the subtitle "An African Novel"), Marinetti's name was already on the lips of the intelligentsia and the middle-class readers of daily newspapers as an agitator, manifesto writer, organizer of exhibitions, host-provocateur of "futurist evenings" (the inspiration for "happenings" of the 1960s), and antiparliamentarian. His trial for public indecency was held in a Milan court in 1910, and attended by a large and vociferous public as if it were one more disruptive performance piece. The proceedings of the trial were published as a kind of declaration of futurist poetics, bound with a long poem of Marinetti's called "Destruction." In his public trial-cum-poetic manifesto, Marinetti was accused of using the French language for his novel to seduce young girls, a charge that he quickly dismissed. Born to Italian parents in Egypt, Marinetti had attended a French-language *école* before departing for the Continent and what would have been the most logical destination for a young poet of the time—Paris. It was not until several years later, at the outbreak of the war, that Marinetti seriously considered the question of his nationality. He fought for Italy and came to construe futurism as a fundamentally Italian movement, even if its roots were obviously entangled with French symbolism and other international modernist movements; in fact, the first manifesto was written in French and published in 1909 on the front page of *Le Figaro*. Nevertheless, the accusation of licentiousness made by the prosecution suggests a certain lack of understanding on the part of the Italian public about what, in retrospect, seems a perfectly logical progression for this deracinated intellectual.

Three essential points of the novel offended the bourgeois reading public. The first was the novel's beginning chapter, titled "The Rape of the Negresses." To be precise, it was not the rape of the Negresses that was offensive, but the pollution that it entailed for the light-skinned Arab soldiers who sank into the "other side" of the boundaries in penetrating the black morass. To the first charge, the futurist Marinetti responded:

> In writing [the novel], I naturally obeyed the highest principles of literature, which are summarized in the expression of one's own dreams with the greatest efficiency, considering images not as mere frou-frou or decorative embellishments, but as essential elements of expression, unconscious instruments for fixing the ungraspable truth and for making the indefinite and the undefinable more precise. That is why I wrote "The Rape of the Negresses," so that the great heroic will of Mafarka could rise up from a huge torrid furnace of luxuriance and filth.[15]

The notion of "high literature" was invoked throughout the trial by various apologists for and including Marinetti. Yet "high literature" seems to have little to do with the actual content of the novel. Instead, what is most important in the contested sections is the compulsion in futurist aesthetics to represent a vertical passage exemplified by Mafarka's solo generation of a son who flies up to and is vitalized by the sun. It is this movement upward, what Marinetti called a poetics of the trampoline,[16] that distinguishes the futurist hero from the swarms of putrid, African bodies below. In other words, if Marinetti had wished merely to narrate an orgiastic rape (the low element in the novel), he would have chosen a European subject — a scene from the Milanese underworld, for example. But precisely the African setting of the novel permits his exoneration from charges of mere pornography, since Africa itself can be essentialized as "heat, filth, luxuriance."[17]

The second problematic moment from the trial turned around a celebration of a military victory during which Mafarka slips aphrodisiacs to a few young girls. The youth and cultural vulnerability of the victims stands in marked contrast to the self-sexualized elements of the novel, the euphoria of male reproduction, and the absolute lack of any real interest in female sexuality per se that might constitute an element of more traditional pulp fiction. Against the charges of rape and lechery, Marinetti did not specifically defend himself, other than in his generic displacement of all listless, oversexed behavior to the Africans. Ironically, though, Mafarka himself emerges from the trial as transcending the boundaries of the dark continent. He "is part of European literature . . . a *human* hero."[18] In fact, Mafarka's identity seems crucial in understanding Italian relations to blackness, precisely because he is created as part of Marinetti's own search for a national self-identity.

The crucial, provocative *idée fixe* in the trial of Marinetti is the physical description of the equine penis—stuffed, consumed, and then regenerated on the Arab king Mafarka. Actually, the penis (called by its Arab name, *zeb*) is the subject of a story told by Mafarka to the enemy black king. Early in the novel, Mafarka disguises himself as an elderly, crippled mendicant and gains admittance to the king's tent. Like Scheherazade in the narrative tradition of the *Arabian Nights,* Mafarka defers a violent encounter with the ruler and dilates time by tale-telling. Framed within a circle of men, all taking puffs from a hookah, the "beggar" begins his tale about a fictional king (named "Mafarka") who had once been a simple horse merchant. One day, the real Mafarka recounts, a demon enters the market and seeks to bid on a stallion. At this point the real black king, Brafane-el-Kibir, interrupts what promises to be a conventional narrative of commerce and evil to inquire about the horse's *zeb.* Upon hearing the question, "all of the blacks erupted in noisy laughter, and the movements of their prone bodies made their dry and wrinkled limbs crackle against the bits of glass and leather sheathes hung from their belts."[19] Appeasing his host, Mafarka responds that the *zeb* was purple, with a head pouring forth saffron, like the *zeb* the girls of Tell-el-Kibir dream about on their wedding nights. The tale recommences, and the king and his men learn that the false merchant of the tale (the demon) buys the stallion and begins to ride it out of town. But the horse is uncontrollable and copulates with every beast it meets so that the demon is thrown from the saddle. Finally, the demon decides to return to the site of the market, where he cuts off the *zeb* of the horse and serves it stuffed to the unsuspecting merchant "Mafarka." Believing that this highly flavorful dish is an exotic fish, "Mafarka" bites into it, "peeling it with his teeth, as one would eat a banana."[20]

Almost immediately, "Mafarka's" own member begins to grow, and he rapes all the surrounding servant girls in a tremendously violent wave of hysteria. He demands that the demon relinquish all of his goods, as he feels power welling up inside him. The demon's trick has failed. King Mafarka's triumph tale is well received by the group of interlocutors, who obviously identify with the monstrous virility of the merchant "Mafarka" and his *zeb*. Finally, after having "satisfied about twenty servant girls and just as many beautiful slaves," "Mafarka," feeling exhausted (*spossato,* the same word used by Marinetti to describe the king Mafarka after the disputed "rape of the Negresses" episode), decides to sleep in the open air, on a bed next to the sea. The sailboats that are anchored in the shallow harbor form a kind of "picturesque roof" over his head, but his eleven-meter-long penis is too awkward, and so he rolls it up "like a cable" next to the bed. During the night, some sailors mistake the *zeb* for a cord, which they use to moor their boat. The *zeb* becomes rigid, now serving as a mast for the sails that carry the unwitting sailors and Mafarka all out to sea. The next morning the boat docks at Tell-el-Kibir, where the reigning king Bubassa is anxious to experience the "virtue" (*virtù*) of such an enormous *zeb*. He kneels down in anticipation, and at this moment, "Mafarka" enchains him and takes over the scepter. Thus ends the tale of a begger-who-becomes-King Mafarka by triumphing over a fictive black African king, told by the real King Mafarka dressed as a beggar, to a real black African king.

The internal narrative of the Arab king's triumph enchants the group of "black" men. They readily accept Mafarka's warning to beware the angry stallion, which is still wandering the land in search of its missing *zeb*. Nevertheless, the blacks indulge in a series of lascivious acts rendering them so weakened and inebriated that they end up fighting and destroying their own army under the phantasm of the great horse. King Mafarka returns to his light-skinned compatriots a true (futurist) hero.

The penis is, then, the nodal point that seduces the black Africans and enfeebles them, while it is also the fictive metaphor that binds Mafarka within and without the narrative he tells. If such narration is a feminine strategy for attenuating time and sapping the male of his violent desire, as in the *Arabian Nights,* Mafarka's enormous member acts as the alibi of his masculine *virtù*.

The central offensive point of both the novel and the trial/spectacle — Mafarka's extraordinary anatomy — may serve as a paradigm for understanding the imaginary relations of the Italian public to the African body. For Marinetti himself, the penis admittedly forms an integral part of the novel because "the virile member, monstrously developed and incessantly operative, constitutes the central, obsessive motif of African life and literature."[21] The tale told by Mafarka, an "African" tale, absolves Marinetti himself from any complicity in bringing the *zeb* to European literary culture. Of course, this is a very old cultural motif, and in one sense Marinetti merely repeats a nineteenth-century bourgeois notion that the very servitude of the Orient, the condition of subjection (figured in "Asiatic workers," as we shall soon see), derives from the East's excessive worship of the penis. Although the subject is distasteful for a decent European public, it was published and made palatable in a discourse of sexologists and ethnologists exploring the degeneration of the East.[22] At one point during Marinetti's trial, it was suggested that if only the Italian version of the novel had included the subtitle "An African Novel," as the French version had, the whole scandal would have been avoided. The court would have read the novel with the appropriate, relativistic perspective. The prosecution would have understood the irony, the distance, that Marinetti, as a European, was himself taking from the offensive descriptions and events. This was Marinetti's ultimate defense, and it was successful in securing him an acquittal in spite of certain inherent contradictions. First, the reader cannot help but read Mafarka as an alter ego of the author. In fact, Marinetti explained that as "*human hero*" Mafarka exemplified all the best qualities of the avant-garde artists: courage, strength, and resistance to feminine sexuality in general. He also exemplifies the avant-garde fantasy of generating life without a female womb.

Yet Mafarka's monstrous body would seem to betray this Europeanism and so reveal a central contradiction facing the avant-garde: how to aestheticize for a more genteel public, with its own conceptions of "primitivism," what was most attractive (for white colonizers) about blackness, namely, the fact that the representation of the black body before a white public helped to normalize white domination. Mafarka was specifically Arab, with all of the cultural connotations this may have had for the Italian public on the brink of taking Libya, but ultimately he was "colored," a figure of blackness with attributes that distinguished him from a white futurist.

To understand the specific meaning of "colored" for an Italian reader, the description of Mafarka from the first chapter of the novel is useful. The hero has just returned to his village after successfully dethroning his uncle in a bloody battle. He stands on a terrace overlooking columns of soldiers who lead along the human booty:

> He had the ease and robustness of a young, invincible athlete, armed to bite, strangle, and tackle. His body so compact, so alive and frenetic under a downy cover and a spotted skin. Like a snake, he seemed to be painted with the colors of victory and fortune like the hull of a beautiful ship. And the light adored him, passionately, since it did not cease to caress his ample pectorals, bulbous like impatient roots, and his oak-like biceps, and the rippling

muscles of his legs, over which his sweat launched explosions. His face was frank, with a square jaw, and had the color of beautiful terracotta. His mouth was large and sensual; his nose, slim and rather short; his gaze was fierce. His eyes, a beautiful black like licorice, flamed violently in the sun, too close together, like those of a beast of prey. But often they seemed to liquify under his eyebrows, exaggerating the opaque pallor of a mild forehead, crowned with the extraordinary will of his thick hair.[23]

Marinetti obsessively links the black body with various geological features of the African landscape: Mafarka wriggles under the animal skin of his own bodily contours, while he melts and liquifies under the sun. Similarly, in his observations of a battle fought during his tenure as a war correspondent in Libya, Marinetti makes an absolute equation between the slain bodies and the land onto which they are fallen. A trench cut into the sand is a vaginal opening, housing the stiff Italian soldiers; the sand undulates as a voluptuous female body; the arrival of an Italian bomber sees the Africans gyrate and quiver into an orgasmic fusion with the land itself.[24] But what is the real importance of this link between land mass and the black body? Is this another example of a Western notion of the "natural" imposed onto a bloody battlefield and consequently onto the subjugation of the native subjects?

The Mafarka paradigm, with its monstrous genitals and fluid, undifferentiated boundaries, recalls very nearly the anthropological figure of the trickster, located in a variety of different cultures from West Africa to the Winnebago Indians of North America. For Mary Douglas, the trickster exemplifies a transformational process, specifically one of cultural modernization. He achieves prominence as a figure for the tribal attempt to grapple with increasingly differentiated economic and sexual models imposed from the outside. He represents ambivalence through his impulsive behavior and his lack of control over passions and appetites, precisely the comportment idealized in Mafarka and in Marinetti's pseudo-ethnography of the African male. In one version of the story, the trickster's body exists in an infantile state of imaginary nonintegration. Like the infant before the mirror stage in Lacanian topology, he wallows in an Imaginary bliss, his intestines and penis wrapped around his body, his scrotum perched on top of his exterior digestive genitalia. His anus is also separated, a further piece of evidence to suggest that these "primitive" myths "are phrased to satisfy a dominant social concern, the problem of how to organize together in a society."[25] Paul Radin, a scholar of Native American culture, recorded the following trickster narrative:

After a while he woke up and found himself lying on his back without a blanket. He looked up above him and saw to his astonishment something floating there. "Aha, aha! The chiefs have unfurled their banner! The people must be having a great feast for this is always the case when the chief's banner is unfurled." With this he sat up and then first realized that his blanket was gone. It was his blanket he saw floating above. His penis had become stiff and the blanket had been forced up. "That's always happening to me," he said. "My younger brother, you will lose the blanket, so bring it back." Thus he spoke to his penis. Then he took hold of it and, as he handled it, it got softer and the blanket finally fell down. Then he coiled up his penis and put it in a box.[26]

Radin notes that the Winnebago mythological cycle charts the development of a masculine trickster whose very identity becomes focused as his virility is established and his penis retracted, fixed on the body. Both Karl Kerényi and Norman O. Brown linked the trickster to ithyphallic figures from antiquity, and to a sacred cult in which this Hermes-like demigod emerges as a "cultural hero" and a mischievous conniver. A common topos from the various trickster narratives is the linkage between sexual potency and cultural or societal differentiation and development. Yet in spite of the anthropological conjunction between trickster and "Westernization," the trickster figure is specifically represented in the avant-garde context as marked by his very non-Europeanism. He must stand as a kind of binary element, coupled with and engaged in a dialogue with a European body.

Whether or not Marinetti studied anthropological accounts of the trickster myth, he clearly was influenced in his depiction by a dominant cultural paradigm that goes beyond the mere assignment of virility to the black male toward a conception of fluidity and lack of specificity. Although *virtù* by itself might seem to coincide generally with a futurist notion of male strength, in point of fact Marinetti expressed a certain revulsion toward the African body in its "slippery" and "prehuman" state. Mafarka's phallus is not really stiff like a futurist machine; it is soft and pliable, wound around the body, and detachable. It is not only an organ of penetration, but also a kind of lazy, loping appendage like the pierced limbs and features of the "primitive subject," ears and lips dangling with heavy jewelry.

In his defense of the novel, however, Marinetti did not make a similar argument. He did not theorize the penis or virility, as I have done in linking Mafarka to the paradigms of the trickster and the Lacanian Imaginary. Instead of covering up the penis or even shrinking it, Marinetti left it exposed in all of its nudity as it would be found in Africa, a cultural space where Western, bourgeois prudishness had not yet intruded into the natural. Stating his case with the utmost candor, Marinetti explained to the magistrates that "in Africa, they aren't priggish like you representatives of the prime minister, and the Africans, whether kings or not, very often keep exposed that thing which is called the virile member, which you, perhaps in homage to your prudishness, have called an equine member."[27] The defense of the penis by its displacement to a form of primitive nudity was clever on Marinetti's part, and also attests to a kind of nascent anthropological relativism within the culture at large. Later, during the 1930s, images of colonized natives with exposed breasts became quotidian in middle-class magazines such as *Le vie d'Italia,* even though, clearly, they are not the same as European breasts.[28] The African breast could be pendulous or pert, anywhere along a spectrum of possibilities, to suit all tastes. There are almost no images, however, of an exposed penis. To show the "primitive penis," soft before the lens of the camera, would be to suggest, however obliquely, that all penises are limp. The threat is too great, and so it does not become part of the photographic iconography of "ethnographic" magazines.

If the African male is made into a futurist, the female is represented as repugnant and vilified. In response to charges that Italian soldiers raped a number of women after a battle in Libya, Marinetti responded that this would be unthinkable. These African female bodies with their breasts "hanging to their waists" stand in opposition to all that the futurists found heroic in the male. "Just try to breathe the fetid odor of their dirty underwear," Marinetti challenged his newspaper readers. "It contains, in baths of pestilential sweat, the richest cultures of cholera, leprosy and syphilis germs." The imagery is altogether familiar from any number of futurist tracts; in *Mafarka,* the king-warrior rejects the feminine altogether for its powers to weaken and drain the male hero of his energies.[29] Specifically, the vilification of the black female during the Libyan conquests represents an early moment in the formation of Italian fascism that will be transformed and deepened during the Ethiopian Campaign and the foundation of the New Roman Empire in 1936. Throughout the *ventennio* of the regime, the futurists continued to explore the contours of the black body, but never significantly departed from the paradigms of Marinetti's early Africa.

Finally, then, I wish to recapitulate the elements that constitute the African (trickster) phallic prototype: The phallus is detached from the body and wound about the male; the male lies on his back to sleep; the phallus becomes stiff and floats above the body; it lifts up the blankets or "takes a trip" away from the body, only to return, soften, and be placed back in its "box" or wound again. What is this African/trickster phallus narrative, if not a narrative of masturbation? Marinetti cannot help but write from the position of a European, from a culture so steeped in fears and taboos that sleep itself becomes subjected to proscribed behaviors and policing (one must never sleep on one's back, because one is liable to have an unexpected erection or because one may deliberately "lift up the blankets" without being noticed, according to a bourgeois, nineteenth-century discourse of child rearing).[30] Marinetti writes from a culture that first linked the primitive and the ape, not only because of certain *facial* features that seemed to suggest the evolutionary inferiority of the black body, but because the monkey was known as the only animal capable of (deliberate) masturbation, a vice assigned to the non-European and the racial other, in general.

Although Mafarka the futurist is a repository for bourgeois fears, he is neither a revolutionary nor a proletarian hero, but a classless vessel. He does not represent anything in particular, but potentially anything that is abject. He encompasses the same sort of contradiction we find in the Nazi persecution of "Nigger Art." He is the opposite of bourgeois values, and in this sense he is a ritualistic, mythic, Promethean figure, all values that would be exploited by fascism as mass movement. But he is also defined as "degenerate" for the masses, and held up as a symbol of all that they should avoid in their processes of Romanization, fascistization, stiffening, defense.[31] The fascists need blackness in order to contain these contradictions; blackness is a dumping ground on which to throw taboos such as masturbation. But as the relation with Africa becomes more concrete, the black body swells with the very same stench that will be used against the bourgeoisie, figured as hypocrites pinching their noses and receding to their antiseptic homes.

Futurist Blackness

How does this narrative figure of the monstrous and taboo become translated into visual language? In the many transformations of Italian futurism, the geometricizing current represented by Depero, Balla, and then by the "second wave" in Milan and Turin adopts the Mafarka paradigm with the greatest relish. Specifically, the futurist aesthetic of pure tone and geometry becomes integrated with a fantasy about the smooth black body that I will discuss at length in this section. The logical relation of smoothness and desire does not present itself at first glance, because the German and Italian racial propagandists condemned *all* representations of blackness as *art negre,* conflating a specific term whose greatest relevance was to analytic cubism, with a generic one without regard for stylistic or formalist criteria. This conflation then spread to a general cultural misunderstanding. Depero, who exemplified the smoothness of the body stocking in various portraits of black men and women, belied this misidentification of the black body with *art negre* in a short piece called "Josephine Backer [*sic*] on the Champs Elysée and Experimental Theater at Montmartre." He describes a stage show with sets featuring the classic emblematic or decorative attributes of blackness: palm trees, cacti, coconuts, and bananas. These attributes alone — regardless of the style in which they were depicted or the elements of the accompanying performance — were enough to label the event as "black." After characterizing the scenographic elements, Depero comments, "I don't love *art negre,* but the savage virginity, the barbaric sincerity of *art negre* and jazz music do overcome me and I am rather amused by them. Magistrally deafening harmonies and syncopated melodies, gurgling, murmurs and tremors transport you in a raucous atmosphere of exotic life, and undoubtedly communicate new emotions of an unexplored life."[32] Swept away by Josephine in Paris, Depero first "blackens" the whole affair (she is black before she is anything; the music is black before it could have any possible relation to the atonal experiments of the futurist art of noise, for example), and then associates it with the only term he knows for a black aesthetic: *art negre.* But what is more interesting about the comment, coming from the pen of a rather wide-eyed provincial Italian craftsman who runs a studio in a small Dolomite town near the Austrian border with his beloved wife, Rosetta, is Depero's absolute insistence on the untried sexuality of the spectacle. Not that he denies this smiling Negress stands for sex — that would be impossible given the cultural saturation of the black female as fixed icon — but he applies his own peculiar form of aesthetic colonialism to the vision before him. Josephine Baker, this smooth figure in a body stocking, is a virginal continent to be discovered, a new life for the provincial, exactly the model of Africa diffused in the popular press and by the pioneers and soldiers who were drawn there, long before the rise of fascism. Disregarding the very questions of aesthetic style that might seem to most preoccupy the futurist imagination — obsessed with manifestos and clarifications of its uniqueness, originality, or national affiliation — Depero's major impulse as a viewer is to assert his own power over blackness, and to appropriate it for his own pleasure. Yet when he himself goes to represent the black body, he moves away from the primitivist aesthetics of *art negre* and makes the black body into a multicolored, smooth picture.

Over time, the "cartoon" features of blackness became codified (and not just in Italy, obviously): large, rounded lips; protruding lower jaw; ingenuous wide-open stare played against cocoa-brown skin tone; ears weighed down by heavy tribal jewelry. Futurist, "cartoonish" blackness has much in common with those caricatures of servility, the American pickaninnies. But in the Italian context, many of these physiognomic details correspond to elements of Cesare Lombroso's nineteenth-century criminal anthropology and, later, to the documents signed by the so-called racist scientists under fascism. In periodicals such as *La difesa della razza,* dedicated to the cultivation of a racial consciousness, the Italian public found photographs of every nature of corporeal manipulation: ear and lip disks, bound feet, hints at unspeakable genital deformation. In fact, the word "deformation" becomes a key term in the fascist educational campaigns, associated with blackness, but also, very concretely, with the *entartete Kunst* that was copied from German publications. Deformation is thus a racist term, but also an aesthetic one. Picasso is the artist of deformation par excellence, and it would be impossible to separate a popular conception of cubism from the discourse of the racist scientists. The foundation for the "modern" science of the fascists lies in the timeless positivism maintained from the nineteenth century in notions that European criminals often exhibited the same sort of anomalies characteristic of "primitive races." Traits such as a flattened nose, an angular skull, the projection of the lower face and jaws (prognathism), and fleshy lips were, in Lombroso's terms, atavistic and shared by apes, Negroes, and criminals.

During the 1930s, the word "deformation" became synonymous both with *art negre* (which the Italians knew about primarily through their importation of documents pertaining to *entartete Kunst*) and with non-Aryanism in general. Depero's plastic, volumetric style was perfectly suited to the geometricization of black physiognomy implied in the racial laws and the manifestos of racist "scientists" produced in support of colonization. But the Negroid lips, creamy-white eyes, and pickaninny features of "cartoon" advertising have little to do with "primitivism" in the aesthetics of *art negre,* fauvism, expressionism, or other movements termed degenerate — *entartete* — by the Nazis, modeled on interpretations of African sculpture and tribal artifacts. *Art negre,* believed to be inspired by an international Jewish conspiracy, and repeated in the cubist planes of Picasso's *Demoiselles,* represents a very sketchy phase in abstraction dominated by vague, shadowy pencil lines that may begin tentatively and suddenly thicken or become emboldened.

Instead, the futurist black body, endlessly repeated and pared down to its silhouette, emerges as just one other version of the *giocattolo futurista,* the

5. Depero's rubber-headed woman.

essere-vivente-artificiale that Depero and others developed in the context of a postwar visual polemic with Boccioni's earlier sculptural forms. A "rubber head" by Depero (figure 5) conflates one of a few traditional colonialist products with this developing geometricization of blackness: the large lips and tribal jewelry stand for a certain hallucinatory relation to the colonized peoples and make the very inclusion of black skin tone itself irrelevant. Like Federico Seneca's animated robots (figure 6) with their towering head-baskets and iconic breasts, Depero's black woman is pure physiognomy, pure

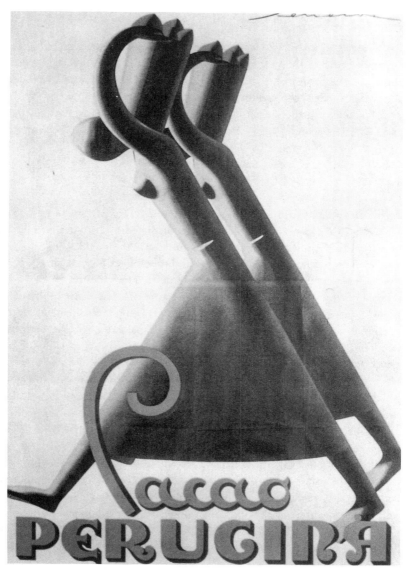

6. Seneca's Perugina chocolate women. (Salce Collection, 21166.)

icon. She is suffused with light, not resting in the shadows or hiding her blackness, her Jewishness, her shame. And as a result of her stylistic boldness there is nothing in her to arouse Aryan nausea. Her blackness reads as an unmistakable sign; she cannot be part of a conspiracy, dreamed up by sick Jewish scribblers (stingy even in their use of color!) in their stinking hovels. Instead, she becomes a legitimate style for advertising products on the open market.

Black and Jew

Neofuturistic advertising art may not reveal anything particular about the fantasies of blackness, because any traces of the reality of African life are elided in the process of graphic abstraction, just as the pseudoscientific language of the racist ethnographers and anthropologists blurred all physiognomic features of the non-Aryan ad absurdum. The vacuousness of fascist science emerges uncannily in a casual caricature of a Jew made in the margin of a letter from Depero to Marinetti (figure 7). Here, again, are the protruding ears, the cigar forming a kind of epidermal extension like the pendent tribal jewelry in so many representations of those other racially inferior types from the African continent. In a picture essay in *La difesa della razza,* black and Jew are classed together as "two typical American types" (figure 8). Both are too lazy to perform the physical labor that has distinguished the Italian proletariat (and enriched the Italian upper classes — the readers of the magazine). *La difesa* is full of intimations that the subjects of Italian colonialism may be biologically incapable of laboring under "normal" democratic conditions of the market. Thus the photograph linking the Jew (the capitalist, the usurer) with the black both plays on certain cultural preoccupations (imported from Germany) of the bourgeoisie, and provides a subtle justification for forced labor in the colonies. Depero's drawing also comes in the context of his experiences in New York, but not all forms of the black–Jewish equation were so displaced. Ethnographers in the 1930s who turned their attention to the Falasha Jews of Ethiopia claimed to notice all of the "classic Jewish features" in these doubly jeopardized Africans.[33]

Generally speaking, black and Jew are both manipulated by the fascists to displace attention from a definition of the Italian race itself. Much of the material in the manifesto of the racist "scientists," printed in 1938, was imported directly from Germany, and it does not address issues of cultural, linguistic, or geographic differences within the Italian peninsula. Instead, Italian racism, which the scientists claim has been a (latent) component of Fascist

7. "The typical New York Jew" by Depero, In *Ricostruzione futurista dell 'universo*. (Courtesy of the Northwestern University Library, Department of Special Collections.)

8. "Black and Jew: Two typical American types." (Reproduced from *La difesa della raza*, September 5, 1939, p. 7.)

Party politics since its foundation, should have an Aryan-Nordic address (*indirizzo ariano-nordico*). This is not because of any documentable links with Scandinavian races, as in Germany's case, but because this "address" confirms the appurtenance of the Italian people with other European races. Finally, the scientists mandate that purely European physical and psychological characteristics of Italians should in no way be altered through miscegenation. But if all of the historical, anecdotal evidence points to a fundamental breakdown in empirical attempts to find points of commonality in non-Aryan features, social and institutional structures such as advertising served important auxiliary functions in the campaigns to construct paradigms of otherness.

Like the black, the Jew is oversexed. In Italy, this theme is expressed in particular through a campaign against Freud. There is one Freud for the small psychoanalytic community in Italy primarily discussed in the *Rivista di psicologia* and the writings of Eduardo Weiss, and another, popular Freud who is caricatured as a highly pessimistic Jew who preaches pansexualism. Like Mafarka's black phallus, Freud's Jewish nose is always poking around where it does not belong, sniffing out the culturally repugnant (which is then utterly denied). Jewishness, like blackness, is a repository for precisely those topics that the middle class cannot itself discuss in any available language. Here is one journalistic commentary:

> I don't know if these [libidinal excesses in Freud] conform to the Jewish idea of man and morals, but most certainly they do not conform to the sentiments common to the Italian people or to any healthy people, and it appears that they are all directed toward justifying incest, which, according to some sources, is practiced on a large scale by the Jews of certain regions for the purpose of maintaining the purity of their race.[34]

Masturbation to the Africans, incest to the Semites! The displaced taboos represent the very threats that the fascist must confront in the colonial encounter. Rather than face the undeniable fact that miscegenation leads to healthier bodies (and not the reverse), fascist science first posits inbreeding as a potential defensive strategy *against* deformation (it helps maintain the purity of the race), and then assigns it to the vilified race itself. The passage begins with the pathologizing of excessive libido (the same quality that held a highly ambivalent position in futurism, as I suggested earlier). But the discourse quickly slips from sexuality (as a personal, moral issue) to demographics (a political one), and then back to incest (a biological urge) in a move that appears utterly ironic against the background of Freud's writings on the incest taboo. At the other end of this absurdly illogical tunnel, it is precisely the purity or consistency of Jewishness that threatens the fascist. The admittance that Jews, as a race, express a capacity for self-generation and reproductive isolation cannot be reconciled with the notions of miscegenation and deformities ascribed to "Jewish aesthetics." If Jews are drawn to surrealism, cubism, and abstractionism, as fascist art critics suggested, then why not also to rationalism and metaphysical painting (the movement associated with Carrà, de Chirico, and Savinio from around 1914 to 1919)? Jews are overzealous in their emotions, hence the lumpy, abstracted bodily forms, the lack of any linear clarity or purity of color, and decoration or "design" in their artworks. But Judaism is equivalent with the aesthetics of "modern art" by 1938, and so it becomes linked even with the high-design styles of minimalism and rationalism in the circles of *Casabella* and *Domus,* even though these clearly present the very opposite qualities from those mentioned as constitutive of the "Jewish abstracting mentality." If the links between *art negre* and the Jewish modernist conspiracy are tendentious in German propaganda, in the Italian translations they verge on the absurd.

To some degree, then, the absolute lack of logical categories or content in Italian racism can be understood to be a result of the awkward imposition of Hitler's programs. Flipping through Italian periodicals of the late thirties, one senses just how cumbersome this whole enterprise was, as if all this material were being hastily printed and distributed to an audience virtually unschooled in its actual significance. An issue of *La difesa* might include an article explaining Mendelian genetics in simple lay terms, along with a profile of several important Jewish writers (exemplars of Semitic pessimism) and a lesson in basic African geography. Each issue ends with a short selection from the notebooks of Giacomo Leopardi, usually a meditation on the Italian spirit, corporeal excellence, the unfathomable beauty of the Italian landscape. The hand-drawn material in this periodical is never graphic or reductive; it has the look of nostalgic sketchbooks (the visual analogue of a pithy paragraph taken from Leopardi), but the photography is surprisingly bold, full of extreme contrasts. A cover montage superimposes a nursing woman of a certain age (presumably this child is only the latest of many; or is this the child's grandmother, just lending a nipple, as it were, for the fatherland?) on a series of oddly slanted buildings (figure 9).[35] The baroque continuum of lower-middle-class apartment buildings seems to engulf this woman. Those towering icons of postwar reconstruction and urban strength might almost seem to conform to the style of revolutionary

9. White woman nursing baby. (Reproduced from cover of *Gente nostra*, February 28, 1937.)

juxtaposition (montage on the Left), rather than an affirmation of a mono-maniacal iconographic nucleus (fascist montage?). There is a distinct link-age, then, between the bold graphics of "disinterested" advertising and the bold photography of fascist rhetoric. I am ultimately suggesting that, al-though the science of race was void of any rigorous thought or logical im-perative, the visual culture that treated the black body was invested with a certain element of the "scientific." I now turn from this general theoretical discussion of racism and representation to a consideration of a number of crucial categories or types.

A Catalog of Abjection

The following survey should not be considered either exhaustive or sys-tematic. My "iconography" of blackness merely provides an opportunity or context within which to view a number of key images.

The Smiling Negress

She offers herself to a viewer, her teeth radiating whiteness against the ex-treme darkness of her skin. She is the biblical Sulamite (*nigra sum, sed for-mosa*), a whole new continent for sexual exploration. She was one of the first types to be classified and represented for the Italian public, as in this very typical description:

> In those young Somalis [This is Brichetti, a military commander, writing in 1899] we discovered a combination of Greek and Roman femininity mixed with the lean profile and the hot and smooth tonality of that particular color proper to Arab blood. Seeing them, I involuntarily compared them to the vivid and beautiful Jewish figures that radiate with loveliness and soft grace from the canvases of Van Dyck and Caracciolo. This is how Raphael imagined the Virgin of the *Marriage,* like Rebecca at the well or Judith with the head of Holofernes. But in the brown and graceful daughters of the sun, blossoming like gentle flowers in those tropical hothouses, we find, again, a mellowness of form, a fullness of lines, and a vague sweetness of expression that rouse the blood with acute fascination ... from the tiny, oblong head, to the soft, ample, and voluptuous curves of their thighs, to their rounded breasts, upright and turgid, which jut forth from the cloths that, in vain, try to constrain them.[36]

It is easy to see how this figure of mythical femininity was immediately translated into visual language and then publicized for male readers of escapist magazines; she epitomized an exotic dream of the tropics, which would prove invaluable in recruiting soldiers. And once this sexual simulacrum had submitted to the troops, she could be reproduced endlessly to sell the very idea of colonialism, as just another of its by-products. Following this line of reasoning, the smiling Negress fits neatly into the logic of the fascist campaign to arouse a colonialist "interest," for soldiers were more likely to go "down there" ("*laggiù*" was the generic term used by Italians to indicate Africa, but it might also be a euphemism for the dark continent of the female genitalia) if they could expect erotic encounters.

In point of fact, once the curiosity of the Blackshirts had been pricked, once they were armed and ready, the seduction/campaign would cease, and another one, making the Negress utterly abject, would take its place. Of course, an epistemology that separates "healthy" heterosexual, libidinal drives from the destructive drives of a brutal war against an entire race may be missing a fundamental point about fascism. The generals, like the foot soldiers who mercilessly bombed and gassed their "own" territory (populated with their "own" women) for over a year, were not engaged in positive sexual experimentation with an exotic, nubile group of women: they

were primarily and utterly hungry for war, and this drive can be understood only in the larger context of the general economy of sexual relations
in fascist society. The facility with which the Negress is shifted from a positive to a negative position can only be explained by a theory of sexuality
that considers the object arbitrary and replaceable. Clearly, the Italian bourgeoisie could not sustain such a notion as law. Yet the Negress, available
and eager in the popular imagery, represents the end (the fulfillment) of
male desire. The threat posed by the Negress to the psychosexual order of
male desire, grounded primarily in the unattainable (white) female object,
is great. In fact, the "total war" of the fascist army seems to gain its strong
(libidinal) drive from the need to wipe out the whole question, to utterly
do away with the Negress and firmly populate the land with monogamous,
middle-class, white families. In the process of the propaganda campaigns,
then, the Negress first entices the soldier with the promise of her submission. But when he has come almost to the point of possession, she is sacri-
ficed in a ritual not unlike the *ius primae noctae* of ancient kings. Ultimately,
the Negress helps the (white) man to circumvent the taboo of virginity, for
she prepares him to enter into sexuality with the (white) woman.[37]

The sexualized Negress is usually found in ads for stimulants: coffee,
chocolate, or perhaps a coffee "surrogate." We meet her early on, as in a 1921
poster by Achille Mauzan (figure 10). The image of "La Torinese" is typical of postwar advertising: a full figure occupying the page surrounded by
decorative motifs, Liberty-style poster graphics, the color coordination between the background and the skin tone of the woman herself. The Negress,
flashing a perfect set of pure white teeth, wears a hat and skirt that transform her into a slightly wilted, common flower. As it happens, the ad is a
sophisticated in-joke between two white viewers: La Torinese is the brand
name, the house name (always feminized in Italian; the adjective means "of
Turin"), in this case a purveyor of chocolates. As it happens, the firm has
offices in Bologna, Padua, and Venice, so the brand name, rendered in the
ad in quotation marks, becomes all the more significant. But where is the
product—the chocolate itself? The chocolate *is* the smiling Negress, we
must suppose, but "La Torinese" is also "the woman from Turin," and so she
cannot be this utterly black creature from deepest Sub-Saharan Africa, the
putative source of the cocoa beans.[38]

On the lap of "La Torinese" is perched an impish, plump white baby.
Indeed, the pose appears most precarious, almost an anti-pietà. The baby girl
is turned toward the background of the image, but her oversized head faces
forward, as if she were twisted around in some torturous, baroque *contrapposto*.

10. "La Torinese" by Mauzan. (Salce Collection, 20421.)

Like the Negress, the baby girl wears a highly exaggerated expression, her eyes wide open; her fingers are spread as if she expects to fall at any moment from her flower-perch, as if the smooth hand of the Negress might at any moment slip from her back. Clearly, the melodrama represented here does not strive for verisimilitude. Mauzan's is a world of fairies and brownies; both the Negress and the girl are cartoonlike caricatures. The relation between them is tenuous, and the artist has made this explicit by drawing them according to different scales. The compositional center of the poster lies at the point of eye contact between the two characters, who in reality will never occupy the same space.

The graphic contrast of white and black tells a complete story, bearing the weight of the whole campaign, whose mechanism is none other than the joke, understood in the sense of a Freudian pact between two parties at the expense of a third. Freudian *Witz*, translated into Italian as *motto di spirito*, bears the sense of *spiritoso*. This adjective is related to spirits and sprites, those little trolls and fairies who populate Liberty and art nouveau advertisements, from the little Thermogène figurines of Cappiello to Bibendum, the Michelin tire homunculus (figure 1). The "Torinese" woman is another of these sprites, of which Mauzan made wide use for a variety of products. She belongs to an archaic, nineteenth-century world of jokes shared by bourgeois readers of humor magazines and purchasers of caricatures. By the 1930s, this kind of fairy-tale scene of exchange will no longer be possible, and the Torinese will be subjected to various mutations. But as long as the scene can be played out as pure theater or fantasy, the Negress will keep holding the tottering child on her petal-lap. Only a few years later, some more stable figure — a white man with a rifle, perhaps — will rescue the girl from her precarious place.

La Torinese exhibits a particular quality of epidermal smoothness. Of all the African women encountered by the Italians "down there," it was almost universally agreed that the Somalis were the most desirable, in a sense because their beauty was perceived to be only an exaggeration of whiteness, and not a degenerate opposite of it. As in Brichetti's account, the Somali is the classically voluptuous whore — sensuous like a Jewess(!), soft, and smooth-skinned. In adventurers' prose descriptions, as in advertising, she stands as a figure for illicit sexuality, and her iconographic counterpart, a white male, is missing from the representation in question. His presence, however, is both presumed and necessary for constructing a full reading of the scene.[39] The black female equals sex, quite clearly, but there is something more to be said about the specific type of the smooth (Somali) Negress. What is important for an Italian audience is precisely what she is *not,* namely, a Hottentot Venus type, "pathologically" endowed with steatopygia, or protruding buttocks.[40] Brichetti and his followers in the Italian colonialist adventure had assimilated the racist scientific discourse of the nineteenth century, which tied a "deformity" of the buttocks to a deformity of the genitalia, and thus linked black sexuality in general with disease. In privileging the Somali, they managed to overcome a disgust for the black female, which they displaced onto the black male. But it is a certain type of female they desire, one that represents only a more extreme version of the classic European whore.

The Somali beauty was legendary in Italy, thanks to a propaganda campaign consisting of firsthand, intimate accounts:

> The [Somali female] body is enclosed in an elastic girdle. You no longer think of the rigid armaments of the bones or of curtain rods or of the volume and wriggle of the muscles ... the tiny, steep breasts, planted nicely apart, at the top of the thorax; and as for their stomachs, completely flat. The waist is highly flexible; the hips are solid but swivel nicely; the lower backs are perfectly hollowed; the legs long and rather subtle and gracefully loose, under their tiny knees; the ankles are dry, strengthened like pure metal from the long walks they take following the caravans.[41]

Except for the final line providing ethnographic detail, this might well be a description of a white model walking down the runway during a 1930s fashion show in Turin. Smoothness is the key term, and nowhere is there ever any mention of the buttocks, so central to the nineteenth-century lexicon of female blackness. In fact, the white woman seems to have everything to envy the black. Whites, too, aspire to silkiness, and that is why the stocking has had such an important place in bourgeois female dress. A women's magazine of the thirties explains:

> We must remember that we live in an age in which black beauty has upset white beauty to which we had previously attributed supremacy: blacks have silky skin, not only on their legs, but on their entire body, like a sweater. Just look at Josephine Baker! She is nude, but her nudity is dressed. And since Europeans cannot transform themselves into Antilleans or Senegalese they invented stockings and they show them with pride.... Oh, competition![42]

Essentially, the stocking is the single motif of sexuality that the white woman allows herself, and it is also a synecdoche for the bourgeois aesthetic, which proclaims that a covered body is more sensuous than an uncovered one.

Bourgeois fashion, or the definition of what is seductive, always works along a hierarchical scale; it always implies competition. If the black body can transform itself into a body stocking, this is also to say that it can sexualize itself entirely, from top to bottom, while the white woman is limited to exhibiting herself as a partial and perhaps fetishistic object. In any case, the smiling Negress encodes the proverbial notion that "sex sells," and this goes for both male and female consumers, once we realize her status in the context of the (white) aesthetics of smoothness.

The link between the smiling Negress and the sale of products is neatly made by another brand of chocolates called "Faccetta nera" or "little black face" (figure 11). The seller is pictured as a rather young woman, absolutely black, with an absolutely white grin. She hardly seems seductive, at first glance, but her iconic status can be understood in relation to the popular significance of her name. "Faccetta nera" was a jingle sung by soldiers in Ethiopia as they sailed on the open seas toward battle:

> If from the highlands you glance down toward the sea,
> little black woman, you slave among slaves,
> you will see, as if a dream, so many ships
> and a tricolored flag will wave for you.
> Black face, beautiful Abyssinian,
> wait and hope, for Italy is drawing near;
> and when we are together with you,
> we will give you another law and another king.
> Our law is the slavery of love,
> but freedom to live and think.
> We Blackshirts will vindicate
> the fallen heroes, and we will liberate you.[43]

This chant could be addressed only to the woman, the *faccetta nera* of Ethiopia, because it is through her that the "new" law and the "new" sexual economy will be enacted. The replacement of a "feudal" order with a new system of sexual vassalage (the themes of liberation and binding) make sense only in an environment where white male displaces black male so neatly that the laws themselves are in fact unchanged. The institutional structures will remain intact; only a new group of individuals will come to fill the positions. "Faccetta nera" brand chocolates are complicitous in this scheme of displacement and conquest.

But in 1936, after it became clear that Italy *would* proclaim its empire, the song was banned by Mussolini, and another one, sung to the same tune, rose in its place:

11. "Faccetta nera" chocolates. (Salce Collection, 12077.)

Black face, get away from me,
I want a white woman, made like me.
I am still a soldier and I go to war
to defend all good things,
but in my heart I carry my bride
because black face is not for me.
I love the national product,
a madonna who protects me from evil.[44]

Now the little black face and her chocolates can no longer signal "sex," pure and simple. She contains a complex multiplicity of meanings related to the changes in the Italian national character over time and, more specifically, to the shifting relations with female sexuality. The satisfaction of male desire through the black body is no longer relevant because of the transference of the libido to fascist military glory. As a spokeswoman for a product, the *faccetta nera* has been changed from temptress to a figure of pathos. Her abjection now stems from her neediness, her imploring gaze. But the fascist is too busy fulfilling his final destiny to take notice.

More recently, the smiling Negress has been nostalgized into a sign of Italy's fundamentally nonracist character. The fact that she appeared in popular culture *at all* is taken to mean that Italy's relation with her was a positive one.[45] She is just another symbol of the imposition of racial laws from outside Italy. In fact, the smiling Negress has a long and complex relation with questions of sexuality and with the way in which advertising manipulates or represents desire for a particular audience. In any case, the smiling Negress is not a willing partner in the enterprise of her own representation, so the kind of thinking that reads her smile as "consent" cannot possibly serve as a valid frame for her interpretation.

The "Asiatic" Worker

When the Negress wears a forced smile or a resigned look of automated determination, she becomes a symbol of slave labor. The black worker in an "Asiatic mode" can be male or female, but is always found in a line with at least two other identical bodies.[46] A chain of copies performs a task, usually carrying something from one place to another—water jugs, a canoe, food. The Asiatic worker is ideal for the purposes of graphic design because the concept involves a single prototype, recopied and reduced: a series of automata forming a harmonious pattern. The figures are docile and decorative silhouettes, but there is something troubling about the mechanization with which they are depicted in movement—unmistakably a sign of the perceived abjection of the Asiatic mode of production, and a more general cultural anxiety about automation, slavery, and dictatorship in domestic industrial production. In fact, the early pioneers who traveled to Africa from Italy and either made deals with the individual sultans, or established trading partners there, did not sufficiently reflect on the larger questions of production that would concern an economic theorist. There was clearly an attempt not to focus on this aspect of life, and issues of forced labor were deliberately left dangling or shrouded in vague language. Moreover, slave trading continued throughout the years of the regime, but the Italian generals tended to look the other way.[47] And when it came time for their own large-scale construction projects—the building of a dam, for example—they invented a highly tendentious language that allowed them to make use of a temporary indigenous force ("for public utilities") without compensation. In part, such language is only another example of arrogance in the face of international humanitarian and political bodies that opposed an Italian presence in AOI; but in part, it attests to something perhaps more troubling, a repression of social issues in Italian labor law itself.

Naturally, the identification of the African feudal order with an automata-like barbarity was above all a justification for the exportation of fascist violence. At the very moment Haile Selassie was attempting to form a modern constitution for his country, the minister de Bono reported back to Mussolini that the Ethiopians "are essentially a semibarbaric nation, and for that reason, what they understand best is force."[48] Tribal brutality and infighting provided the moral authorization for war, but the threat of the disappearence of such internal strife was also the motivation for military mobilization. Finally, however, this projection of feudal abjection onto the African body was related to fears about Italian workers, and also served to rationalize violent antiunionism in the industries at home.

If questions of forced labor, feudalism, and despotism trouble certain sectors of the population in Italy, the very ease with which slave labor is translated into a strictly Italian graphic language makes an uncomfortable proximity between colonizer and colonized. In one of Seneca's advertisements for Perugina chocolates, women workers are streamlined to the point of stiffening (figure 6). One can no longer confuse them with the ideal of those seductive, silky-skinned Somalis offering themselves up for the service of Italian soldiers and functionaries. Seneca's "chocolate" women are small steel machines; their breasts are gyrating cogs; their heads are balloons inflated with air pumping from a fan belt; their baskets bearing coconuts have been welded into place, assuring that the carriers will go perpetually back and forth, delivering their cargo with robotic rhythm. In their "natural habitat," these bodies also speak eloquently about the aesthetics of modern industrial production. Two palm trees sketched tentatively in the background to the right of the figures seem a titillating afterthought, for even without them we would, of course, recognize the scene as Africa in all of its vast, yellow emptiness. And there is something menacing about the tiny palms, because in spite of the very direct iconicity in the association of Africa with chocolates, Perugina-Buitoni is one of the largest firms in Italy, a powerful producer of two central products in the regime's autarchy campaigns: alimentary paste and chocolate, turned out in the factories of northern Italy, the locus of the machines themselves.[49]

There is a specific geographic–ideologic relation, then, between those iconic palms and the feudal laborer. Sometimes it seems that the only traces left in Italy of the imperialist legacy are the palms. One sees them in the North, jutting up from the front yard of a bourgeois villa, where they have been transplanted from somewhere else and inscribed as a sign of Mediterraneanism. In the late nineteenth century, while the military kept up attempts to penetrate the continent through Ethiopia from the Red Sea, the Italian parliament wistfully dreamed of a Mediterranean conquest — the dream of centuries, the revival of the Roman Empire — and East Africa seemed like a second-rate compromise. The popular imagination was not captured by Africa, and instead, the phrase of one dismayed observer seemed to confirm the lack of interest: "A slip of deserted coast, two palm trees, a couple of ostriches and 160 'subjects.'"[50] Are these two palms of desolation the palms of Seneca's Perugina ad?

An impressive group of palms line the square in Sabaudia, once a fascist retreat built on reclaimed land, now a fashionable seaside resort where television stars sun topless. The trees form a lovely shaded park, but the perfect geometry of the landscaping gives it all away — the myth of indigenous palms. And so the palms in Seneca's advertisement, which seem to be casually drawn in to fill up space in the composition, are really the iconic key to reading the whole image. The ad informs its readers: You have your empire; you have feudal subjects; and you have a modernized, industrial base in northern Italy. You have a bourgeois class in the North that is the hidden basis of fascism, and you have workers and machines that are subjected to that class. The palms behind the Perugina women are the clear signs of the relations between the geopolitical poles of North and South, which cannot be pronounced loudly; instead, they arouse a mild sense of pleasure in the consumer, linking the brand name of Perugina with a vague sense of power, alterity, exoticism.

While the mechanized slaves of advertising culture are clearly abject in one sense, they also represent a certain order, a highly aesthetic and graphic scene of nobility, as opposed to the decadence of the black body when it is left "loose," left to collapse in the liberal-democratic state. The American black, for example, lacks any of the upright dignity or geometrical clarity of the Asiatic worker. When free to wander, he falls into the hands of other undisciplined types such as the Jew (figure 8). The fear of decline and the desire for order may explain why so many advertisements for insurance companies make use of the black body.[51]

As an invention of the modern state, insurance is for something tangible, but ultimately it is for class affiliation, and, as in a "give-away" watercolor for a mortgage company, the "pretty picture" (you can hang it up in the kitchen) implies that a careful plan combining savings and borrowing — investment in a piece of domestic property — also *insures* the continuation of the feudal order of the empire (figure 12). The scene is superficially pretty, but its message is nothing short of insidious: invest at home and your place (as white) in the global economy is assured. The fascist, dressed in colonial khakis, stares into the sun. His pose, with head thrown back, shoulders open, chest forward, will become emblematic during the period for a new kind of optimism about the future that Boccasile prophetically represented in 1930. The Asiatic workers in this insurance picture are carrying *fasci,* or bundles of grain, the symbol of the regime itself. Six years before the conquest of the empire, this advertisement speaks to the heart of the matter: the regime guarantees your home loan, your place, your colony, and your race, just as the palms lurking behind Seneca's workers guarantee the continuation of the subjection of the South (or the land "down there").

In images like Seneca's chocolate workers, the figure of the Asiatic despot himself is effaced. The workers labor under his gaze, and, in a sense, they reflect it; they define its shape, as Lacan might say. The despot, the gaze (the Lacanian *petit a*), surrounds and shames the workers, but it has no particular identity. There is no iconography of the despot to which we can refer in a study like the present one. In part this can be explained by the fact that Italy was an observer of the mode of production, but was never quite able to take the place of the gaze, or to become it, in more concrete terms. The inability of the Italian state to become the Ethiopian state, for example, was related to the perpetual military dimension in the fascist conception of government. Mussolini and his generals insisted that there was

12. "Insurance" by subjugation. (Salce Collection, 03082.)

no national consciousness among the colonized subjects. They recognized only fragmentation, tribal economies, individuals who would turn against one another; and when Britain raised the theme of nationalism during the thirties, Italy declared this a mere "fetish."[52] But as long as he deferred the possibility of nation status for the colonies, Mussolini could never become the Despot, ordering "Asiatic" production.

The Silent Arab

Unlike the "difficult" Ethiopian, the Arab seems somehow more docile, and he always appears either under long flowing robes or veiled (figure 13). He walks with a certain dignity that distinguishes him quite clearly from the subjugated "Asiatic" type. He never grins like the Moor, but bears a solemn expression of one who has seen much and has accepted his colonizers, his destiny. I have found him in the usual colonial advertisements, but also more commonly selling the Lottery of Tripoli or various gasoline and oil products, probably because, among other things, Libya had practicable roads in place. The question of penetration into the hinterland of East Africa was a very touchy subject for both military and political leaders beginning around the turn of the century and leading up to the conquest of Ethiopia. Only after 1936 could transportation-related items be marketed comfortably to the Italian public under the general rubric of imperial product.[53] But Tripoli was safer and more knowable because Italy's experience of colonization there was vastly more "civilized" than in AOI. Racial propaganda and fascist science portrayed the Libyans as further evolved (possibly because they were farther north, in the Mediterranean basin) than blacks of East Africa. The prefascist victory had been won along the consoling coast, and a long-standing cultural tradition construed the sea approach — the reversal of the movement of Italy's founder father, Aeneas — as manifest destiny. In the nineteenth century, in a famous speech before the Italian Geographical Society, one early colonizer expressed what would later become a cultural cliché:

> Africa attracts us invincibly. It is our predestination. For so many centuries we have looked toward this blank page, this mysterious horizon that closes up the semibarbarous space of the Mediterranean, which forces Italy to exist at the edge of the civilized world ... Africa, always Africa! ... We have looked toward it, but until now it has been out of reach.[54]

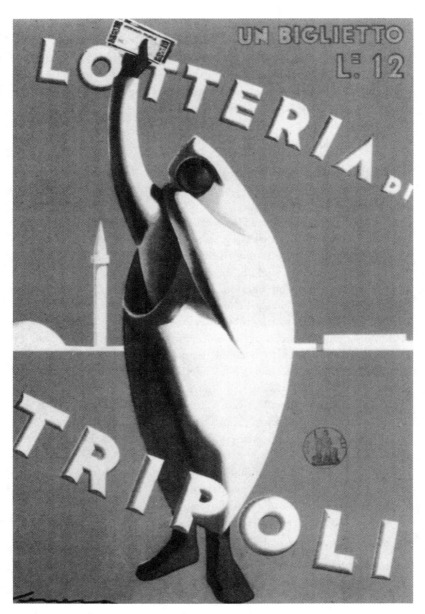

13. Veiled Arab by Seneca. (Salce Collection, 08507.)

As I suggested in the beginning of this chapter, the inevitability and attraction of colonization were not diffused in the culture until decades later, but what the Society members understood from the speech was essentially a question of space and closure. Conquest of Libya would represent above all the formation of a circle, a cradle for the sea whose very color served as the sign of Italy's land (Italy's national color *azzurro,* the blue-green of the Mediterranean).

Aside from these cultural and geographical myths that play strongly on the imagination, there are strictly tactical reasons for the association of the Arab body with the strength of the closed, circular matrix. The Libyan conquest was accomplished during the Giolittian, parliamentary era, which saw a tremendous increase in industrial capital and the creation of a mass proletariat in northern Italy. Giolitti himself was a product of the liberal-democratic state, interested in economic progress above all. The traditional historiography makes him a rather unwilling, or at best passive, partner in the Libyan war. Giolitti declared war to pacify a rising nationalism on the part of conservatives and syndicalists, but, at the same time, he declared universal suffrage in Italy to pacify the socialists. His duplicitous political maneuvers and lack of mystifying rhetoric distinguish the earlier war from the one in the 1930s. Italy seems to glide into Libya without the propaganda campaign to build up the enemy, rendered unnecessary because of the "inherent" logic of capitalism itself.

One of those young socialists who opposed the Libyan conquest was Benito Mussolini, and when he came to power, his attitude toward the North African territory was much more liberal than his attitude toward AOI. He tolerated the Muslim religion, and Libyans had special status as Italian citizens within their own country. The lack of any real propaganda campaign against them is one historical explanation for the iconography of the silent Arab. Even more important is the fact that colonization of a Muslim country allowed Italians to construe their activities as a latter-day crusade supported by historical precedents and a sense of spiritual inevitability and destiny. Because of this cultural contextualization, and because of the longer-term presence of Italy in Libya, the Arab body attained a certain degree of familiarity among the broader public. The utter blackness of sub-Saharan Africa — the Africa of fascist Italy — never aroused the same sense of comfort and domesticity.

The body hidden under robes and veils is not the same kind of threat as the exposed skin of negroid blackness. In addition, although the exoticism of the (unattainable) Arab female is certainly attractive, she never emerges from the advertising as a sexualized type like the smiling Negress, the *faccetta nera*. She remains respected and hidden from view, and in this sense she does not pose an overt threat to the structures of the Italian nuclear family. In fact, the head-to-toe veil of the Arab woman could be considered as a form of defiance, a rejection of (male) scopic desire that has been considered the dominant paradigm of all vision (particularly in advertising culture) in the West. Writing not about the manipulations of graphic design, but about the "objective" camera lens, the art critic Malek Alloula has maintained that

> the whiteness of the veil becomes the symbolic equivalent of blindness; a leukoma, a white speck on the eye of the photographer and on his viewfinder. Whiteness is the absence of a photo, a veiled photograph.[55]

In theorizing the *actual* encounter between photographer and photographed subject, Alloula finds that the colonized Algerian women who stared out from under their veils mimic the eye at the viewfinder and subvert the project of "cataloging" the sexual attributes of the East. Of course, the photographer, like the graphic designer, felt empowered to strip models of their veils and to photograph them in more precisely "Western terms" under the protective aegis of what Alloula calls the "ethnographic alibi." But the silent Arab was often represented in the 1930s outside of considerations of gender and sexuality, almost as if the Italian designers hoped to maintain a category that would be pure, uncontaminated by desire itself. Ultimately, of course, such boundaries cannot stand.

The Moretto

The little Moor is an impish, docile figurine with a large white smile and some form of exotic dress, often a grass skirt or an effeminizing pantaloon. He appears in the usual advertisements for coffee, chocolate, and bananas. Boccasile made frequent use of him in ads for Ettore Moretti, a manufacturer of waterproof fabrics, raincoats, and other resistant materials (figure 14). In developing the ad campaign, the urge to pun on the industrialist's last name (Moretti = little Moors) was irresistible, and so what seems like an absolutely logical link was made between blackness and these products, made to serve the regime in its colonialist enterprise. In other words, the importance of marketing the raincoat or waterproof tent as a specifically imperialist product, resistant against the threats of blackness and the unpre-

14. Ettore Moretti tents.

dictable and savage weather of East Africa, seems to be imperative in the ads. Obviously, however, there could be many other ways to market these products in a purely domestic, middle-class context. Nevertheless, Boccasile's little Moor became an indelible mark for Ettore Moretti, a play on words and a visual pun, with all the pleasure that can be expected to accompany such mechanisms in mass culture.

Sometimes the joke of the little Moor resides entirely in his utter feminization (figure 15). He wears an earring and lipstick, and he looks suggestively at the viewer out from under the dangling cord of his fez. He parts his lips suggestively, calling the consumer to take him and the product, too, both irresistible in the context of the politics of expansionism, but both, ultimately, wearing their dependency and their pathos like a mask. What kind of a document is this? In Africa, clearly, the Italians found solace in *female* blackness, and the general public was sympathetic, given that so few white women ventured there until the late 1930s. An article in the magazine *Lei* even laughs it off: men will be men, and in point of fact, by taking on these "short-term wives" they actually perform an invaluable civilizing mission. The black women will return to their "tribes" and help temper the savagery of their "real" husbands. One can easily comprehend how the ideal "female masochist" would not only tolerate, but even promote,

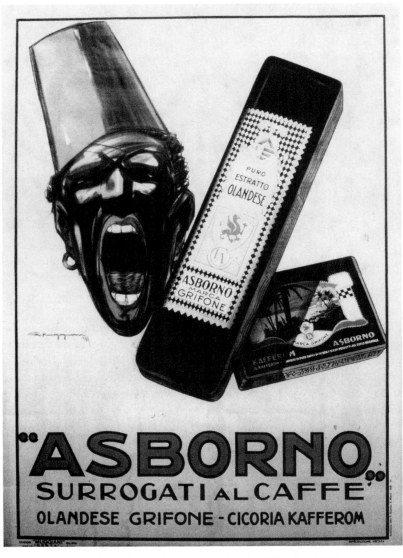

15. Feminized Moor figure from coffee surrogate ad. (Salce Collection, 04668.)

relations between white and black in such a context. But in this discourse of tolerance the existence of male prostitutes, the *messieurs* who must have had their place in the village along with the "civilizing" *madames,* goes unremarked. And since there can be nothing more humiliating than the degraded, effeminate Moor, why put him in an advertisement meant to associate positive and healthy sentiments with a product?

The Moor who gives himself up — not just to the viewer, but to his own soft inner core, to his sickening femininity — represents a figure of no resistance. During the 1930s, as Mussolini and his ministers moved toward total war and then toward the inevitable coexistence of colonial occupation, this kind of figure offered a tacit but reassuring sense that, ultimately, the Africans could not help themselves. There was a growing hope that they would melt before fascist force and serve with docility, precisely because this was perceived to be their nature. Of course, this notion really contradicts another ethnographic discourse asserting the barbarity, the cruelty, and the frenetic aggression of the natives that was widely diffused in Italy at the same time through periodicals, photographic essays, newspapers, and other popular forms. As the decade progressed and the nation had to face up to an imperialist status for which it was extraordinarily ill prepared, the little Moor, sometimes no more than a young child with a sparkling gold earring, peered out from advertisements, winking and acknowledging his own weakness in an invitation to take the product (coffee, investment in a savings account, and so on) in exchange for the utter submission of the colonial subject.

At the time of this writing, it still is quite normal to find "Moretto" candies for sale in Italy, and they have not been censured by any voices of "political correctness" as one might imagine would be the case in the United States, for example. Whatever the effect of removing the cellophane wrapper and spreading out the highly articulated graphic image of the Moor's head, he is associated with childhood, with sweets, and he is consumed within the context of the *pasticceria,* an institution found in every Italian town, no matter how small. The pasticceria is open on Sunday morning, while every other place of business except the newspaper stand keeps its shutters barred. One may dip into bins of brightly colored candies sold in bulk, a glittering treat to bring when one is invited for a lunch date. And here is where the Moor ends up, the brown skin and white teeth mixed in a bottomless pit of sticky confections and compensatory treats.

The Black Baby

A variation on the little Moor, the black baby is a smiling, bouncing, fleshy little ball. He stands for the future: not his, but that of the new Italian order. He appeared in a great deal of regime propaganda specifically created for children — on notebooks, postcards, board games, and in other popular forms. On one hand, the black baby attests to the importance the regime placed on the consensus of children in the colonialist enterprise. If fascist youth would stand up and salute the "rescue" of the black baby, it would be much more difficult for parents to express "antiquated" liberal oppositions to the war. On the other hand, the black baby circulated in forms specifically addressed to adults. He loses his gaminlike status and enters yet another position of abjection. Quite a number of representations of Haile Selassie came in this cartoonish, "infantilized," caricatured form. His cheeks are slightly puffed out, his body shortened, and his eyes enlarged, but he still retains recognizable, adult features.

The black baby is found riding on a blunt instrument formed by the letters INA (an abbreviation for the state insurance agency), his earring gleaming as he stares into the sun (figure 16). The text reads: "INA will grant you a 5 percent, 15-year national loan for life insurance. It is your duty ... And it's in your *interest*" (emphasis added to highlight a play on words in Italian, as in English). The INA logo cuts apart the chains that bind the white farmer in the background. The baby, turned toward the sun, is the key to the economics of personal security. In a similar advertisement for a savings bank in Treviso, a white baby shows a black baby how to put coins in a piggy bank (figure 17). Patriarchal tutelage starts young. The ad includes the motto: "And my well-being lies in savings" ("E nel risparmio è il mio benessere"). The "I" of the utterance is clearly the young Balilla, who holds open a book (perhaps a manual) for the black boy. Ironically, the black is shirtless, wearing only a striped and "exotic" loincloth and a Balilla tie around his throat. Although he smiles as he prepares to let the coin drop into the gaping mouth of the fascist bank, a rifle points directly at him, posed on an open book. Savings, then, is part of a larger routine that may include teaching the indigenous boy to read, threatening him with a rifle, and dressing him up in the costume of a fascist youth. The equation makes sense in the context of regime propaganda, but why, and how, should children be asked to hold up this immense responsibility?

One thing to note is that in this particular iconographic type, the little baby is always separated from his family or any fixed national or institutional

16. Insurance baby. (Salce Collection, 18822.)

17. Children play out race relations in Treviso savings bank ad. (Salce Collection, 13202.)

identity. He is alone on the INA bulwark. He bows before a white baby just around his age, perhaps surrounded by a few other little Moorish play-mates. He sits in various ads abandoned by his mother and father who have gone off to work in the nearby fields or factory. In general, apart from race, there is something menacing about the image of a baby left alone, disjointed from the nest of home, from the nexus of family relations that the regime sought so intently to regulate on Italian soil. As a symbol of "futurity" the lone baby signifies the eventual absence of the parents, themselves the readers of the image. In other words, he figures their very disappearance, as he sells the abstract commodity of continuation, security, and stability. He stands for the (newly acquired) sense of inevitable economic progress in which each generation is expected to surpass the one before it. The baby always represents a sacrifice in ads of the 1930s, something given up in the service of the ideal of a fascist future. But at the same time, the black baby in particular threatens through his potential dependency, his lack of a family matrix. Will the Italian motherland be forced into raising it along with her own offspring? Must she give her breast to nourish this mischievous pickaninny, in an ironic role reversal with the indigenous wet nurse? In spite of pacifying words such as "insurance," "interest," and "capital appreciation," the black baby menaces a viewer. He serves as a cuddly reduction of the black male, another example of his deflation for the Italian public. But he also raises a troubling series of questions about patronage, responsibility, and government that remained unresolved before, during, and after Italy's "moment in the sun."

The various body types detailed here all suggest a series of contradictions centered on the question of distance. The native should be, above all, marked as different from white, so that he or she can remain absolutely inferior. This was Mussolini's explicit desire, and it is sustained within various representational codes. Nevertheless, it is a documentable, objective fact that white males in Africa were inevitably, almost fatally, drawn to black females. Once the gap had been breached, fascist disgust at this contact with the abject seems to break through the surface of the images in uncanny flashes. "Madamism," a term imported into Italian from the French colonial experience, produced its share of mulatto children as the irrefutable signs of contact. And if ocular testimony found these children to be attractive and healthy, miscegenation was twisted around in regime propaganda until it became synonymous with incest. Both miscegenation and incest, coded as simultaneously "black" and "Jewish," were incorporated into a discourse of physical and mental degeneration. And although official racial language states that erosion is unidirectional (it cannot reverse its course and act upon the Aryan), there is clearly a fear in Italy about protecting the boundaries of the state/body.

To stem the tide of (nomadic) degeneration, Italian culture of the 1930s included many representations of the positive, "civilizing" benefits for blacks of their contact with whites, even to the point that their bodies could be transformed and whitened. Nevertheless, by law such contact was strictly taboo; a constant motif of ethnographic and pseudoscientific writing was the possibility that whites might be dragged down by their "civilizing" mission and wallow forever at the level of the putrid swarm, never finding the spring of Marinetti's trampoline. The cracks in the wall of segregation cannot be explained by the liberal antislavery lobby of the turn of the century, or with the Catholic missionary's benevolent, paternalistic hand-holding. Instead, these moments of contact attest to a magnetic pull exerted on both sides. There is no question that the images seen here both struggle to be complicitous in the creation of an ideal distance, and reveal the contradictions, the slippage, between black and white. Ultimately, the absolute, Manichaean categories of fascist ideology do not hold.

Marinetti's abhorrent descriptions of a black orgy in *Mafarka* reveal a central preoccupation with the question of boundaries and separation long before the reality of imperial Italy. Hundreds of delirious Arab soldiers swarm around in a putrid green pool. They breathe each other's odors until there is no distinction between one body and the next. Mafarka must use his sword to separate two generals fighting because their bodies seem to flow into each other. On a cover of *La difesa della razza*, a sword separates the black and Jew from the Roman (figure 18). A clean cut is essential to be rid of flowing, boundaryless forces of attraction that are coded as "feminine," "oriental," "communist," and perhaps "nomadic" threats to the (Oedipalized) male ego.[56] The very facility with which the abject (masturbation, incest, sterility) can be transferred to the ethos of blackness attests to this permeability between the two sides. In fact, after the time frame that is the subject of this study, in the early 1940s, one would most certainly be able to document an increasing cultural anxiety about how to separate (and of course, since this is fascism, to bind) black and white.

For the 1940 Triennale exhibit in Milan, a display called *Colonial Equipment* was mounted. The Triennale was primarily a showcase for the products of national "ingenuity," grouped under a variety of themes and displayed in pavilions. The principal architect of the colonial exhibit, Carlo Rava, explained that his purpose was not to introduce ethnographic details to the public or to arouse a "colonial consciousness" (the fascist project of the early 1930s), but to solicit designs for furniture and other practical tools to be used by Italian families and military personnel in Africa. The exhibit specifically avoided anything like a folkloric appreciation of local culture; it focused instead on the application of European, functionalist, high-design

18. Knife cutting Aryan Italian from degenerate others. (Reproduced from cover of *La difesa della razza*, September 5, 1938.)

style aesthetics to items such as foldable beds, plastic stowable dishware, and compartmentalized and resistant suitcases for strapping on a camel's back. The problem posed by Rava did not primarily address military or tactical needs, but rather "how to maintain the dignity and culture" of the Italian way of life in a primarily "barbaric setting." Solutions were seen to lie in "the coexistence of an elaborate modernity with an acute understanding of the needs related to the climate and latitude."[57]

Rava's project description makes ample use of the dreaded word "modernity"—once a key term in critical language for its putative relation with Judaism and an international aesthetic conspiracy against geometrical forms. For the colonial exhibit, "modernity" was retooled in the context of a Morrisonian International Style, but also specifically tied to national ingenuity. The "equipment" displayed was all easily movable ("*di movimento,*" Rava says)—an indication that Italian presence in Africa was still unstable and insecure. The exhibit, with its "solutions" to the "problem" of preserving "culture," is, in fact, extremely uncanny. Although the designers involved in the project could have created something like a hut environment to display their furnishings, they chose to leave the pavilion structure intact, but to break up the space with screens and low divider walls. The effect is highly orientalizing, something like a faux Japanese interior, rendered in calming, *noton* tones (figure 19). Scattered about the rooms are a few potted palms,

19. Triennale colonial decor. (Courtesy of the Triennale Archive, Milan.)

suggestive of a tropical milieu. The modernist, oriental minimalism of the Triennale set is momentarily confusing, for it looks like nothing that a public might associate with the Dark Continent or with the black body. The exhibit does not invite the spectator to enter: the space is cold and forbidding, and resounds with an eerie emptiness.

But even before the postconquest period captured in the purity of Rava's "African" house, the black body becomes banalized like wallpaper; and Italy already had witnessed the translation of an atrocious war into high-bourgeois style in Boccasile's 1936 advertisement for Ramazzotti bitter aperitif (figure 20). A white woman in the foreground in a stylized version of colonialist khaki and safari helmet stares off into the sun, as a female Moor figure stands in the background holding a serving tray. The putative link

20. Boccasile's transvestite drama. (Salce Collection, 03097.)

between the product (an extremely well known bitter, here advertised as particularly thirst quenching when mixed with club soda) and the scene of power relations might seem arbitrary. Ramazzotti had been sold, after all, in an extremely varied series of campaigns and had been connected with the widest imaginable variety of images. The only fixed element in the company's advertising history is the foregrounding of the bottle itself, whose label is unchanged to this day. The decision to sell the product through the juxtaposition of a haughty sun-drenched white body with a servile Moor amounts to this: the victory in Ethiopia was the most significant event for a whole generation of Italians who had come of age during fascism. Very simply, the equation of leisure time—the woman is enjoying a vacation in the sun, the drink is a late-afternoon luxury—with the pleasure of colonial domination now seems almost inevitable.

The scene is pure fantasy: the white woman will no more find herself in Africa than the smiling Negress in black tie and bare breasts will find herself in Italy, first serving aperitifs in an open-air café, then putting on a pressed uniform for the first time and working her way up from barmaid to petty bourgeois consumer, all the while sincerely intent on bettering herself and assimilating into the middle class. This is, quite simply, not an Italian narrative. The foregrounding of the bottle of seltzer is ironic, since the spritz action of the tap is associated in some advertising with masculinity itself, with the kind of primitive power of micturition that put out the fires in psychoanalytic legend. The transvestite drama not only reconfirms the strict regulation of gender roles (because femininity is displaced only for a moment, and in a highly theatrical way), it also draws racial boundaries as sharp as the silhouettes of the graphic forms themselves. Only because the two figures are so utterly separated in reality can Boccasile permit himself this fantasy proximity in an advertisement that equates "taste" with whiteness, above all.

The illusion of the ad is the same one that sustains the link between the clever foldable beds and ingenious little multitiered sideboards with the harsh life of the colonizers, or the continuation of guerrilla warfare in AOI long after the "declaration of fascist peace." (The Triennale design "solutions" actually end up on the terraces and in the gardens of the Italian bourgeoisie: sleek, stylized lawn furniture filling the pages of home and decorating magazines beginning in the late 1930s.)[58] In the images of the colonial exhibit, we witness the start of a slippage from the colony as foreign dominion to the colony as domestic space reserved for leisure.

Legacies of Blackness

Ultimately, Boccasile's serving Moor is also a fantasy that displaces another class reality: the subordination of southern Italians (called "blacks" or "Moroccans" in slang, even to the present) to northerners.[59] The regime may have managed to suspend temporarily the southern question by pointing its magic wand elsewhere and casting a spell of national, racial identity over Italy, but it was inevitable that the wounds would be reopened. With the loss of the colonialist euphoria, especially during the postwar years, reconstructionists had to deal with the havoc wrought on the Italian countryside by the regime and its lack of any coherent policy. In fact, during the "boom" years of the fifties, it was the southern Italian peasant "black" who would come north and serve the powerful elite. In its fascination with the black body in all of the various incarnations I have discussed here, the regime managed to move the gaze of the public "down there"—beyond the failed land reclamation programs in Sicily, beyond the impoverished feudalistic villages of Calabria—to Africa. But the southern question is by no means resolved even today. The various northern leagues that have enjoyed stunning political victories in recent elections, with their platforms of separatism, racism, and of plugging the drainage of government funds to aid programs for the South, have helped bring the gaze back to Italy itself.

The question is, what has happened to blackness in the meantime? Would an image such as Boccasile's staged power play still work in the context of the postcolonialist market? Or is it inevitably linked with the historical moment of colonization?

If the reduced, servile bodies of the 1930s now strike the eye as "kitschy" or provoke a slight sense of embarrassment, perhaps it is because they have generally been replaced with more "European" black bodies in mass culture—bodies dressed up in Benetton, in youthful Bata sneakers, or even in high fashion. The only traces left of Africa are the colorful ribbons or vaguely "tribal" jewelry that is, in any case, assimilated into the fashion vocabulary of the West. Blackness has been co-opted by a new youth-oriented target for which "being in fashion" also means having some relation (but is it a truly serious one?) with issues of world peace, the environment, and multiculturalism (figure 21).

This is the thrust of the "United Colors of Benetton" campaign with its obsessive insistence on the "one of every color" variety. Ironically, of course, this multicoloration of the advertisements is really a reference to

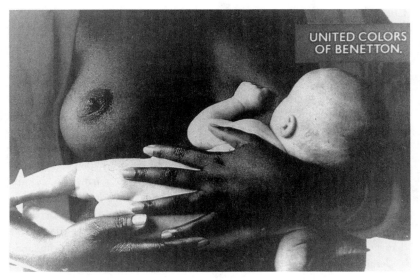

21. United Colors of Benetton nursing black mother.

the mix-and-match stock of colors available for the consumer of clothing. In its elegant store displays, Benetton offers a limited number of patterns or shapes, but a large array of dyes during a given season. The eye is attracted to the stacked sweaters in a store window. Items are exhibited strategically to persuade the consumer into buying an ensemble — a series of shaded layers, a bright clash of scarf over vest. In this context, blackness is only one of a whole series of colors. But this proposed all-inclusiveness masks the single most significant binary opposition of colored/white and empowered/subordinated on which the real economy of the international clothing and textile industries is based.[60] The positive, youthful association of the Benetton name with a new world order of global unity is also another way of forgetting the colonialist legacy and, by association, the very mechanisms of power forged under the regime, which still persist at some level in contemporary Italy.

This is not the place to discuss current forms of racism in Italy. Complex indeed are the problems associated with the unification of the European Community; immigration quotas; the public deficit; favoritism and parasitism; the "blackness" of the Mafia and Sicily. Local officials debate municipal laws against African street peddlers, or "*vu comprà*" (a shortening of "*vuoi comprare?*" — "Do you want to buy?" which the vendors of lighters, batteries, plastic toys, sculpted camel caravans, and other merchandise seem to yell to passersby). Just as the market in the 1930s, marching inevitably toward maturity, helped in the process of arousing a "colonial interest or will," so the market today helps to efface the traces of this passionate moment in Italian public consensus. Perhaps, finally, the strongest factor linking the earlier graphic forms with more current mass-cultural ones is precisely the black–white distinction as a mechanism for displacing a disturbing discourse about class in Italy. Boccasile's serving Moor and haughty woman in safari garb hardly make sense today, or at best they have achieved the status of kitsch inasmuch as their bodies are posed as part of a theatrical piece whose very narrative structure resounds with "nostalgia" and a sense of "otherness" or "pastness." These bodies exhibit the flavor of old memorabilia, which always convey a vague sense of pleasure, but are not linked to any historical atrocity. Finally, then, the representational codes of blackness derive from a critical historical moment in Italy; but perhaps because they do not "read" immediately or primarily as objects of fascist culture, they have not been examined with the appropriate degree of seriousness. In the next chapter I treat bodies that often are quite recognizable as "fascist bodies"; as such, they may be more comfortably considered as "horrific" documents of an ignoble past.

3 / The Fascist Body as Producer and Consumer

Toward a Theory of the Fascist Body

In the previous chapter I focused on how representations of blackness helped shape national identity in Italy. In shifting now to the white body I will raise questions of how categories of class and gender contaminate the "Italian" body of fascism. The mid-1930s, the period of the Ethiopian campaigns, marked a fundamental change in the intensity and direction of control exercised by the regime over public discourses, including advertising. As advertisers became more sophisticated, more "rationalized," and more powerful, the regime kept a closer watch over the kinds of images and texts that dominated the urban landscape; print culture; public transportation; and various other spaces. But this extensive regulation did not result in an out-and-out conflict between private enterprise and public consensus. On the contrary, the urban advertisers, particularly those working in Milan and Turin, collaborated with explicit economic and social programs of the regime hierarchy based in Rome. As I have insisted all along, the modernization of mass media in Italy is inextricably bound up with its very fascistization. The general aims of "publicity" cannot be separated from two significant, larger goals of fascism: to create a classless consumer who would inevitably identify his or her needs with a national economy rather than with a particular class-based commodity culture, and to create a rationalized (working-class) producer.

In this chapter I explore how this "new man" is constructed within advertising, and how his body is a locus for either incorporating or resisting strategies of control. A fundamental question concerns the representation of consumption and production in graphic design. On a purely stylistic level, one may ask how it is possible to translate something like a repetitive action or a kinetic, biochemical transformation into a necessarily static language. And this is to say nothing of the question of the aestheticization of complex economic factors such as the labor theory of value that are central to an understanding of "rationalization."[1] My aim in this chapter is to provide a context in which to view bodies under different conditions of labor and repose. In fact, the very techniques and shortcuts used by artists prove quite revelatory when attempting to interpret the limits of fascist control.

Since, in part, the bodies in this chapter may be seen as oppressed, as literally pressed down by the weight of the pact between the state and capitalism, it seems important to stress that the economic history of Italy under fascism can only be studied in relation to the global depression that marks the decade of the 1930s. In Italy, the crash of the American stock market on Black Tuesday was experienced in a continuity with a recession brought about in the wake of Mussolini's 1926–1927 efforts to stabilize the lira. By 1935, the regime could boast of increased production in certain sectors, but the depression also saw higher unemployment, a lowering of real wages, a diminution of work hours, and a decrease in quality of life. Fascism itself, in other words, is not a cause of these trends, any more than its vast bureaucratization of various aspects of social and work life was unique: all the developed nations found new forms of intervention in production necessary during this period. Construed in this key, fascism *is* modernization; it represents motion forward along a global continuum rather than an aberrant, ideologic regression. But in order to survive under the new rules developed between the two world wars, Italy obsessively directed energy toward its own so-called autarchic position in the global economy through a campaign that specifically effaced the international crisis. Thus, producing and consuming bodies represent themselves as specific to an Italian national context even though the graphic design styles may derive from an international, modernist one. The viewer should remain skeptical of the exclusive nationalist paranoia implied in the Italian autarchy campaigns. If Italian bodies are subject to oppression, one must guard against the temptation to regard this oppression as a global conspiracy against the regime, a theme embedded in fascist rhetoric.

Leafing through any number of volumes of poster art from the turn of the century through the 1930s, one notices that labor, per se, was almost never represented as part of any kind of advertising strategy. Only occasionally does one get a glimpse of the machinery or handwork that lies behind the making of products; distribution, the third term (along with production and consumption) in traditional economic exchange, is simply never represented. It seems that both production and distribution are often elided precisely because of the graphic, enticing nature of posters as an art form. Products are represented in a highly tangible way, lined up for immediate consumption; they could almost be plucked from the wall as if from a store shelf.[2] The poster is often utilized as a point-of-sale display, rendering the product in full color and detail, in all of its sensuality, available on demand, with no spatial or temporal division between the moments of beholding and holding the merchandise. In this sense, the modern poster renders production and distribution obsolete, functionless. It is not the case that fascism insidiously attempts to obliterate a preexisting visual language of production. In short, that language has never been part of the visual rhetoric of persuasion associated with bourgeois consumer goods.

As the cultural critic Judith Williamson points out, advertising often functions by hailing or, in Althusser's terms, interpellating a subject as part of a group structure. But that group is rarely allied with an actual social class or with shared labor practices. Instead, group identity is constructed around "totemic" signifiers bearing no logical reference to any existing social condition. Advertising, then, amounts to a form of false consciousness:

> Advertisements obscure and avoid the real issues of society, those relating to work: to jobs and wages and who works for whom. They create systems of social differentiation which are a veneer on the basic class structure of our society. Advertising refers only to consumption, to a sort of a perennial leisure time.... It emphasizes what you buy, which in fact means you have to work harder to earn the money to buy.... you do not simply buy the product in order to become a part of the group it represents; you must feel that you already naturally belong to that group therefore you will buy it.[3]

If on one hand, production is elided from a visual vocabulary, on the other hand, in fascism *consumption* becomes the object of obsessive probing.

The body—along with all its processes of incorporation, adornment, and acquisition—forms an intrinsic part of the so-called totemic equation within which individuals recognize themselves as subjects. But here I insert a note of caution, suggesting, along with Deleuze and Guattari, that even this focus on consumption is a chimera, because for the authors of *Anti-Oedipus,* "Everything is production."[4]

One real danger of fascism, from the liberal-humanist perspective, lies in the state appropriation of consumption through its own apparatuses. The pretense to study consumption by itself, as in a wide variety of fascist discourses, and then to use the knowledge "gained" to help individuals lead a better life, is riddled from the start with contradictions. In propaganda (and also in advertising of the "free" market), the regime tried to make something "natural" and universal out of consumption. By disseminating information in a variety of campaigns, brochures, scientific bulletins, handbooks for fascist youth organizations, and even school textbooks, fascism tried to pass itself off as a maternal entity, taking over the functions that previously had been assigned to a logic of "old wives' tales" and domestic common sense.

But one of the persistent themes raised by studies of fascist institutions and organizations is that in assuming the role of "domestic economist," the regime actually risked emphasizing, rather than glossing over, class differences. In her *The Culture of Consent,* Victoria de Grazia insists on this contradiction within, for example, the development of the Opera Nazionale del Dopolavoro (OND, the national network of fascist "after work" organizations).[5] As an antidote to potential class consciousness, the regime specifically pursued the creation of a mass consumer market with particularly nationalist overtones. Products such as the radio were marketed to appeal to this classless consumer-patriot. So what had been an element of the leisure culture of the bourgeoisie that saw itself as "European" and sophisticated was now a form of state-sponsored coercion (I will say more about this in chapter 4). The idea of such a revision was not to create conspicuous consumers who would expend vast amounts of energy or capital on consumption and have nothing left over for production, but to promote the "modest" accumulation of "durable" domestic products that might in turn reinforce the "cult of the home." A thrifty housewife was the model citizen, and women were particularly subject to restrictions on the consumption end of the economic equation. While negating the female's place in the national scheme of production, manufacturers began to realize that women were in practice often responsible for making decisions about consumption. The advertising strategies of the corporate culture assume that the model of "consent" dominant in fascist theory works unproblematically in the reception of images, but as I have suggested, this logic precludes unconscious mechanisms of reading and viewing.

I would like to add a cautionary note here about the dangers of presuming this control over consumption as a necessarily evil force imposed on innocent (female) consumers from the regime hierarchy. Indeed, the female target might be imagined to *revel* in the address of a discourse of thriftiness. Perhaps her experiences as a good fascist are enhanced by the attention paid to her economizing desires. It would be a mistake to explain away the fascist savings campaign as a form of "female masochism," pleasure through a deferral of the attainment of capital goods.[6] As I suggest later in a discussion of representations of "savings," home economics is also a way for women to exercise their own control, even if this sense is ultimately illusory, a kind of false consciousness of the mechanisms of capitalism. In a larger framework, the bodies in this chapter represent compromises, or forms of adaptation, to various institutions and ideologies of the regime.

Now I would like to pose an obvious and perhaps banal question: What does a fascist look like? Does he stand rigidly behind a factory, his gaze focused and intense, his youthful body trim like a Roman statue, his muscular arm outstretched, forming the fascist salute and the gesture of autarchic supremacy? Or does she sit in a wheat field, fertilizing the land, her plump bosom bursting from her shirt, her cheeks reddened by hard work and exposure to the elements? Both the resistant, "phallic" body and the bosomy peasant-mother belong to a traditional iconography of fascism. But what is the relation between these two images and the lived reality of consumption and production—the expenses of energies that do determine, ultimately, the shape of the body?[7] And is a gender division necessary here? Is the female fascist really a soft, rounded, and maternal body—does she wear her consent on her hips, so to speak? Are the phallic bodies strictly speaking "male"? The gender division stands categorically for different states of being recognized as functions of production and assigned by the regime to biologically different subjects. Nevertheless, difference is categorical *only to the degree that sexual reproduction is in jeopardy*. The "true" body of the fascist is the phallic body, existing in a state of preparedness for war. It was possible for women to occupy this position at certain moments in the history of the regime, as long as they were relatively malleable, capable of moving back to the mystical place reserved for maternity. Men, however, maintain only one position, and their form is absolutely fixed. In short, male identity is legislated; female identity is subject to change.

The discourse of fascism is full of anecdotes of the perfect, consenting body: the young woman who faints when she sees the Duce in person; the infant from Ancona who is born with a mark of the *fascio littorio* (the fascist emblem of grains wrapped around a sword) imprinted on her skin. (Apparently the mother had a kind of visionary moment before an illuminated *fascio* in the city's main piazza when she was pregnant; while staring at the emblem, she pressed her stomach — hence the mark. A photograph of the fascist miracle baby was sent to Mussolini for his "collection.")[8] Of course, the Duce promoted his own body in this context, the prototype for all males. Mussolini's body is promoted to such an obsessive degree that one might well say he becomes not-body, always already a representation, one step removed from corporeal presence.

The question of a fascist body is deeply rooted in popular culture. I use the term "popular" not in the official sense of the Popular Culture Ministry set up to oversee the dissemination of certain aesthetic and behavioral principles to the working classes, but as a set of practices making up the fabric of everyday life. A fundamental Marxist notion suggests that separate individuals form a class only to the extent that they carry on a common battle against another class. Since the regime sought to create, in effect, a classless body, it is precisely in retrieving the gap between the presentation of the body and the lived reality of bodies that something like a fascist unconscious may be located. (But the question of how to gain access to this unconscious level remains vexed.)[9]

A brand of humanizing history of fascism will try to redeem the "real" body from the ideal of bodies pressed together in a mass. This is what Ettore Scola does, to some degree, in his film *Una giornata particolare* (*A Special Day*), which I will invoke again later.[10] The housewife and baby machine played by Sophia Loren seems to collapse into a crumpled rag heap after her numerous children and husband march off to the parade welcoming Hitler to Rome. Through a series of long shots, the camera reveals streams of conformists rounding the bends of the metallic stairways in a working-class apartment complex. Alone, the woman is finally "herself," a limp and haggard figure, in contrast to the phallic, public *dramatis personae* who go outside of the domestic sphere. Her relation with a homosexual antifascist played by Marcello Mastroianni is also construed as "genuinely" maternal. The film reveals the truly illusory nature of the "fascist persona" through traditional cinematic and narrative techniques of identification. But at the same time, I would argue, the bodies swarming off to the Führer's parade are also "real" bodies. They live out this "special day" with just as much authenticity as the bodies of the two (highly sympathetic) protagonists. Moreover, the mother cannot turn back or erase the fascists she has produced, whereas the homosexual will never (re)produce. His legacy for Italy, then, is nonexistent. He has no imprint on the future generations, and for this he is subject to a special "celibacy tax" that literally "wipes him out," financially and juridically. One might say that the mother is "reduced" to her function as Fascist Mother, and this is highly dehumanizing, but the homosexual literally pays off his identity, as one cancels a debt.

In addition to a gender division centered on the producer/reproducer binarism, another, perhaps nonparallel, distinction presents itself in a study of the fascist body: the leader and the follower, the dictator and the consenter. Which one is more essentially fascist, and how can it be represented?[11] In popular mythology, there is a confusion between the types of the fascist as *dictator,* and the fascist as anal narcissist.[12] I suggest that this same confusion is perpetuated at various levels of misuse today, and so I will be clear in stating that what really interests me in the context of this chapter is not the psychosexual or body ego dynamics of the dictator (the penetrator, the parental over- or under-stimulator, the toilet trainer), but the "child," who is subjected to a kind of control and who often adapts to it by withdrawing into a state of narcissistic regression. Ultimately, the figures of the passive consumer and the aggressive producer of fascist doctrine may be merely accommodating metaphors, but they should not be taken as necessarily complementary terms in a dialectic. Likewise, in Freudian thinking, sexuality is not absolutely or necessarily defined by a passive (feminine) and active (masculine) element interacting. Both sexuality and fascism are broader than this dialectic, and yet the terms "active" and "passive" remain useful for comprehending something about the way regimes are lived out by bodies. (And of course, it is understood that when the child grows up, he takes the place of his father.)[13]

Consumption: Sugar, Stimulants

It has been suggested that modernity (and again, I mean popular modernity, not modernity in an elite or merely aesthetic sense) signals a transformation of eating patterns. Could this provide a biochemical explanation for fascism itself? Well, perhaps this seems extreme, but suppose it were agreed that one distinguishing characteristic of the modern age is a shift from a national diet based on complex carbohydrates (pasta in all its many forms, or rice) to one based on simple carbohydrates (sucrose) as well as a wide variety of high-calorie, nonnutritious "fillers." This thesis is promoted by the anthropologist Sidney Mintz in his book *Sweetness and Power*.[14] A dietary shift can be verified in the futurists' banishment of pasta from the dinner table, and their embrace of stimulants, including the free nervous energy associated with the consumption of sugar.[15] In its efforts to overcome "backwardness," Italy recognized progress mirrored in its consumption of sugar; the nation was literally "stimulated" by self-sustenance, by economic autarchy, as well as by the biological effects of an increased consumption of sweets. The ability to satisfy internal sugar demands, or even to export sugar-based products was of the highest order for national self-esteem. An editorial in the dessert industry monthly asked rhetorically: "Who, moreover, better than the dessert industry, benefits from the prosperity of our nation? Isn't this, precisely this, one of the most obvious signs of the degree of civility and prosperity of a people? ... it [sugar] is becoming an alimentary product [as opposed to a luxury good], little by little, as buying power increases and taste becomes more refined."[16]

Both export and internal consumption of sugar are signs, then, of a developed economy. And sugar is, of course, a stimulant whose place in the economy must be studied within considerations of nationalism and colonialism. Stimulants keep the body alert and productive, but only at the cost of addiction, which is primarily supported and encouraged by the exploitation of indigenous labor. Like other colonial products, stimulants valorize merchant capital and the particular forms of profit-taking involved in their sale. For Italy, on the brink of conquering its empire, this was obviously a highly positive sign.

Stimulants also hold an important function for the domestic workforce. Wolfgang Haug understands sugar as functioning to help "guard against uncontrolled libidinal outbreaks that might threaten their adjustment to office life." And as office work becomes increasingly mechanized, specialized, and tedious, "The capitalists compensate with pleasure highly suited to their bourgeois activities."[17] For Italian fascism, this had very particular implications. The first part of the equation, the addictiveness and the "nervous energy" produced by stimulants, was theoretically desirable, especially within a futurist-revolutionary rhetoric. Hot cocoa was promoted by the dessert industry as a "healthful, nutritious" drink not only in winter, but also in summer, when we have a greater need for "not only muscular, but also nervous sustenance."[18] All manner of sugar-based products stressed the pos-

itive value of "nervous" energy, which came to be construed as the antithesis of the torpor of the liberal state. The problematic nature of Italy's
dependence for sugar on foreign sources was raised during the early years
of the regime, in the context of the colonial question and the rhetoric of
national inferiority. But rather than resulting in a critique of stimulants, the
dependency question only meant that commodities such as sugar would be
endowed with a particular ambivalence that would seem to emerge in advertising.

Once again, because the question of sugar production and the origin
of raw materials is problematic, consumption becomes the obsessive preoccupation of language and images for public use: "Tennis requires an expense of nervous energy in addition to muscular energy. Just a few cubes of
sugar in your drink is enough to reestablish your balance and to maintain
full efficiency during play," reads an advertisement sponsored by the Italian
sugar industry.[19] In the context of this collectively financed campaign, sugar
is represented as one of the building blocks of biochemical energy, formed
into spiraling cubes like genetic material, a mysterious blowup of the basic
units constituting the body politic (figure 22). The individual body itself is
made transparent, all of its processes exposed to the viewer's eye. The tennis ad appeared in conjunction with a series of ads, all of which focus on
traditional bourgeois activities such as tennis, golf, or motoring. This particular selection is extremely important, because unlike the classless, paramilitary sports of the regime's physical culture, tennis is directly associated
with the consumption of leisure, and so it pulls attention away from production. The image of the transparent cube and the terse body corresponds
perfectly to the poetic slogan of the fascist dessert industry:

> The Italian sun, assimilated in the fields and the plants, is found in
> all the products of the dessert industry, which has as its indispen-
> sable and irreplaceable basis, sugar, a sovereign element of our
> organism.[20]

In point of fact, the sugar that was promoted in the collective campaign of the thirties was not just any old sugar, it was sugar extracted from
beets grown on home soil. Sugar was also, however, a generic commodity
promoted on the basis of its uniformity and adherence to international
standards. No brand name is mentioned in the tennis advertisement because this is one of the ads generated for the entire Italian sugar industry
(similar campaigns were run by the beer industry, rice growers, pasta makers,
and so on), and not for the product of any particular factory. In order to

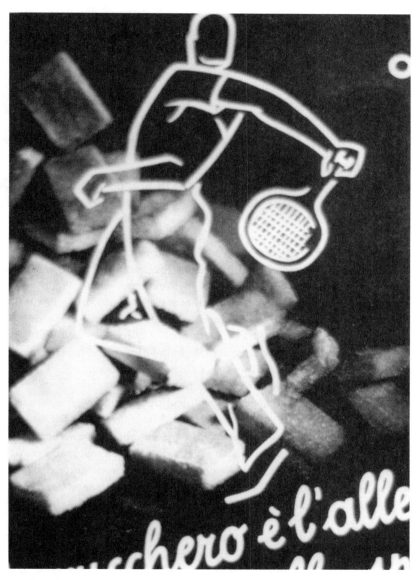

22. Sugar body without organs.

succeed, the ads in this series had to be general about the positive benefits of *Italian* sugar (since it is, precisely, *Italian sugar* that is at stake), and had to mask the particular source of the sugar (because the entire argument rested on the assumption that Italian sugar is equivalent to sugar produced from cane cultivated in a tropical, colonized state, and because various national growers and manufacturers had agreed to finance the campaign in exchange for this generality).

In declaring sugar an autarchic product, the regime consequently raised its price and retooled its status within the "domestic economy" of each Italian household. One of the primary goals of the campaign was to remind consumers of the importance of sugar—at its new price—for the daily regime. From the point of view of the individual consumer (not to mention allied industries that relied on sugar as a raw material), autarchy often resulted in a price increase, a sort of luxury tax. The ad campaign very cleverly marketed this commodity as if it could increase leisure consumption (in Veblen's terms, specifically, the materialization of the distance of the body from labor). In fact, however, the campaign was really all about increasing commodity consumption (labor translated into material form). Finally, because the particular commodity at stake here was, once again, a stimulant, it therefore related to an economy of quick fixes and bursts of energy rather than sustained development of industries. The cubes of sugar superimposed on the athlete thus make a perfect, metonymic equation between the individual body and the body politic.

The dessert industry in Italy, which had traditionally been associated with luxury rather than with necessity, found itself constantly fighting to increase consumption. No sooner had the New Roman Empire been declared, than "research" was initiated into the potential for growing cocoa beans and sugar cane in the Ethiopian highlands. At the same time, then, the industry began to speculate about the possibilities for increased consumption on the part of the *indigenous* peoples. One economic analyst lamented the fact that the Ethiopians did not keep records on such things as annual consumption of various products, but he added, "We must expect that the opening up of a new life and a more intense rhythm of civilization will rapidly increase the consumption of sugar, which is highly prized by the natives. Hence the necessity to respond to these new needs."[21] (The new bodily economy will have to exist in a reciprocal relation with modern statistics and the quantifying of bodies so central to the utopian graphic language of isotype, for example.[22] As individual body shapes shift, so will the idealized, universal representations of the body in a numerical set or series.)

In the economic analyst's quotation, the general tendency to displace focus from production to consumption is revealed at a linguistic level. The "new needs" posited for the colonial subjects literally take over the narrative of this article, which is otherwise optimistic about the potential for cultivating various raw materials.

The problem, in essence, is not the productive labor of the colony—that is a given—but the cooperation of the *land* itself. If the land was figured as a reproducer, then this was also a way of shifting the blame for relative infertility away from the fascist producer, the male. In addition to sugar, the dessert industry was concerned about chocolate, since cocoa beans were imported from nations adhering to the League of Nations' sanctions against Italy (primarily from the Gold Coast, then under British control). As I suggested in my reading of "La Torinese" and the "Faccetta nera" chocolate women in chapter 2, the cultural preoccupation with cocoa and economic autarchy was figured in the sexual submission of the black female. Italy's sense of inferiority was shifted from a discussion of the potential productivity of actual bodies into the realm of the natural, which must be subjugated to its will:

> If there is, then, a possibility of emancipating our country from this importation, so as to make it [cocoa] an object of large-scale production for the continuing increase demanded of the chocolate industry by all of the European countries, the Italian dessert industry must also answer "present!" to the call for the empowerment of Ethiopia. And as a collective group, we must study the initiatives necessary so that cocoa can be grown and can represent one of the sources of wealth and of work for Italy and for Ethiopia.[23]

It is understood that the consequence of increased productivity is not only the support of the regime for the industry—in this sense, the article itself constitutes a form of lobbying—but an increase in domestic consumption: "We can certainly hope that soon Italy will be able to consume cocoa produced totally by her own sons, and that as a national product chocolate will be more popular than it is today."[24] In this optimistic picture, consumption emerges as the final term in the economic equation.

Ironically, during the 1980s, another collective campaign for sugar was launched, repeating much of the older language. Each advertisement features a short text framed by a thick and thin blue line, the same design found on "Italian" sugar packages on the supermarket shelves today. Below an explanatory text praising the nutritional value of sugar for a properly balanced diet, a youthful individual with arms raised leaps joyfully in the air. The slogan "Sugar is full of life" is found on each of the ads. In other words, sugar is being sold in this campaign as a "natural" and "necessary" product for confronting the stress of everyday life, in strict opposition to those artificial sweeteners "born in the laboratory," which have no part in the scheme of essential food groups. Sugar is "the most modern resource" that *nature* offers. Once again, as in the 1930s, any reference to protectionist measures is eclipsed. The rhetoric of the 1980s collective campaign still attaches itself to an autarchic or nationalist production only through its subtle use of a graphic layout, the thin and thick blue lines of "Italian" sugar. The single most important code in both the 1930s text and its later incarnation is the association of sugar with energy and lightness, while the nationalism of the product is masked; the overlay of a rhetoric of individual bodily energy eclipses another discourse about national strength that cannot be uttered as part of advertising language. Without a brand name to distract the reader (and to reveal the profit motive behind the advertisement), the campaign passes itself off as the expression of a nutritional authority, a kind of public service message. This practice of demonizing production (as the profit end of the equation), and then erasing it from advertising altogether, begins in Italy under fascism, but continues to be effective for any product whose price structure depends not on brand recognition, but on fidelity cultivated through uniformity or conformity.

The fascist sugar campaign displaces a possible language of production with a language of levity, leisure, and energy. Yet the so-called modern diet of the futurists (repeated in the 1980s sugar campaign) is precisely the opposite of what current nutritionists recommend. This only demonstrates beyond a shadow of a doubt the purely cultural or conventional dimension inherent in the hierarchy of acceptable foods at any given historical moment.[25] The fascist sugar campaign takes its product as an essential building block of the body, one that actively consumes its own distance from labor, and so imitates a body specifically coded as bourgeois. Of course, our latter-day nutritionists would probably suggest a plate of pasta in order to keep up the level of energy even *after* the tennis game, since sport is only one part of a daily regimen that also includes mental and sexual acts, resistance to the stress incurred during a day, and so on. Contemporary science argues against stimulants that only fuel the body long enough for a game, but then leave it drained and unproductive. Complex carbohydrates have become a key term in a current discourse that equates eating with morality (be "good" to your body), but also with "the new," with youth and energy.

If morality is supposed to be fixed — transhistorical and transgenerational — eating habits, on the other hand, are decidedly cyclical, and are ultimately related to production or the availability of certain ingredients. The rhetoric of advertising invariably reshapes the body, while the body also shapes advertising; both factors engage in a give-and-take at the level of individual and collective economies. This fundamental problem is displaced also by a series of strategies played out in relation to a severe shortage of grain during the 1930s and a growing desire for isolationism among the Italian public.

Grains

Like sugar, grain was fascistized. While sugar maintained a place of high prestige, however, the consumption of grain was viewed generally as a sign of underdevelopment by economic theorists who regarded richer countries like France with envy.[26] In the 1932 manifesto of futurist cooking, Marinetti called for the abolition of pasta. It is, he stated, "forty percent less nutritious than meat or fish," and with its "massive heaviness" it "shackles" the energies of the body "with a ball and chain." Although the pasta industry had hired guns with academic titles to defend the merits of the national dish, Marinetti termed them "melancholic," evoking again heaviness, antivirility, passivity. And it might be said that futurist cooking — with its restaurants and traveling banquets, and its publication of recipes, manifestos, and menus — was the most successful of all the futurist activities at truly penetrating into the sphere of popular culture. Even though the banquets were elite affairs, they were publicized in newspapers along with many anecdotes that in turn provoked activities in the public arena: Housewives in Aquila had signed a petition in favor of pasta; photographs were published of Marinetti eating spaghetti, but it turned out they were only doctored photomontages in the tradition of the worst libelous journalism.[27]

The futurist meals led to the kind of productive bursts of energy suggested by the sugar campaign: eruptions of violence, manic music and skits, brief ejaculations of erotic vigor, unsustainable levels of activity. In a short narrative piece titled "The Dinner that Stopped a Suicide," the futurist artists Fillìa, Prampolini, and Marinetti made an edible female "aerosculpture" to compensate Giulio Onesti, a jilted lover contemplating suicide. Their creation was composed of various ingredients, some "colonialist," some homegrown — all plentiful and "obedient," to use the futurist terminology. Ransacking the kitchen of a large, northern Italian villa, Prampolini shouts:

> Our ingenious hands need a hundred sacks of the following indis-
> pensable ingredients: chestnut flour, wheat flour, ground almonds,
> rye flour, cornmeal, cocoa powder, red pepper, sugar and eggs. Ten
> jars of honey, oil and milk. A quintal of dates and bananas.[28]

Clearly, abundance of these materials is a way of overcoming (male) depression, and this in turn reflects a larger cultural paradigm. The link between
the *copia* of materials and copulation is not merely metaphorical:

> In fact the flesh of the curve signifying the synthesis of every move-
> ment of her [the sculpture's] hips was even appetizing. And she
> shone with a sugary down peculiar to her which excited the very
> enamel on the teeth of the attentive mouths of his [Prampolini's]
> two companions. Higher up, the spherical sweetnesses of all ideal
> breasts spoke from a geometrical distance to the dome of the stom-
> ach, supported by the force-lines of dynamic thighs.[29]

As in the sugar campaign, the expense of energy required for production is
matched by an exhaustion of calories requiring immediate consumption:
"With the mouths of friendly cannibals Giulio Onesti, Marinetti, Prampolini
and Fillìa restored themselves with a tasty morsel of statue every now and
then."[30] The kind of geometricized, sexualized body they have constructed
is intimately linked with the question of national dominance I raised in
chapter 2. In fact, this sculpture, made from readily available, even eager,
personified materials appears "inoculated with the gentle magnetism of the
most beautiful women and the most beautiful Africas ever dreamed of." In
these passages we notice, again, the conflation of geometrical forms, blackness, and feminine sexuality in general. And as if this slippage between
gender and nationalism were not clear enough, the description goes on to
make a perfectly legible connection between Italian industrial production
and colonial domination through sexual potency. The "sloping architecture
of soft curves following one upon the other to heaven concealed the grace
of the world's most feminine little feet in a thick and sugary network of green
oasis-palms, whose tufts were mechanically interlocked by cog-wheels."[31]
The female body contains the palms of the colony, and it is linked with a
process of (fascist) domestic production.

Finally, unable to contain himself, Onesti devours the aerosculpture
from head to toe. He then takes a walk through a nearby park, utterly revi-
talized, feeling "unencumbered, liberated, empty and bursting.... Unique
and complete."[32] The adjectives might well have been lifted from one of
the sugar campaign advertisements. Like the ideal producer in fascist rhetoric,

the futurist feels his superiority in the ability to go beyond exhaustion, to expend surplus energy, and to figure his body as a machine. What lies at the base of all of these various food campaigns is not ultimately the putative desire to overturn passé ideas of what constitutes a good meal, but a new concept of production that could be linked with any particular food concept within a standard rhetoric of energy expense.

At the same time that the futurists linked slower productivity with the overconsumption of pasta, the regime worked in the opposite direction, addressing its publicity skills to the full-scale *battaglia del grano* (battle of the grain). During this campaign, the land was figured as a body that had to train and discipline itself in order to become a better fascist producer. In addition to propaganda that raised fears about a hypothetical future war and inevitable shortages, the regime awarded prizes for high yields (just as it would later, for the high-yielding female body).

At the same time the regime's agricultural branch cultivated the productivity end of the equation, the propaganda offices launched a campaign to promote rice over pasta, reeducating vast segments of the population to accept the former as its national dish. During these years when rice production was particularly strong, the regime and the industry cooperated by promoting the grain to housewives as a nutritious and filling food staple. Maternal guilt was the primary thrust of such educational campaigns. Without rice, children will remain unfulfilled and be subject to colds and — the unspeakable — tuberculosis.[33] Apparently, not all mothers of the previous generation had passed what in Italy might be called a "rice culture" on to their daughters, so the manufacturers routinely gave away recipe booklets in rice packages, and sent rice press releases to women's magazines. The press, in turn, cooperated with explanatory spreads and recipes, linking rice dishes with images of warmth, wetness, the hearth, the breast. An ad campaign exploited the elliptical slogan: "Rice: from production to consumption." These two economic terms grouped together were presumably enough to sell the product, without any further persuasion, visual or linguistic. The brief motto suggests the interiority and autarchy of rice, with the imperative: "Buy Italian!" understood as an unstated given. The pleasures of economizing, serving the fatherland, and creatively engaging in making rice palatable with various recipes and surprising combinations are all bound up together in female subjectivity as constructed by fascism. One might ask, then, what equivalent pleasures were available to the male, and the answer, rather obviously, would seem to lie in the promise of fulfilling military service. If the female can make herself into an organized, economical, thrifty consumer by cathecting her daily routine, the male can look forward to a similar channeling of desire into the structure of combat. The pleasures may ultimately be the same, regardless of the gender division, and this is reflected in the homogeneity of the language used by the regime: the battle of rice, the battle of the grain. The link between the domestic battle and the international, political one, went beyond a mere linguistic coincidence.

All three of these contradictory campaigns—the futurist anti-pasta manifestos, the fascist grain battle, and the rice promotion—amount to something like the logic of the teakettle in Freud's definition of the defense mechanism. In his famous analysis of the dream of Irma's injection, Freud posits several (contradictory) defenses against his own incompetence, and these remind him of a parable of the man who returned a borrowed kettle in damaged condition. "The defendant asserted first, that he had given it back undamaged; secondly, that the kettle had a hole in it when he borrowed it, and thirdly, that he had never borrowed a kettle from his neighbor at all. So much the better: if only a single one of these three lines of defence were to be accepted as valid, the man would have to be acquitted."[34] Acting independently, the futurists responded to a crisis in production by fantasizing absolute independence and supranutritional energy; the regime attempted to remedy the shortages with land reclamation, economic incentives, and quantity prizes; finally, a new product was introduced to take the place of the one threatened by "natural" and economically created factors. All of these strategies were played out in the mass market through a rhetoric strictly related to the fascist body. Eventually, in the course of the 1930s, grain production would increase, and then a new series of campaigns, linking pasta with levity, invention, playfulness, and modernity, became necessary to reintegrate pasta into the national diet.

Digestion, Automatism

The waistline, particularly in the case of the female body, often serves as a site for negotiating minute details of the economy, and for either emphasizing or effacing issues of class according to particular needs. "Scientific management" (of the bourgeois body in particular) is somehow oddly detached from concrete realities of consumption and production of energies, and emerges at its most disturbing in the haunting language of purgatives. Pills are marketed within fascist "science" as a kind of morning-after solution for consumptive binges. One can slim down instantly by ingesting a laxative, as if the temporal and spatial dynamic involved in eating could be utterly eclipsed. Purgative blood cures are recommended for

> anyone who suffers from gastrointestinal disturbances, lack of appetite, constipation, hemorrhoids. They are also a real providence for women who have irregular and painful menstrual disturbances, menopause, or are at that critical age, in nervous individuals, especially when their nervousness is characterized by asthenia, cerebral weakness, a heavy head, obfuscated vision, dizziness, insomnia, and so on.[35]

As in Marinetti's futuristic pill diet, the body can be purified in a single gesture, and all foreign agents removed on a cyclical basis. The instant cure proposed by the maternal voice of fascism is something to write on the calendar like a periodic checkup. In this sense, the body is reduced to a machine that can move in reverse, a technique associated with modern cinematic experimentation, and also with a certain kind of comedy of the automaton that will be important throughout this discussion.

A wide variety of products were advertised in the context of slimness. The fascist really wants to become two-dimensional, even if such slimness is problematic from the point of view of maternity.[36] Like the sugar ads and the futurist anti-pasta campaigns, the collective campaign for beer touted its slimming properties, the ability to purge the body of calories that might otherwise be converted to fat. Again, the ads efface the fact that the beer in question is "Italian" beer, a product lacking in tradition or prestige within the national culture. Laxatives were advertised, especially to women, not as medicinal antidotes to an occasional stopping-up of the system, but as a daily routine for slenderizing. If today's experts would recommend building up the fibrous bulk in the diet in order to regulate the intestinal tract, such a strategy would have aroused a deep anxiety during the 1930s.

Consider the poster by Fortunato Depero for the laxative Magnesia San Pellegrino (figure 23). Even today, this product is marketed with a double entendre: the *pellegrino* (pilgrim, traveler) needs a laxative, since it is well known that one often experiences symptoms of constipation while away from one's familiar surroundings. But the product itself is also a pilgrim, working its way through the intestines and arriving at its destination, having purged the system. The intestines are a metonym for the movements of the individual body as well as the body of the industrialized, fascist state.[37] The robotic man, which Depero repeats endlessly in so many of his designs, is here a plumber who purges his own internal (autarchic) pipe with

23. Depero's Magnesia San Pellegrino poster. (Salce Collection, 12859.)

a plunger. The bulk, the mass, the heaviness of whatever substance is clogging the machinery must be expelled quickly so that the machinery can function at full, streamlined efficiency.

In spite of the cheerful colors and ludic spirit, there is something very sinister about this image. Defecation, after all, represents the last stage of a rather long and complex process that involves the breakdown of the digestible item, but not its utter disappearance. In *Crowds and Power,* a book I consider essential in understanding fascist "ideology" as well as the power formations specific to fascist regimes, Elias Canetti writes that defecation is a sign of murder. Tracing certain forms of the exercise of power as they begin in the primitive "pack," Canetti discusses a psychology of the hunter that is pleasure producing. Archaic acts of seizing and incorporating prey still exercise influence on so-called civilized social formations. Using hands, teeth, and later, weapons, humans come to "possess" the trapped animal and incorporate it into the narrow opening of the mouth. The process of digestion, which strips the animal of anything valuable and then rejects it as stinking mass, is central to a conception of human power, especially in a fascist society. But this origin of power must be suppressed for moral reasons, and the equation of excrement with the exercise of power has long been buried under the deposits of advanced societies:

> The excrement, which is the remains of all this, is loaded with our whole blood guilt. By it we know what we have murdered. It is the compressed sum of all the evidence against us. It is our daily and continuing sin and, as such, it stinks and cries to heaven. It is remarkable how we isolate ourselves with it; in special rooms, set aside for the purpose, we get rid of it; our most private moment is when we withdraw there; we are alone only with our excrement. It is clear that we are ashamed of it. It is the age-old seal of that power-process of digestion, which is enacted in darkness and which, without this, would remain hidden forever.[38]

Depero's equation of the process of digestion, transformation, and expulsion of waste with a fast-moving pipeline is not merely to euphemize a scatological discourse for a polite audience; it is also a very literal identification of the body with the state, in full collaboration with the regime's economic policies. This ad realizes the absolute coincidence of later futurist aesthetics with politics. The little plumber serves to displace the bloody, archaic narrative of the pack and the hunt that lies below the figure of fascist violence in Canetti's schema. The plumber winks and transforms the dark process of seizing and incorporating into a game. However, as Andrew Hewitt has suggested in a discussion of the essential relation of fascism and modernism, the apparent aestheticization implied by a figure like Depero's plumber does not simply mean "the false reconciliation of social contradictions at the level of the aesthetic." For the futurists, such reconciliation is not offered "as a social facade, imposing a false aesthetic unity on an unruly political situation. If a model of harmony and social cohesion is being produced, it is produced only by the invocation of its opposite, by an aesthetic of aggression, opposition, and disunity."[39] The precisely aggressive nature of Depero's "journeyman-craftsman" persona will figure in a later discussion of the artisanal body. The body of the plumber stands for the futurist body in a larger cultural narrative of the avant-garde and its relation to the fascist state.

Depero's plumber also expresses another fundamental ambiguity between what Hewitt terms "an ideal of discipline and an ideal of liberation."[40] For the plumber's motions are both restrained and playful, as he works diligently to move the bottle along through the intestines. Locomotion and freedom in motility (even in a mental sense) are involved in a child's mastery of bowel "movements," according to Freud.

> Defecation affords the first occasion in which the child must decide between a narcissistic and an object-loving attitude. He either parts obediently with his faeces, "sacrifices" them to his parent, or else retains them with the purpose of auto-erotic satisfaction and later as a means of asserting his own will. If he makes the latter choice we are in the presence of defiance (obstinacy) which, accordingly, springs from a narcissistic clinging to anal eroticism.[41]

Defecation is a game, then, but one in which the child works out a relation with the figures of authority governing his or her body. Depero's "state" is one in which the plumber follows orders to cleanse away the blood-guilt represented by the feces. If the body does not comply, it must be purged.

In Freud, a dictatorial parent might be imagined to enact a severe "sphincter-morality," arousing guilt complexes in the child. Later, such guilt may lead to symptoms including the inability to feel deep emotions. Life is experienced as a kind of boredom or dullness — the life of fascist production, in short. What does it mean, then, to represent the (happy) movement through the intestines as effected by a colorful, toy robot-plumber? Like the anal period, the period in which a child plays with toys represents a transitional moment toward object relations. As the child moves about the domestic space with brightly colored objects, he or she learns about motility, unless this process is somehow disturbed by an aberrant or even "pathological" parental situation. The fascist parent attempts to control the toy, like the father of Daniel Paul Schreber, who figures prominently in many discussions of fascist subjectivity. In a book on child-rearing practices, Dr. Schreber the educator wrote: "Do not allow the child to occupy himself with more than one toy at any time.... Pay heed that the change is made only after the child has used sufficient energy (physical or mental) on the given toy.... Above all, toys offer the opportunity of turning cleanliness, care for property, and tidiness into firm rules."[42] It has been suggested that for the child the result of such control is an inhibition of movements in later life, exemplified by Schreber himself; he remained motionless for "long periods" in his asylum.

Wilhelm Reich seems to have been correct in identifying Schreber *père* as an emblematic fascist father, one who demands control over the space in which the child develops a sense of body identity that includes processes of excrement. But in a less extreme version of this case, the capitalist-father purchases the toy in exchange for a particular value to be redeemed in educational capital. As Pierre Bourdieu suggests in *Distinction,* toys may appear to be leisure objects, purely pleasurable, but they actually serve to challenge and provoke, training and improving the child, in rituals of self-betterment.[43] Depero's image reconnects anality, something quite far from adult, or "civilized" behavior, with transitional objects, and ties the process of (bowel) movement to play. Moving toys around displaces interest from bodily openings and functions by providing a new source of pleasure in motility for the child. This is the regressive attitude figured in Depero's "adult" joke.

What, then, are the larger cultural implications of this constipation? As I suggested earlier, the fascist character type is often linked with what Freud listed as the three principal components of anal narcissism: orderliness, parsimony, and obstinacy.[44] These qualities are prominent, Freud notes, in certain patients who, it can be proven, have suffered some disturbance in childhood experiences of toilet training:

> Now anal erotism is one of the components of the [sexual] instinct which, in the course of development and in accordance with the education demanded by our present civilization, *have become unserviceable* for sexual aims [emphasis mine]. It is therefore plausible to suppose that these character-traits of orderliness, parsimony and obstinacy, which are so often prominent in people who were formerly anal erotics, are to be regarded as the first and most constant results of the sublimation of anal erotism.[45]

This text goes on to suggest that these characteristics — (negative) signs of a repression having taken place — would be expected to be absent in individuals who *have,* in fact, made anal erotism serviceable for sexual aims. Indeed, Freud writes, practicing homosexuals tend *not* to express these negative signs. Of course, this is a highly problematic statement, and the relation between adult "character types" and the development of homosexual tendencies in childhood experiences of viewing remains unresolved in the Freudian corpus.[46] Nevertheless, what is interesting for the present context is the implicit relation between child-rearing practices and the degree of repression of anal erotism that is achieved. In "On the Sexual Theories of Children," Freud wrote that many children who are involved with the birth of a younger sibling suppose that the fetus is expelled through the mother's anus, thus allowing for the hypothetical possibility of male pregnancy. Such a belief is not considered "dirty" by the child, since in early life, "the child was still not so distant from his constitutional coprophilic inclinations. There was nothing degraded about coming into the world like a heap of faeces, which had not yet been condemned by feelings of disgust."[47]

I now wish to put this scheme of civilization-through-anal-control in a historical context. The regime rewarded a woman with money for the babies (equivalent for the child with feces) she was able to produce. Although, obviously, the regime made a distinction between female reproduction and male production, it might be supposed that a child would have a more tactile and immediate comprehension of the former, which was, after all, carried out in the home, under the child's own nose. The demographic campaigns not only dehumanized woman by reducing her to a womb (this is the most obvious critique one could make), but they also must have had a profound effect on the psychosexual makeup of the children born into a condition of quantification. These effects are evident, once again, in what I consider to be a profoundly humanist film, *A Special Day.* In the first scene, Sophia Loren, a tired womb, moves around the house tidying up, as a series of brown ("Mediterranean," but also brown-shirted) children fall out unexpectedly from sheets, from beds, from behind drapes — like turds falling from a closing and opening anus. The effect is meant to be comic, almost as if this maternal figure cannot keep track of her offspring and has lost any connection to them as individuals. Finally, the children dress in their freshly ironed Balilla uniforms and parade out into an endless stream of brown shirts. Later, when she is alone with her homosexual neighbor, the mother explains that she has six children, and that a seventh would mean a special demographic award for her family. The equation of children with feces with money is complete.

Various followers of Freud have continued to view toilet training as a process in which a child is coaxed into giving a gift to a parental figure (defecation, but at a particular time and in a particular place). The child often confuses this offering with the act of giving birth, just as he or she confuses the anus with the opening of the birth canal, or the vagina. In addition, the child associates his or her own fullness of feelings with the image of the pregnant mother's inflated stomach. In a society where making the offering of a (little brown) child is the ultimate gift a woman can give to her Father, and for which she is widely rewarded, the child on the toilet cannot help but associate what he or she does with a similar oblation.

In his discussion of the drives and of Freud's essay "Instincts and Their Vicissitudes," Lacan focuses on the rimlike structure that is characteristic of all erogenous zones in the body (comprising both vagina and anus, as well as others). This formation is not casual (it is not simply that humans are biologically prone to be stimulated at the points where the body exhibits "openings"), but related to the intrinsic structure of the drive as it turns out from the body, circumvents some object, and then moves back on itself, receding once again in the body where it achieves "satisfaction." The degree to which the rim structure is metaphoric in Freudian thought, or really expresses an empirical pattern, remains problematic after many readings of Lacan. Nevertheless, his text is quite suggestive for a discussion of the body in its relation to the so-called anal drive. For if the movement *outward* from the body represents only a partial drive, what happens when the anal drive returns and folds into the body? Moreover, who, or better, what, is the object around which the anal drive is turned?[48] Although the notion of a self-reflexive anal drive may sound absurd, Lacan refuses to dismiss the secondary "backward" motion under the presumption that all of the drives share a set of fundamental structural properties:

> *Se faire chier* has a meaning! When one says *here, on se fait rudement chier,* one has the *emmerdeur éternel* in mind. [Translator's footnote in text: This sentence is strictly untranslatable on account of the play on words. *Se faire chier* means literally "to get oneself shitted." "*Tu me fais chier*" has the sense of "you make me sick." "*On se fait rudement chier*" means "we were bored to death." An "*emmerdeur*" (literally, a "shitter") is a "bore."] It is quite wrong simply to identify the celebrated scybala with the function given it in the me-

tabolism of obsessional neurosis. It is quite wrong to separate it from
what it represents, a gift, as it happens, and from the relation it has
with soiling, purification, catharsis. It is wrong not to see that it is
from here that the function of oblation emerges. In short, the object, here, is not very far from the domain that is called that of the
soul.[49]

Lacan links a number of important themes here: the rim structure of the
anus, the "eternal bore," boredom, and the constitution of the soul in its
relation with defecation. The sum total of these elements corresponds to a
clearly fascist subjectivity.

During the 1930s, a laxative with the brand name "Rim" was sold as
an antidote to overconsumption. Consumers were encouraged to take a
few Rims before going to bed so they would wake up "like new." In Italian, the word *rima* is used to denote the rim of the anus, but only in a
technical sense. The product takes a term from medical language and trans-
lates it into a "foreign" language as Rim. The advertisements featuring
slim-waisted women bear all the ambivalence of fascist economics: on one
hand, purgatives can help resexualize the female body by forcing it to "make
a sublime offering" of feces, just like the excessive gifts of multiple births
mandated by the regime in its propaganda for women. On the other hand,
though, the slim, phallic body pictured in advertising is a threat to the
regime and to masculinity. The laxative ads seem to appeal to a female target, in defiance of regime maternity standards. By purging herself too fast,
the woman risks losing everything at once, and her orifices become mouths
that can devour and castrate the male. The rim is the site where these body
problems are all negotiated, but not necessarily resolved, because, ultimately,
they are problems of the regulation of the drives. Subject to overcontrol, it
is possible that the anal drive, for example, folds in itself, and *on se fait chier* —
boredom — results.

In this discussion of the body as consumer, which I have chosen to
center on Depero's San Pellegrino man, an uncanny sense of the mechanistic emerges. The expulsion of excrement should be a natural process, but
above all, it should be private. There is something "wrong" with Depero's
plumber boldly pushing the excrement along through the pipe. Depero's
robotic figures in general recall an earlier aesthetic form: the automaton. In
the eighteenth century, Vaucanson and other inventors traveled through
Europe displaying their curiosities for court audiences and upper-class sa-
lons. Eventually, automata also surfaced as middle-class forms of entertainment. One of Vaucanson's greatest successes was his mechanical duck. This

spring-drive figure took a grain from the hand of its "trainer," swallowed, and then seemed to "digest" and defecate. In reality, the grain was probably stored inside the duck while some other material, in a more pulverized form, was substituted for it during the process of "passing" through the digestive tract.[50] But what is interesting about this particular cultural phenomenon of spectatorship and public fascination is that of all the "natural" kinetic acts that could be mechanized with the spring technology, defecation should have been given such a historically privileged position. Vaucanson went on to invent a number of industrial machines, including a type of cloth loom. Ultimately, then, automatization, linked to a *philosophical* discourse about self-determination and human capacity, had practical implications for the industrialization of labor. Moreover, the connection between the venture capitalization of defecation and of other "productive" machines seems far from arbitrary. During the eighteenth century, the automaton may have been a specular figure of human folly within a certain kind of discourse, but it was primarily a device to make money, and its value was strictly linked to the degree of realism of its movements.

The specifically automatic and mechanistic quality of the act of excretion is underscored in Depero's consuming and producing body. Its inner mechanical workings are exposed, not hidden, and it is recast in the bright colors of the playroom. Ultimately, though, this "game" of consumption masks the depth of control the regime attempted to exercise over the most private moments of the private body. Or rather, in figuring the process of movement as a game, Depero complies with a certain mechanistic language that characterizes regime propaganda.

The White Homunculus

The figure of the Michelin tire man, Bibendum, predates fascism and emerges from the late-nineteenth-century world of sprites and puppets exemplified by artists such as Mauzan and Cappiello. These *lares* and *penates* helped to domesticate a whole series of products, and to blunt the edge of the hard sell inherent in modern advertising. The advertising industry understood the importance of employing humanoid "spokesfigures" early on. Such figures could attest to the positive qualities of a product, in a way that appealed to the inherently antimechanistic bias of middle-class culture. The bodies I am considering in this admittedly artificial category are white, puffy, reduced cartoons like Bibendum (figure 1) and, in a more recent incarnation that should be familiar to most readers, the Pillsbury Doughboy. Sometimes the white man smiles (Doughboy does when you poke him in his yeasty, pasty belly), but often he merely lumbers along, a strangely automatized and faceless puffball.

The early incarnation of Bibendum sold bicycle tires. In fact, his inventors, the Michelin brothers, conceived of him in the 1890s after they spotted a pile of tires stacked up to form what appeared as a "little man." Bibendum's original physiognomy and comportment were based on a beer hall advertisement. Smoking a cigar, perched on a two-wheeler, he was identified with a jolly, avuncular type of sales pitch (see my remarks on the "salesman" in chapter 1). His inventors gave him an aristocratic pince-nez, later removed in an effort to popularize him. Bibendum models traveled around France promoting Michelin products and highway development legislation. They appeared at small fairs and large urban rallies. In short, Bibendum was part of one of the very earliest broad-based marketing campaigns.

Beyond his function in a modern economy, however, there is something quite disturbing about Bibendum: he can remove cross-sections of himself (one or two tires at a time), and, indeed, his entire body is composed of bulges like the fecal column itself. I am not implying here that Bibendum *represents* a form of anality, only that his capacity for self-vivisection and his ridged, segmented form are highly disturbing when viewed as *body*. "Nunc est bibendum ... ," ran an advertising slogan. "That is to say: To your health. The Michelin tire drinks up any obstacle in your way." Retaining his puffiness, the white man drinks metal objects from a chalice while his rival tires lie deflated and limp at his side. He always keeps his shape. He pokes a finger into his hollow inside like a Doubting Thomas, and then puffs on his cigar, puffing up his insides.

The current tire man, reproduced on road signs and garages and made into highly collectible dolls, has a vastly reduced number of ridges. The individual car tires composing his body are blended together so that he is less segmented, and unlike his predecessor from the turn of the century, today's Bibendum cannot remove tires. His eyes are more rounded, more friendly; in short, he is no longer the slightly oddball uncle, but a family toy, a puppet, and a smooth, elastic organ. He no longer threatens a viewer's sense of bodily integrity through his self-decomposition.[51]

In a 1933 advertisement for a "modern" pasta manufacturer, the white homunculus rides on the back of a pasta horse (figure 24). Wielding a knife, setting out on his own personal "grain battle," the pasta man wears a jolly expression. The ad was probably meant to appeal to mothers in search of products that would puff up their children and keep them within the

24. Pastificio Moderno white homunculus. (Salce Collection, 00791.)

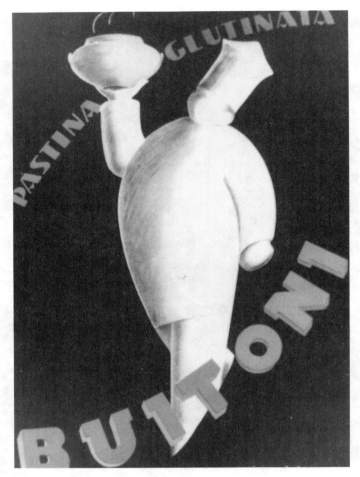

25. Seneca, Pastina Buitoni.

ethos of the home. A similar figure appears in one of Seneca's brilliant ads for Buitoni, in which a puffy baker waits on clients (figure 25). The pasta man is the antonym of the slimmed-down bodies of the sugar campaigns that either skip the stage of consumption altogether, or enact it so quickly that they remain flattened and productive, never filled with mass. Like Bibendum, the pasta man appears to be an organ turned inside out, the smooth side of the intestine where food lingers in a more comforting and regressive period of life. He represents fullness, satisfaction of instinct, drowsiness, comfort—all terms that have been banned from the ethos of the fascist male (and the female inasmuch as she equates masculinity with her liberation). In short, the white homunculus signifies maternity. But to the degree that the female target, the domestic consumer, associates these qualities of full- ness with her own subjugation, they come to be transferred from the fe- male body onto a puppet, a plaything, who bears them with a kind of stoic pathos.

Women and children do appear, without disguises, in advertisements for Buitoni Pastina Glutinata, a form of pasta made with gluten flour rather than semolina and marketed for babies and convalescents:

> Buitoni Pastina Glutinata, prepared with special processes that pre- serve all the protein in the glutens, can be substituted for meat and eggs by anyone with a weak stomach; it nutrifies without weigh- ing down the stomach, it favors the renewal of tissue, and it's gen- tle on delicate digestive organs. For this reason, Buitoni Pastina Glutinata is the only product designated for baby food whose com- position is regulated by law. Listen to the advice of famous doc- tors.... Buitoni produces "the best products of the regime" [a double entendre — the word, which is the same in Italian, refers to the fascist regime and to the daily diet].[52]

Dictated by law, the pasta of regression, of the periods when bowel control is lacking, also utilizes the rhetoric of fascist purgation. Pastina Glutinata does not weigh down the stomach; it revives tissue; and so on. Pictures ac- companying this campaign foreground a hot bowl of pastina served by a cheerful apron-clad mother to a group of small children in a cozy kitchen. (One ad focused on the royal family in just such a domestic scenario!) In any case, there is never any male present, as if the product were ashamed to associate itself in any way with virility. If the female consumer can tolerate this evocation of the warmth of an infantile Imaginary, it is perhaps more difficult to market adult products under this same sign, and this is where the white homunculus enters the picture.

Not only does the white homunculus take on maternity in order to displace fullness from real female bodies, but he also assumes a class burden. Encoded in the "full" body is a working-class taste that lies outside the acceptable parameters of fascist discourse. Just as the female consumer may enjoy a regressive fantasy about fullness that coexists with a resistance to over-regulation, the white homunculus provides an alibi for the work- ing class to recognize itself as a class. As Bourdieu remarks, even in a demo- cratic society the professional classes tend to eat lighter foods, for which they claim to have developed "a taste." In reality, however, this "taste" for slimness is related to unconscious issues of body image and ideological stance, encoded in a classless fascist body with national overtones. In the working-class meal, that which fascism tries to efface,

> "elastic" and "abundant" dishes are brought to the table — soups or sauces, pasta or potatoes ... served with a ladle or a spoon to avoid too much measuring and counting, in contrast to everything that has to be cut up and divided, such as roasts.[53]

For the working class, "Food is claimed as a material reality, a nourishing substance which sustains the body and gives strength (hence the emphasis on heavy, fatty, strong foods, of which the paradigm is pork — fatty and salty," whereas for the bourgeoisie, "The priority given to form (the shape of the body, for example) and social form, formality, puts the pursuit of strength and substance in the background and identifies true freedom with the elective asceticism of self-imposed rule."[54] Figures like the white homunculus take up the former position in fascism precisely so that the latter position can persist in images of the body that pass themselves off as transcending class affiliation. But the notion of these puffy men, these sympathetic toys, as martyrs sacrificing their own dignity in the service of fascist ideals does not seem to fully explain their continued popularity in visual culture.

One might consider the possible place of these figures in a more general economy of production and consumption through Bergson's influential essay "On Laughter." The comic element that coexists with the pathos of the white homunculus seems perfectly captured by Bergson's notion of the laughable as related to an absence of feeling, an emotional smoothness. Bergson begins from the assumption that laughter is a kind of humanism, an essential element of socialization (intersubjective communication), but not linked with any specific subjectivities. Comedy is not an inherent quality. Rather, laughter derives from the sensory perception of objects (and these can be human objects) in an environment where the subject has been stripped of emotion: "something like a momentary anesthesia of the heart."[55] The laughing subject is always part of a group, and this has ramifications for a reading of the white body inasmuch as advertising is a public discourse addressed to readers in some group formation (on a crowded bus, in a town square, and so on). But Bergson's analysis transcends mere reception of an object by the senses; he understands the cathartic moment of laughing as itself formative of a subjectivity characterized by shared responses, as a "secret freemasonry, or even complicity."[56]

Once the social significance of laughter has been established, Bergson goes on to attribute to *all* comic situations the quality of an unexpected (nonhuman) mechanical elasticity. In fact, the essay on laughter has been brought into proximity with Chaplin's characters, particularly in the relation of the body with the machine in *Modern Times*.[57] In short, Bergson's formula suggests a relation between automatism and laughter itself. For Bergson automatism ought to be compensated by elasticity and adaptability in a "well-balanced" individual who is capable of social adjustment (humor). The automated comic object is that which seems absentminded, "as though the soul had allowed itself to be fascinated and hypnotized by the materiality of a simple action."[58] And again, although Bergson does not take this into the realm of social critique, it seems clear that this kind of absence is precisely what characterizes the "productive worker" in the rationalized factory: Chaplin fails in the factory because of an overabundance of elasticity (and, it is understood, humanity). He is laughable, however, to the degree that his "body reminds us of a mere machine."[59] Figures like the white homunculus (and there must be others) disguise themselves to provide a catharsis for the machine age. Automatism is anathema to a "humanist" thinker, whether this is understood in strictly productive terms or in terms that privilege the human in relation to concepts of metaphysical importance: élan vital, memory, duration.[60] When Bergson's social individuals laugh, they are also psychologically compelled to watch out for themselves, to make themselves less rigid, more "human" — hence the redemptive, moral dimension in the comic genre as aesthetic category.

In essence, Bergson's invocation of a dualistic morality that elevates the soul to a position of élan vital (because we "disregard in it the elements of weight, of resistance, and, in a word, of matter)"[61] is mirrored in the fascist science of bodily purgation. But unlike the discourse of fascism, Bergson's philosophy is not content to leave the question of materiality in suspense. He returns to the body and asks:

> Suppose, however, that our attention is drawn to this material side of the body; that, so far from sharing in the lightness and subtlety of the principle with which it is animated, the body is no more in our eyes than a heavy and cumbersome vesture, a kind of irksome ballast which holds down to earth a soul eager to rise aloft. Then the body will become to the soul what ... the garment was to the body itself—inert matter dumped down upon living energy.[62]

This seems to me to be a precise description of the position of the white homunculus in the large scheme of body management I have been tracing in this chapter. In relinquishing its hold on the higher functions of humanity (the soul), the white homunculus arouses a sense of comedy in a group of viewers, who then also solidify their (human) identity as a group. Simply put, the white homunculus sacrifices its humanity in the service of a positive social (and humanizing) force.

Bergson considers a body "comic" if there is some concrete disjuncture between its surface or crust and what one imagines to lie beneath. This perception is certainly possible in the white man; we need only think of Bibendum — the certainty that he is massive and solid contradicted by the knowledge that he is formed by a series of bicycle (or later, automobile) tires that cover a hollow inside. This characteristic of the comic as "disjointed" matter can be transferred from the individual body to a larger disjuncture between social ritual and natural behavior; that is, to a moment when the solemnity of a social act is broken apart and revealed as travesty or delusion. Taking advertising as just such a social moment (the ritual involved in beholding an ad and then being "persuaded" or becoming "interested" in an economic sense), it is easy to understand how the white body fits within a scheme in which pleasure or laughter is released. I have focused on Bergson's tract and given particular emphasis to its aphoristic logic because it seems to be the same kind of logic involved in the early forms of advertising — in particular, in the use of what I term "toy" bodies (for lack of a more inclusive word). And the effect of such images is not limited to readers who are theoretically knowledgeable about the antimechanistic bias of humanist ideology: "A kind of dim, vague instinct may enable even an uncultured mind to get an inkling here of the subtler results of psychological sciences."[63] The white man seems to be a point of convergence, then, between the uncanny, the automatic, and the toy. It straddles the line between the human and the humanoid. To use Bergson's words, it is like a person that gives us the "impression of being a thing."[64]

To further clarify the relation between automation and salesmanship in the white body, Baudrillard's "three ages" of the simulacrum may prove helpful. The first age, spanning the period from the Renaissance to the industrial revolution, is characterized as *contrefaçon,* a form of wit or playfulness. The automaton, that eighteenth-century curiosity that can digest grains of corn and defecate, play a tune on the flute, or generate texts on a machine, belongs to the second age: the order of *production.* To some degree, the automaton attempts to imitate human motion, human form, and in this sense it introduces a slight sense of discomfort or menace. On the other hand, the robot that emerges in the third age after the establishment of a capitalist market no longer bothers to interrogate the relation of reality to appearance, of science to the "marvelous." The only truth of the robot, Baudrillard claims, is "mechanical efficiency."[65] The white homunculi of the Italy of the 1930s might be said to lie on the border between the second age—that of production—and the third age, in which the logic of the market collapses and is replaced by *simulacra*. The automaton always involved a narrative of disclosure or trickery; either its mechanism would be revealed, or it would continue to exercise its power of fascination over its public. But the robot does not even aspire to such gimmicks: it simply works. The robot "no longer resembles or disresembles man or God, but an immanent logic of the operational principle."[66] The robot can be constructed in a series of identical machines or simulacra, such that production as a force, so essential for Marx's thought, loses all meaning; what matters now is reproduction, the stamping out of indistinguishable workers whose form is not even grounded on an "original" or prototype to which they may refer.[67] Baudrillard admits a critical tendency to draw an analogy between the automaton and the robot on the basis of a humanist, antimechanistic bias. As in Bergson's definition of the comic, the primary response to both of these "inanimate" types is potentially laughter. But the robot moves beyond caricature; it is a being that labors, even if its gestures are mechanical. The robot cannot be confused with humanity, nor does it arouse a sense of the *Unheimlich* as in Freud's reading of the animated Olympia.

The white homunculus seems to me to exist in a no-man's-land between these two types sketched by Baudrillard. On one hand, it lacks the spring mechanism, the trickery behind the automaton—the being that strives to recognize itself in the image of a god, but finally reveals its own subhuman status. On the other hand, it lacks the streamlined determination of the robot—the worker—characterized in Baudrillard's pessimistic postmodern ethic. Perhaps what distinguishes the white homunculus from either the modern or the postmodern automaton is the introduction of the category of gender, which occupies a charged space between Baudrillard's spheres of production and reproduction. The white homunculus takes up the bulk that is purged from the body, and it wallows in its own slowness—a sign of regression that may be understood in phylogenetic or ontogenetic terms. He appeals to both men and women through his comic inelasticity, and he

evokes a sense of nostalgia for some safer time. Only by reading him in relation to representations of "real" gendered and classed bodies can one understand his status as alibi within a fascist ethos.

Agricultural Production

Unlike the uncanny white homunculus, bodies associated with the agricultural sector tended to draw on a conventional and realistic visual language.
In fact, there is no significant stylistic distinction between the codes employed in propaganda addressed to peasant workers, and in selling the farm
products of a given region to a larger base of consumers. The fulsome
peasant woman offering her gifts, her maternity, her fertility, was recycled
as a national emblem for targets that cut across class lines.

Agrarian bodies exhibit solidity and mass. Many of the posters figure
children against the background of wheat *fasci,* the young bodies soft and
plump, not stiffened like the phallic soldier. The grain campaign specifically marked this style as appropriate for the peasant class, just as it marked
the reduced, geometrical bodies as appropriate for an urban population. In
the "battle of the grain," the body is never shown toiling, but simply brimming forth with fertility. An equation is made between the fertility of the
peasant body and the earth itself: sheaves of wheat blossom forth from a
woman's lap; an enormous ear of corn juts forth from a man's crotch; bodies embrace the earth and glow from the nurturing sun; "a good inseminator" sows his seeds, a specter that haunts a young girl (figure 26). Such images are not really examples of sexual *symbolism.* They represent agricultural
production and sexual production as the two languages are truly linked in
the fascist mind-set. The fascist makes no distinction between the peasant
womb and the land; nor is he interested in cultivating either one or in having any sort of proximity to it, only in dividing it up, quantifying it, and as-
signing prizes for the highest yields. The fascist wants to empty out the
cities and move the productive force into an anachronistic, idealized world
that can only exist, by nature, in representation. The image that is used to
sell the products of the land has nothing to do with production, and the
capitalist will wait until the agricultural commodity has been transformed
into (clean) capital before he takes hold of it.

Representations of the agricultural ethos seem to exist in a realm of
soft-washed realism that exhibits none of the pathological symptoms of the
reduced, geometricized bodies — such as the white homunculus — found
in other sectors of the economy. The reason for this has more to do with

26. "He who saves is a good inseminator." (Salce Collection, 0583.)

the definition of an appropriate style for *addressing* the peasant than it does with something like a "normalcy" or "well-adjusted" attitude toward the farmer on the part of the market. For the fascist, the idealized countryside is full of associations with the "sane" and "healthy," hence the desirability of linking various types of production that *make use* of raw materials with the agricultural. Consumers must be made to understand, for example, that "the dessert industry is truly an eminently agricultural one, and that its products do not belong to the category of luxury goods."[68]

Mussolini's particular obsession with idealizing rural life has been well documented. The conflation of the *strapaese* ("super country") movement in the visual arts with political ideology results in stylistic consistency for this area of popular imagery.[69] When Mussolini takes a vacation in the Romagnule countryside in 1926, he insists on strolling over toward the fields and taking his place atop a tractor pulled by oxen. As is often the case, he is photographed, and the event is captured for the popular imagination—for urban newspaper readers. After two hours, the tractor (coincidentally branded with the name *Italia*) is brought into its shed where Mussolini is surprised to find "his own portrait with the salute of the agricultural worker, his brother in the great undertaking."[70] This scene can only be staged, reported, and represented because of the actual distance of the reading public from rural life; as in the advertisements for agricultural products, production itself is a monumental parade through fields that has no apparent relation with the expenditure of energy.

The *battle* of the grain, represented in high, heroic style, followed along these same lines. As more than one historian has noted, this campaign, begun in 1925, did not strive to improve the economic standing of individual farmers, whether in the organized North or in the impoverished South, as much as it sought to solidify the power of the rural bourgeoisie, those provincial landowners who sponsor a conference on "Dentists for Dante" in Pasolini's wicked scene from *Hawks and Sparrows*.[71] Fascist agricultural policy ended up devastating the land, severely reducing animal husbandry, and favoring the landowner over the peasant laborer. The battle did little to improve technology or to introduce more effective methods of crop rotation, which would have benefited the South in particular. So when artists represent the happy peasant in the middle of vast fields of golden grain, they are repeating a myth very much tied to nostalgia and nationalist sentiments—a myth that *specifically* serves to avoid any discussion of the reinstallation of feudal relations of dependency. More significantly, the origins of the return to an "interest" in peasant culture on the part of the regime also displaces the reality of northern wealth, inextricably tied to the military-industrial complex. Images of agrarian fecundity are a distraction from class difference, which was quickly becoming exaggerated precisely because the *battaglia* and land reclamation projects widened the gap between the industrial North and the agricultural South. In effect, the battle saw to it that "agriculture was placed in a subaltern position with respect to industry."[72]

Although the terms of the *battaglia* promised that advanced machinery, chemicals, crop rotation, and other forms of "progress" would mean a reduction in difficult labor associated with farming, a decrease in agricultural labor power explicitly contradicted Mussolini's politics of ruralization — the utopian absorption of labor from the overcrowded cities into the countryside. Unstated and unrepresented in the images of agricultural production is the cultural technophobia, the fear of large masses of unemployed or disenfranchised urban workers who had formed one of the core groups of communists in Italy, along with migrant workers. The stable, full-time farmer, entirely dedicated to rural life, is the exemplar recycled over and over in both propaganda and advertising. In actuality, however, the *ventennio* witnessed mass internal migration to the cities, the very centers of marketing that contributed to the making of rural images. If one cannot read a particular pathology into the images of the land and its products, it is because that area of life is so wholly closed off from any disturbances that might puncture its seamlessness, so very alien to the urban centers of design.

Industrial Production

The Body and the Hand

During the course of my research on "producing" bodies, it became quite apparent that one particular figure was recycled frequently. Instead of a body working, say, on an assembly line, artists would often represent a hand, either superimposed over a machine cog, or looming beside factory smokestacks like a specter. The producing hands of various industrial advertisements are always cocked and rigid; they sometimes form the horizontal bar around which the cogs themselves turn. Sometimes the outstretched hand is a figure of paternal protection, holding the tiny bodies of workers or serving as a comforting cover, but always it is larger than life, severed, and masculine (figure 27).[73] A hand, glowing with a holy aura, represents the regime itself as intervening to save the family or private enterprise.

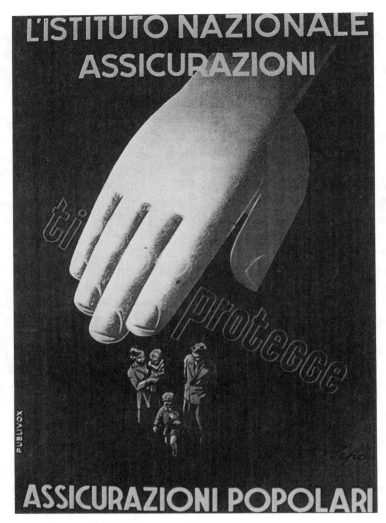

27. Insuring hand. (Salce Collection, 3722.)

Often one finds multiple hands, those belonging to the workers, who form part of the body of the state. There are many, many more examples of the hand and machine motif from advertising of the 1930s. Of all the iconographic topoi repeated during this era, the hand holds a place of the highest importance, and one need only flip through the collections of advertising art for confirmation. This topos is not limited to Italy: the hand is an irresistible motif in modern poster art from a wide variety of social and political formations.

My first reaction was to read the producing hand of Italian advertising as the visual synecdoche for the arm of the Roman salute. Extended, firm, also phallic, the hand would stiffen next to the machine, fascistizing production, inserting a firm support. If there was one thing Mussolini hated it was a limp hand, especially the kind wearing gloves and offering itself to another hand in the context of weak, bourgeois social relations. (He even outlawed the handshake. One wonders: would this be punishable, after a certain number of offenses, by the removal of the felonious organ?) Nevertheless, when I stepped back from this initial reading, it occurred to me that the dismembered body part, the synecdochal hand, was also a fragment, a possible sign of castration anxiety. "Watch out!" warns a worker-safety propaganda poster. "Your limbs can be severed if you aren't careful." "Workers! Wear goggles! Your eyes are at risk!" "Italians, remember!" — this is the only text included on a 1924 advertisement depicting a man falling from a bridge. The industrial risk here is not anything particular, but then, it is something quite particular: communism. One poster says, "Workers! Watch your sickle!" — and hammer, we understand (figure 28). This image includes a "good" man with bound sickle on his way home from the fields, and a "bad" man about to decapitate his little daughter, who idles dangerously close to his unprotected blade. This poster belongs to a national worker-safety campaign that was waged throughout the 1920s and 1930s; interestingly, nearly all of the images are rendered in that nostalgic, "easy watching" watercolor style of the agricultural propaganda. Bodies outlined in black, filled in with a watercolor wash; no bold colors, just soft, blended tones without a trace of the graphic stiffness of the industrial hand motif. In short, the worker-safety, anticastration campaign is based on an assumption about working-class taste and about the legibility of images. Perhaps these particular posters, whose very slogans are so blunt, so highly obvious, are essentially free of the anxiety that plagues the geometric, high-design–style hand-machine images.

The hand motif, so popular in modern advertising, constitutes a literal translation of "manual labor" (in Marx's distinction, *Kopf- und Handarbeit*) into visual terms. If manual labor and intellectual labor must be brought into harmony in Marxist thought, they must remain all the more separated for fascism to survive. Taylorization and other rationalizing sciences of production were essential to the fascist economy, and they are being sold in the industrial production advertisements, along with the given product or

28. Worker-safety poster in agricultural style. (Salce Collection, 07373.)

service. In his biography, *My Life and Work,* Henry Ford wrote that humanity is made up of only a few heads but many hands. As long as the market
forces an absolute division between these two spheres, it will always be the
heads who become cognizant of their position, because the head is the seat
of consciousness. So although Ford's statement appears objective, the very
recognition and repetition of such a notion preclude his own appurtenance
in the former group — the "heads." A working-class "uninformed" viewer
might understand these hands as a glorification of manual labor and all that
it can accomplish. But as I suggested, given the stylistic matrix of the images, the real target for such ads is not the worker or even the petty bourgeois consumer, but the intellectual laborer, the scientific manager, the *Kop-
farbeiter.* His job is to see to it that the "hands" of production move with
such force and efficiency that they will have no time to become conscious
of their status as "hands."

In fact, throughout Europe, as factories became more productive under
systems calculating units of time, owners ended up with a surplus of goods.
On one hand, the fascist desire for productivity promoted male under-
employment in favor of cheaper female and child labor. However, such desires came into direct conflict with deeply entrenched values of masculine

subjectivity. Thus, in spite of the benefits to the Italian economy of indus-trialization and progress (at any cost), Mussolini feared both female labor and machine production as they were linked with (male) unemployment. In a 1930 article, "Machines and Women," the Duce addresses the issue of world depression by stating that both machines and women castrate men, making them feel "useless" and impotent, both in terms of their broad identity and their sexuality in particular.[74]

But scientific management made it impossible to slow down or even to regulate the rate of production: time units were fixed for a given unit of labor or motion like a natural law that workers had to obey, even if it meant that factories now existed outside of an economy regulated by mar-ket demand. I see the severed hand on the cog, then, as a symbol for this fixing of productivity. And the anxiety that it generates is related to the alienation of the manager from this inevitably forward-marching process. (In *Modern Times,* Chaplin creates a comic inversion of the forward march in his routine at the steel mills. The assembly line moves from right to left like the teleological narrative of Western development. Chaplin's worker is supposed to remain fixed in one spot, using his hands and arms to tighten screws on a plate. But he cannot help but feel his entire body swept up by the motion of the line. Over and over he is thrown to the left and must work his way back toward the right, undoing the narrative of productivity. He cannot isolate the movements necessary to perform the task from his total body movements. His "fault," from the managerial point of view, is *not* that he moves too slowly, but that he moves too quickly.) During the twenties and thirties, a new term entered the economic vocabulary of in-dustrial production: bankruptcy. This happened not when a factory could no longer live up to demand or move fast enough to compete, but when it was stuck with surplus merchandise because of new efficiency.

This, finally, is the fear encoded in the fragmentary hand. The hand is a figure for the body (the body politic, the national body, the body of the enemy, the body of workers), but it is also a figure of great ambiguity and vulnerability because of its position as an extremity of the body. If the hand were to grow a brain, says the factory manager, evoking a surrealist fantasy, it would become communist.[75] The rest of the body can be elided in this formulation, precisely because of the rigid binary thinking at the basis of machine-based manufacturing. Severing the hand from the body accom-plishes the desired bracketing of sexuality and corporeality, which slow down productivity; but as a fragment, the hand loses its human anchoring and takes on the overproductive qualities of the machine. This is why the hand appears in advertisements for autarchic products and services, whose consumption is deemed the highest priority for the survival of the capitalist.[76]

Representing Taylorization

The vulnerability of the market to overproduction raises the question of how a very important moment in fascism may be represented in visual language. Taylorization fundamentally changed the shape of the body in modern times, and one need only study the industrial magazines to verify this. The body was broken down into its smallest component parts; each part was analyzed according to fatigue quotients, subjected to complex numerical calculation, and then reassembled as a highly efficient machine. Every bodily function was included in the new science—not just those directly involved in production such as turning the arm, lifting, and bending, but even pausing, inhalating, stretching out, walking to and from the water fountain, swallowing, urinating, defecating, scratching an itch, and rubbing one's eyes.

The new rhetoric of efficiency was filled with terms such as "comfort" and "humanism," as if these were to be considered the guiding principles of office and factory management. The popular understanding of the inhumanity of efficiency management is represented in *Modern Times* when Chaplin's worker punches out and goes to have a cigarette in the bathroom, only to be discovered by the capitalist who watches on a television monitor. Although this scene seems like a critique of the company intervention into "private" matters, Chaplin smokes only once again during the film, when he steals a cigar in order to be arrested along with his gamin. He is not a habitual smoker; he only uses the cigarette as an excuse to avoid working, or to elicit the gaze of the factory owner, to taunt him. Chaplin's hero is not a revolutionary, but by his resigned and ingenuous actions he helps make the power structures of the factory stand out in relief.

Given the inevitability of mechanization, one must make the body adapt while preserving its essential nobility. The human body is not a piece of wood, reasoned one technician of production, so it is best to let workers sit unless their particular tasks actually require an upright position. Standing consumes more calories than sitting, and those calories saved by taking this "comfort measure" can be invested into the product itself.[77] This rhetoric of natural comfort divides all human activity into kilocalories, the smallest knowable unit in the chain of production and consumption. But more importantly, this "humane" form of management helps us forget that the body in its erect form is really the most "civilized" body, the most developed and "noble" one. So the manager who advises his workers to sit is really forcing them into a position of regression. Learning to walk upright is probably the most important moment in the child's individuation from his or her primary parental figure, according to Margaret Mahler and other child analysts.[78] To deny the "child–worker" this freedom goes beyond a question of humanist values or tolerance to deeply buried psychic interests. But this rhetoric of "comfort" and the "natural" only masks the fact that the movement toward an erect posture has *always* been linked with power, and in Freudian psychoanalytic terms it is related to a diminution of anal eroticism, the first stage in the infant's "civilization" (and the "sign" of his developing heterosexuality).

Elias Canetti equates the act of standing up with individuation of the ruler's body, its separation out from the crowd:

> Our pride in standing consists in feeling independent and needing no support.... When someone gets up from a sitting or lying position his standing is the result of a specific effort by which he makes himself as tall as he possibly can.... The stiller he stands, the less often he turns and looks about him, the more impressive he is. He shows that he does not even fear an attack from behind, where he cannot see.[79]

What happens, then, when even time spent in the bathroom is subject to strict managerial controls? The answer is, clearly, a form of regression to the anal stage, which I have been suggesting as a crucial reference point throughout this chapter. Standard psychoanalytic thinking holds that such overregulation leads the child into a state of extreme narcissism or defense, during which everything literally turns to shit, that is, to a dirty, undifferentiated mass. The body under any totalitarian system of controls is often said to undergo a kind of soul murder, an existence characterized by an obsession with cleanliness and order, and also by a hypnotic repetition.[80]

But my question is, again, not whether such an effect might have aroused diffidence among the humanist critics of mechanization in Italy, but to what degree the mechanical could be represented in the marketing of the products themselves. If a Taylorized worker cannot be represented, this is perhaps because the real "value" of these rationalizing processes lies in the comportment of the producer *after work,* when he is transformed into a consumer. Fordism, for example, was strictly related to the American situation under prohibition, and to the relatively high salaries paid to workers. In the minds of European intellectuals, Fordism was closely associated with dubious forms of control and surveillance of workers. Nevertheless, as Gramsci wrote, the European tendency to equate rationalization with (hypocritical) Puritanism, fails to perceive the importance of "the *objective reach* of the American phenomenon, which is *also* the greatest collective effort realized until now, for creating, with unprecedented speed and singlemindedness, a new type of worker and man."[81] In Italy, where the cultural and social situation was fundamentally different, the force of rationalization did not exhibit such strong Puritan characteristics, because it was directed toward the larger cultural aims of control exemplified by the Dopolavoro. And these aspects, particularly the sexual question, which Gramsci saw as essential to both Fordism and Taylorism, *are,* in fact, legible beneath the surface of representations of the laborer.

The ideal Taylorized worker—a woman selling a Dopolavoro-sponsored cruise, for example—is almost never shown performing the particular time-unit task for which she has been mechanized (figure 29). Instead, she has been "reassembled" by consuming leisure and enjoying the reification of the distance from her own labor value thanks to the benevolence of the regime, which allows her to imitate the class that had previously enjoyed such benefits exclusively. This robust worker triumphantly raises the ship and the flag as she stands under a stream of sun rays. The rays fill her with health, and yet they sap her of whatever made her particular within the taxonomy of Italian bodies, like the cruise itself with its "single class" (*classe unica*) ticket. The workers on the deck of another ship (figure 30) are also wiped out by the blinding sun; lined up like the Asiatic workers of Africa, they are nearly reduced to the simulacrum threatened by the very technique used in their (photomechanical) reproduction.

The cruise may present itself as pure pleasure (*vacatio*) to the worker-consumer, but it also represents a form of extreme regulation of the body typical of rationalization. Irene Brin describes a variant of the *bourgeois* cruise as it sanctions conformity. Young women are shown various brochures, and,

> after having opted for the first or the second [of these cruise destinations], there was nothing else to do but follow, docilely, an organizer-windbag, who took care of the transportation, food, tourism, refreshments. The unexpected was abolished: numbered

29. Ideal Taylorized worker holding cruise ship. (Salce Collection, 02210.)

30. Taylorized workers on cruise-ship deck. (Salce Collection, 19663.)

like sheep, stunned by the extremely rapid changes of horizon, restored and sent to bed by the highest orders, the tourists had just enough strength to send some sensationalist postcard with a portrait of *toreros* or fishermen: "We are having the time of our lives, we just arrived at B. and tonight we leave again for C."[82]

But when this particular form of bourgeois pleasure was retooled for the working classes, conformity seems to take on the cast of coercion, albeit self-imposed or interiorized. Indeed, as Gramsci suggests, the repression of instincts, which is fundamental to the rationalization of production, proceeds historically through the imposition of force. But in various epochs of history, once an initial phase of exterior coercion has been normalized, workers will subsume and self-regulate various repressive practices.[83] To suggest that the cruise should be viewed within the larger frame of the "sexual question" is to take nothing away from the immediate pleasure experienced by the worker on a Dopolavoro-sponsored vacation. Pleasure, in this sense, may derive from the possibility for workers of transcending their traditional class activities by choosing from a number of exotic destinations. Unlike the typical bourgeois woman of the 1930s, this Dopolavoro worker holding a toy ship is stripped of all the trappings of femininity, as if she existed outside of any class or gender affiliation, not showing herself to any gaze, but simply enjoying nothing. There is something extremely unnerving about this image, in my view, and I locate it in the representation of the sunlight on the planes of this "perfect" working-class body. There must be a "humanizing" impulse behind this advertisement, to show the body under conditions of repose and pleasure, but the image moves beyond the pleasure principle, annihilating the self in a wash of blinding brilliance. What is represented in this image *is* Taylorization inasmuch as this can be conceived as a kind of repression of sexual and nervous impulses.[84] As I will reaffirm in chapter 5, the body exposed to rays — here, of the sun, but they might be emanating from any number of sources — begins to disappear. The new rationalization, then, is not necessarily represented in the iconographic terms of the robot or machine-body parts, even though these mechanisms exist on the surface of Taylorization (labeled as vulgar Americanization) and pose an overt threat to the European humanist intellectual tradition. Instead, consensus is formed around a picture of happiness and stability. In facing the sun, however, the body is sapped of its force — whitened and immobilized in a state that corresponds to the soul murder of the daily work routine.

Office Work

One sector of the Italian economy that was greatly affected by rationalizing techniques was office work. In Italian the workers of this sector are not designated by their "white collars," but are simply called "employees" ("*impiegati*").[85] Aside from its status as a name for this particular labor class, *impiegato* is also an adjective meaning "utilized," "adopted for a purpose." The body of the *impiegato* is "folded in" (*in-piegato*) on itself and "in use" as a time-saving measure. During the *ventennio*, *L'ufficio moderno* championed time-saving devices and procedures with almost an aesthetic fervor. The rhetoric of office technology suggests that profit making should never be the goal of labor, but that individuals should work together with team spirit, and that "the working day consists in specialization, in loving and becoming passionate about one's own work or career, whatever that may be, so that one does not become unhappy or envious of another."[86] There can be no question that the rational office — with its endlessly segmented categories of automated accounting devices, folders, sorters, printers, hole punchers, and so on — caused a shift in productivity at the level of service industries, but it is rare to find this shift represented in advertising for the services. What accounts for the undesirability of selling efficiency with the "product," or is rationalization simply not representable in the language of graphic art?

First, consider the most monumental shift within office rationalization that might affect the behavior of consumers: compensation based on productivity rather than hourly wages. In practice, the latter remained standard for many firms, but the very introduction of the former as a possibility, and its link with a rhetoric of the "happiness" of the worker, poses a significant rupture with the past. As I will propose later, hourly wages are linked with the antiquated prestige of the coin over paper money, which will have implications for the way capital itself is embodied in visual imagery. The new worker is supposed to draw satisfaction from his new efficiency, and he is theoretically going to bring his rational faculties to bear on his consumption of goods as well. Production-based wages promise something like a perfect alliance with consumption, and they represent the utopian hope of the future. The rationalization of the office justified, in part, the use of stark, modernist graphics for a wide variety of products addressed to individuals in the service sectors. But in another sense, the rhetoric of office rationalization masked two significant social realities: first, the vast intervention of the state into the service sector, and second, the lowering of real wages in tandem with a push to increase productivity. The new *impiegati* were highly conformist and were shaped in their work habits during the period after World War I. But it was precisely because this new class of workers might actually begin to view itself as a class — technically skilled, well adapted to the structures of the fascist government bureaucracy, subjected to questions of rationalization and time management — that the regime was nervous about interpellating them as a potential bloc of consumers. This fear goes a long way toward explaining the lack of any particular representational code for the new office labor.

Office work could be considered a phase of "civilization" in the ontogenetic development of humanity. In fact, many of the *impiegati* in the public sector had left their rural, ancestral villages to join the new urban expansion movements under fascism. As for the private sector, *L'ufficio moderno,* as already noted, strongly promoted the "comfort value" of sitting. The office was promoted as a more "advanced" phase in human development; the phylogenetic evolution from upright labor in the fields to "desk jobs" was crucial for this generation.

In certain archaic social formations, sitting is the privilege of the ruler, and is constituted as a form of divine leisure. Sitting, Canetti writes, is always a form of pressure on an object, a subjugation of that object and so an exercise of power:

> When we sit we make use of extraneous legs to replace the two we relinquished in order to stand upright. The chair, as we know it today, derives from the throne, and the throne presupposes subject animals or human beings, whose function it is to carry the weight of the ruler.... To sit on a chair was originally a mark of distinction. The man who sat rested on other men, who were his subjects or slaves.[87]

Standing is power and individuation, two states that are inherently disruptive of the smooth operation of the office procedure. But another thing that the fascist bureaucrat may have feared was precisely allowing any kind of link between sitting and the experience of a privileged class *as class.* Thus he makes a point of incorporating sitting into his new science, as if he had invented it himself, tailor-made for the modern office.

The "new" nobility of sitting is played out in the codes associated with the office environment, which clearly allies itself with the most modern work habits and their corresponding design initiatives. In a sense, the whole design ethos that lies behind the geometricization of forms and the "modernized" international styles of the 1930s *does,* in fact, amount to a representation of the office, which also produces advertising; the spaces and forms of advertising, however, take their distance from labor practices through their very overdetermination of the machine. Time is saved, or better, time is reified, in the empty spaces of the rationalized office buildings, with their darkened windows and neatly organized desks. The office is evacuated, and all workers may be presumed to be on vacation, but before this narrative is reconstructed, the initial visual impression is of the purity of form and the starkness of the environment, uncluttered by the worker himself.

An ad by Boccasile for Cervo hats seems to exemplify the *impiegato*, without actually picturing him in a situation of labor (figure 31). A highly "neutral" and conformist style of headgear is modeled by a mannequin, his features wiped out and reduced to planes of color. The image is elegant, but there is something quite eerie about the stark coolness, the reduced and geometricized physiognomy. Behind this perfect worker is the ghostly white outline of his very body, interrupted only by a dash of color—the green hat folded in his pocket. Taken together, these two figures—or rather, the same figure at different moments—form a narrative of disappearance. Moving from a sphere of presence (in the foreground) to one of absence, this urban office worker reflects a cultural fantasy of leisure. The disappearing act, paralleled by the removal of the hat, takes the *impiegato* literally out of himself, out of his class status, out of the reality of daily work routines. In absenting himself, this worker theoretically moves toward a moment of leisure, but one in which he is paradoxically self-effaced.

The Artisan-Producer

During the 1930s (and even to this day), Italy's economy was characterized by a large stratum of individual, artisan producers. Their handicrafts—including cloth, lace, furniture, clothing, specialized alimentary products, and liqueurs—were made available for both domestic use and export, and offered an important contribution to the gross national product. Many of these lower-middle-class producers were early supporters of fascism; they saw their wages decline in the years following World War I, and they were eager for a revolutionary turn of events. In spite of the wide variety of industries involved in this level of production, and the lack of any real geographical or institutional center associated with the artisanal effort, it could be argued that every autarchic advertisement touting Italian excellence was also an advertisement for the artisanal product, functioning almost like a collective campaign. Sometimes, in fact, artisans did group together for

31. Leisure-seeking office worker with Bantam hat. (Salce Collection, 03058.)

exhibitions and markets, effacing their particular productive labor for a larger regional theme, or advertising under the rubric of "fine handiwork" for petty bourgeois consumers.

Collective advertisements would sometimes focus on a particular product, but if there was one sign to be equated with the general category of artisan production, it might be that of a body emerging from a private space (a house-cum-factory), as in this ad for a 1926 exhibit (figure 32). The image is striking because of the reduction of a complex economic category to a simple ideogram: the enclosed space and the body with no mediating institutions, no Dopolavoro or policed physical-education activities, no machines or tools. The artisanal emblem seems to represent, then, an antithesis to the regulation of the body I located in the worker who effaces herself in the sun on the deck of a cruise liner.

In fact, in Italy, the artisan image is linked with particular intensity to a certain nostalgia for a precapitalist moment whose traces are visible everywhere in the medieval foundations of the cities. Many economic centers of the productive, industrial North were founded when feudal laborers left behind their vassalage, learned a trade, and amassed enough capital to own their own homes and instruments. Even if these individuals were dependent on the market economy that established the prices of their goods, they were essentially "independent," and unlike the Taylorized workers of fascism, they did not overproduce. They were "masters" of their trades, and so they established their own normative times and "units of energy" involved in their particular tasks. This information was not entrusted to a management team of intellectual laborers or "heads," but was passed down orally in the form of common sense from master to journeymen. In many cities, the signs of the early modern artisan revolution still are visible — in guild-sponsored architecture, in statuaries depicting patron saints, and even in the codes utilized by the tourist industry to promote regional crafts. In fact, the fascists themselves recycled some of this artisanal visual symbolism in store advertising, in the print culture of relations between small business owners and their clients, and so on. Fascism may have harnessed artisanal production for its own nationalistic ends, but the general culture also saw in the handmade object a possible escape from the controls of rationalization:

> The artist generally comes from the humble and poor ranks of the people: thus, his language and style are those of fresh and instinctive spontaneity. The artist is also (and perhaps before all else) an artisan, because he loves materials and work and he is not afraid of fatigue.[88]

32. Body emerging from artisanal space. (Salce Collection, 03507.)

These are the words of Fortunato Depero. His concept of the workshop or *bottega,* echoing William Morris, allowed him to occupy the spheres of both the artist and the artisan. This duplicity resulted in an interesting set of contradictions that emerge in his highly crafted self-presentation. After a number of years as a futurist in Rome, that is, as an individual agitator-artist,

Depero turned away from the revolutionary and destructive mode of self-promotion, while retaining the label of the movement that had helped launch his reputation. Working from his home in the provincial town of Rovereto, Depero produced designer items such as furniture, pillows, and clothing. He employed a small team of women, led by his wife, who were responsible for all the cloth manufacturing, from weaving to sewing and embroidery. A team of men practiced woodwork and construction, and this idyllic work environment was publicized along with the various products.

Depero invented his own form of furniture lacquer called "Buxus," which he marketed as a strictly autarchic product, exemplifying the marriage of artistry with artisan production. Although Buxus was essentially a wood finish, it should only be applied with "art," Depero wrote in his advertising material. "Thus it is a joy for the artist and a joy for the artisan; thanks to an autarchic product these two meet on a fertile and direct path which is essentially fascist."[89] Buxus was an exemplary "modern" invention, and its bright colors and cheerful shine link it with the automata and puppets of Depero's early futurist period. The product underscores an essential connection between the machine as game, or perhaps even idyll, and the serious business of fascist industrial production.

And so this cottage industry, this provincial, domestic scene, is framed by a rhetoric of virility, violence, and futurist aesthetics in Depero's self-advertising. Depero included the "casa d'arte" logo—the little woman working in the house—on a variety of printed materials, including announcements of exhibitions, postcards, and invoices (figure 33). The logo was even printed on stationary bearing the motto "The most violent art," which was used for aggressive letters to other futurists, for minimanifestos directed toward further refining the goals of the movement, and even for performative utterances—futurist proclamations of anger in destructive prose. The graphically arresting "casa d'arte" logo embodies the domestic artisan ethos of Depero's workshop, but its potential displacement to a document of antibourgeois aggression perfectly captures the contradictory position of the futurist in the thirties.

Depero's various artisan items sold, in part, because of the artist's reputation as a member of an established movement specifically directed toward destroying bourgeois values. Yet his theory of *auto-réclame* suggests that, in order to be compensated for his creative labors, the artist must engage in elaborate self-publicizing campaigns that often are inextricable from his other "disinterested" work.[90] The artist's activities for the Campari company exemplify this kind of engagement to such a degree that his mechanistic

33. Depero's multipurpose Casa d'Arte logo. (Courtesy of the Museo di Arte Moderna e Contemporanea di Trento e Rovereto. Copyright Fortunato Depero.)

human figurines, developed from a futurist idolization of robots and machinery, became exclusively associated with the drink products, and the company redesigned its very containers to conform with the artist's logo — his ubiquitous homunculus. Depero's own body, endlessly reproduced in the "Pubblicità Depero" logo and other self-representations, becomes this same bottle, this same homunculus ready for consumption by an endless assembly line of waiting figures who themselves turn into consumable products. The contours between self and product, between "disinterested" or pure art and commodification, are continually blurred.

The implications of the publicity of self can be understood only by reviewing the conventions of futurist self-representations, both visual and discursive. Although the futurist continually places his body into a mechanical context (he attempts to relegate himself to the status of a robot on an assembly line or the cog in a generator), a contradictory relationship with capital emerges. For while the body tries to disappear in a lineup of identical robots, the artist calls attention to his singular self as worthy of reward and as author of the very machine depicted. These contradictions are inherent in Depero's letters and sketches. The futurist ego is nourished, precisely, by his sense of belonging to something utterly modern and industrialized, but at each crank of the generator, the boundaries of the (bourgeois) self are also drawn with greater precision. The futurist tries to throw his body out into the world of machines and masculine social relations: he imagines himself on a stage, in a parade, traveling the world in a speeding car, seducing women in exotic locations. But this is very far from the reality of the artisan-producer who appropriates the futurist label in the period between the wars. Depero gravitates toward the home as an ideal, and in this sense he is no different from the working-class individual who retreats further into the domestic space in order to escape fascist control over various aspects of social and working life. In his home, this artisan repeats the paternal paradigm of fascism with his "corporation" of workers, but he is also protected, and preserves a sense of autonomy to which he had grown accustomed in his early days as an agitator, interventionist, and revolutionary.[91] I am focusing on Depero here because it seems to me that he represents a return to artisanal production, which is made possible under fascism, and which, incidentally, represents a phase after the revolutionary, "avant-garde" moment of futurism has already been suppressed.[92] Depero, like the other surviving futurists, adapted to the conditions of the regime; the retreat into the house is an exemplary image of self-engulfment. Depero's figure at work in the enclosure of the *bottega* imitates medieval miniatures of the artist's studio such as the "painter Marcia" topos.[93]

Psychoanalytic language also treats this topos of the enclosed within the context of regression. During the anal stage of development, the child begins to feel its own body as an entity with doors that shut and with real boundaries. The process of self-mastery over the sphincter is important for becoming a self-sufficient adult, and in various clinical cases of anal narcissism, the bathroom takes on the signifying power of a little "house" where the individual is "closed in" and protected. In his studies of anality, Leonard Shengold finds many patients who can defecate only in their own private bathrooms. His powerful explication of the narrative of Caspar Hauser makes the undeniable link between the enclosing space and the space of defensive instincts. The tiny house that encloses the figurine at work cannot be separated from historically determined imagery of the artisan who, through his specialization and technique, gains "mastery" over the market in its transition to capitalism. But at the same time, I would see these images in a relation to a regressive psychology of survival, adaptation, and nostalgia under the fascist regime.

Representing Capital

Along with the parsimony of defecation, Freud's anal narcissists exhibit symptoms of stinginess in their relation to real currency. In this light, I explore representations of money as a body from the *ventennio*. The very idea of a campaign to promote a particular currency suggests a situation of transition in the very status of money. Beginning in 1924, the Italian lira lost value against British and American currencies as inflation increased. At the same time, imports were an increasing threat, primarily because of a poor harvest and the need for certain raw materials. Consequently, in 1925 and 1926, years when Mussolini was attempting to consolidate his party power and personal prestige, the Italian public saw a rise in prices and a decline in real wages. In 1926 Mussolini called for a radical revaluation of the lira, because he understood that the very survival of the regime depended on it:

> My examination of the exchange rate has led me to this curious conclusion: when the budget was in a deficit, the circulation of money was equal to or greater than it is presently; the interallied debts had not been paid off; and the regime was just beginning to gain strength — the exchange rate was good, or at least discrete.

> Now that that budget is balanced, circulation is diminished; for-
> eign debt has been taken care of with notable reduction; the coun-
> try is calm and is working as never before — the exchange rate has
> worsened.[94]

This passage is revelatory for the present discussion since it demonstrates
that autarchy, or real independence from foreign debt, was not enough for
the Duce. He wanted the lira to transcend its function in relation to other
currencies, to take on the value of his own aura and vice versa, for domestic consensus. Of course, this desire for affirmation at home reflects a sense
of Italy's inferiority in its relations with other nations. The fascist ego would
only be built up by gestures of symbolic currency revaluation:

> Do we have a program? [Mussolini asked] No. Saying that we
> want to stabilize the lira doesn't mean a thing. It is the level of sta-
> bilization and the *modus procedendi* that count; there is backward
> stabilization and forward stabilization.... There is no doubt of our
> preference. We must resolutely adopt the latter method of stabi-
> lization, because the former leads to the abyss.[95]

The ideal of an exchange rate of ninety lire to the pound was considered
too low by the regime hierarchy, and too high by the industrialists. Finally,
in 1927, Mussolini's "quota ninety" won out, but this rate continued to
hurt workers, and contributed to significantly higher unemployment. Working against his block of capitalist supporters, Mussolini waged a campaign
for the "quota ninety," appealing primarily to the middle classes, who were
desperate for some stability after the war. By pegging the lira deliberately
high in relation to foreign currencies, Mussolini helped create the *impression* of a strong Italian economy. In point of fact, with exports down, Mussolini's decision helped bankrupt many companies; increase dependence on
American banks; and create a widening gap between industrialists capable
of consolidating their factories into larger productive blocs and the workers
themselves.

Contrary to this history of consolidation and deliberate raising of the
value of the lira, in propaganda for this "battle," capital is figured as a sexless
homunculus, a flattened body ascending a sheer mountain face (figure 34).
Fighting against the forces of inflation, this little naked god pushes a roll of
accounting paper (but could it also be toilet paper?) wound around a roll of
the *fascio.* This image effaces the fact that the state can control the level of
the currency along this "stairway" of value; in fact, the regime could have

34. Lira as ascending homunculus in propaganda. (Salce Collection, 12994.)

pushed the lira to an even higher place (with respect to other currencies) except that this would have meant a diminishing return in international prestige. "Capital-man" appears in an ad for a financial magazine called *Progress,* as if currency fluctuation were something to be learned, cultivated. But in reality, progress is a matter for the state to manipulate.

Significantly, the god of capital deals in paper, and not a mound of coins, for example. As Canetti suggests, the coin can be a potent symbol of and for mass consensus when it is heaped up in the form of treasure — a totality that is, nevertheless, composed of "individuals" with well-defined borders, bas-relief monuments or faces, and a determinate weight or "character."[96] On the other hand, paper money lacks this "friendly," immediate, and weighty quality, so it does not arouse the same sort of mass fidelity as the coin. In everyday life, piecework, or even hourly, wages were still calculable within the range of coins during the 1930s, and so the coin retains a particular place of importance within the cultural imagination. Nevertheless, paper money clearly represented "progress" exemplified in the naked god and his uphill battle to "save" the Italian currency. Canetti writes: "If the coins of earlier days had something of the strict hierarchical organization of a closed society, modern paper money is akin to the inhabitants of a great city."[97] In the *Progress* image, the lira clearly exists in a certain relation to a monumental, rational structure that obliterates the old-fashioned forms of monetary (and social) exchange centered on the coin.

As in many other examples of fascist propaganda, greatness here develops at the expense of the individual and his obsolete forms of individual accumulation. The lira exists outside of any reference to class or region; it is an "every body," a demigod. The makers of capital — the workers in the stock market — also are slatelike and identical, absolutely without volume, paper cutouts (figure 35). One could read Sironi's ad for this daily financial newspaper as an ironic commentary on the uniformity of the capitalist enterprise, an early version of the "man in the gray flannel suit." But what seems important here is not the conformity of these bodies, but the equation of capital with paper. This image is clearly addressed to urbane, sophisticated readers who would have been able to appreciate the modernist style of these bodies clamoring for a piece of the action on the market floor. The legibility of these bodies is limited to viewers who understand the world of abstract money and who have transcended the value of the coin.

35. Cutout paper traders on the stock exchange. (Salce Collection, 12436.)

Savings

In the late 1930s, the regime sponsored an annual "savings day," promoted primarily in the context of family values, and through the rhetoric of future stability. A father might be shown helping his son put coins into a piggy bank, or, in another version of this paternalism, a white boy teaches this same action to an infantalized black *moretto* (figure 17). In a 1937 poster for the annual savings day, an entire geometricized family stands with their backs to the picture plane, gazing off into the blinding sunlight (figure 36). Light is reflected on the giant savings-account passbook that floats before the family. As in the image of the perfect Dopolavoro worker, the sun is an apparent symbol for the future and the continuity of the regime, but it simultaneously obliterates identity. It is a Mediterranean, life-giving force that elevates this petty bourgeois family above the quotidian conditions of their labor, and conveys them to a higher plane. Their thrifty habits are rewarded with this transfiguration, and the viewer of the poster is positioned right behind them, bathed in the glow of whatever light shines forth around the edges of the picture plane. But again, the extreme, almost extraterrestrial brilliance of the light and the effacement of the bodies shown here appears extremely disturbing; a sort of Oedipal-drama, close-encounter-with-an-alien-presence narrative. The Hollywood version of this story would have the freshly landed alien at first threaten, but then confirm, the family romance; he is either adopted as a grotesque but lovable pet (or perhaps as a son, depending on the degree of anthropomorphism), or he returns to his planet brimming with the love he witnessed on Earth. If his presence brings a momentary uneasiness, he never breaks the bonds (in this case, savings bonds) that the family group always depends on providing for the next generation.

In another variant of this Oedipal image, a mother holds her newborn son up to the sunlight, the great life-giver and obliterator (figure 37). So bright is the day that it essentially blinds us to the boy's genitalia, cleansing the image and rendering it holy. But what is truly horrendous is not the little penis that we (do not) see, but the (hidden) gaze of the mother, directed as it is into the child's anus. The mother effaces herself (saves herself, economizes herself) for the sake of the future (soldered in the heroic relation between the child and the sun, which decapitates her). But it would be wrong to suppose that this image represents the eclipsing of the maternal by the new generation of fascist males. Although she is made acephalous by the sacrificial baby, the mother exercises a form of sphincter

36. Savings-day (Oedipal) family campaign. (Salce Collection, 16970.)

37. "Basic fault" ad with mother and child. (Salce Collection, 04098.)

control that parallels the dictatorial relation of the Duce with his subjects. Like the biblical sacrifice of Isaac, the offering of the fascist baby empowers the parental figure. Here is what Canetti writes about the horrors of maternal control:

> The concentration of the appetite for domination on such a small organism gives rise to a feeling of superiority greater than that obtaining in any habitual relationship between human beings.... It means that a creature is kept prisoner, even though in this case genuinely for its own advantage; ... she can enforce *growth* — something to which rulers only approximate by conferring promotions in rank.... There is no intenser form of power.[98]

In citing this passage, I do not wish to give the impression that the savings day subverted fascist authority by conferring extraordinary power on women. Rather, the mother takes over state functions in her relation with the child, and so ultimately strengthens the hierarchy of the regime itself. If the regime went to the trouble of sponsoring this campaign, and collaborated in the creation of this kind of heliosacral imagery, the family needed to be persuaded to save. Something was threatening the pact by which parents always provide for their children in exchange for the children providing for their own children, and so on, endlessly, into the future. Yet the image does *not* represent the producer, who makes this relation ultimately possible.

Material Metabolism

Perhaps the repression of the unspeakable truth of "productivity" in so many of these images can best be understood in relation to a more general theory of economics. In the *Grundrisse,* Marx critiques the political economists' discussion of production as something distinct (and natural, universal). Such an idealization allows the economist to sneak *bourgeois* production into this scheme of "natural laws" as if it belonged there inextricably. Marx's definition of production, on the other hand, is "an appropriation of nature on the part of an individual within and through a *specific* form of society."[99] There can be no discussion of production (or consumption, for that matter) in the abstract, and so no opportunity to slip the particulars of bourgeois production into the general definition.

In a section of the *Grundrisse* titled "Capitalism, Machinery and Automation," Marx states that automated machine production, an inevitable feature of advanced capitalism, does not transform or "dehumanize" labor, it actually takes over labor altogether. In this sense, mechanization is not so much dehumanizing, as it is organicizing (of machines). Just as the human consumes various products, more or less transformed beyond the stages of "raw materials," so machines consume coal or other fuel, what are called by Marx *materières instrumentales*. This relation is not merely metaphorical or coincidental: both machine and human consumption are mediated by production, which is, in turn, regulated by laws of consumption in a cycle of material metabolism. It is the "head" (the scientific manager) who stands near the machine and regulates the rate of metabolism. In its anxious use of the "hand" motif, Italian industry anticipates the disappearance of the human form altogether from production. In fact, it is the "head," objectified in the machine, that will take over, pushing the body to the side, reducing it to the role of occasional intervenor, an overseer who adjusts the machinery when necessary. At the moment of fascism, though, this replacement is not absolutely complete, so the "heads" and "hands" continue to battle for hegemony.

Although fascist production is not entirely automated, it is moving inevitably in a direction that will absolutely alienate the producer from his products. In the midst of this transitional moment, then, the homunculus figure pops up, like an uncanny jack-in-the-box, to mediate between (human) labor value and the displacement of labor by its capitalization. Marx writes: "The appropriation of labor by capital confronts the worker in a coarsely sensuous form; capital absorbs labor into itself—'as though its body were by love possessed.' "[100] In this poetic phrase, Marx figures the demonic embodiment of labor into the machine; and the visual analogue to the process can be located in the many (mechanical) bodies that populate mass culture and advertising (figure 38). The body possessed by love cannot shake off the exterior forces that assault its boundaries. This body stiffens and becomes a spectacle (it gives itself to be seen—*se donne à voir,* to use a term from Lacan). So on the one hand, the homunculi of advertising are humanizing "salesmen" that ease the culture toward its late capitalist phase; they are also the visible signs of the moment of possession, the erection that holds itself indefinitely.

38. Body as machine.

4 / The Body and Its Armors

Advertising and Gender in the 1930s

Theories of advertising commonly assume that the female body and feminine sexuality are used to sell products. For the male consumer, this is supposed to work as a mechanism of pure seduction or attraction, and it presupposes the supremacy of the male gaze as a universal model for vision. Advertising figures prominently in feminist studies of visuality, and has been taken as the exemplary standard of the object-position of the female body.[1] Within this same paradigm, the image also works, conversely, to create a sense of envy or lack in a female viewer. Although some thinkers recently have called the asymmetrical, male-dominated, dyadic structure of visuality into question, it seems clear that this kind of paradigmatic sexism of the market was squarely in place during the 1930s. If the notion that "sex sells" is valid within normative capitalist culture, it falls apart to some degree in the fascist market populated by bodies that have been stripped of gender and suited up in coats of armor. And the kind of rational logic that might lead a manufacturer to commission sexualized female bodies — the kind of masculine "knowledge" that *L'ufficio moderno* promotes with a wink — seems to lose its ground in a series of images that I will present in this section.

The market, under normal conditions, obeyed the fascist state in taking "as axiomatic that women and men were different by nature." For the historian of fascism, Victoria de Grazia, this led the government to politicize difference "to the advantage of males and made it the cornerstone of an especially repressive, comprehensive new system for defining female citizenship, for governing women's sexuality, wage labor, and social participation."[2] The language of advertising makes light of this axiom through a pleasant, jibing sort of humor that ultimately reaffirms the commonsense, ahistorical, and cross-class values of difference. "The Boccasile woman exemplifies that highly attractive Junoesque form which is often used these days," says a blurb from *L'ufficio moderno.* "And the manufacturers, or at least certain among them, think that the more the bust sticks out, the more likely the public is to buy their aperitif, to sample their cheese, to wear their shoes. Naturally, these are folks who understand a lot about advertising."[3] The magazine, with its obsessive insistence on "rationality" and "rationalism," repeats proverbs and adages related to a kind of *inter hominem* wit of which this is only a mild example. But the "Boccasile woman," best known from the covers of Pitigrilli's pulp magazine *La signorina grandi firme,* was also a troubling character whose ultra-slim "crisis" (*"crisi"*) waist troubled Mussolini, and whose disproportionately long legs threatened to distract the serious fascist from the serious business of production.[4]

Nevertheless, the new "science" of advertising, which was also the "science" of psychology, and thus linked with a certain notion of progress exemplified in American, French, English, and German culture, felt compelled to make use of the human figure. And if the psychological mechanism at work in this compulsion is one of identification, the female body seems to perform a positive function for both genders, just as the Boccasile woman both attracts men on a purely visual level and satisfies women's fantasies on a narrative one. The pseudoscientific program of advertising through female sexuality is summarized in one of the earliest Italian tracts of a practical nature, Roggero's *Come si riesce con la pubblicità* of 1920:

> The human figure retains its sovereign position in the modern poster. It is certainly true that if the golden age of the Greeks left us the pure white forms of their Venuses, we will leave trichromatic prints to our great-grandchildren, illuminating with the sweet feminine smile and the sexy torso of a *demi-vierge* the miraculous properties of our mineral waters, our vermouths, and our sparkling wines.... The human figure, then, and especially the woman, now

forms an impressive component of the multicolored world of the
poster.... such a varied, female, seductive, and inviting world ...
attracts all the various social classes.[5]

Roggero's invocation of modern advertising as a new classicism whose iconography centers on the human body as a *popular* aesthetic ideal contrasts ironically with Marinetti's dismissal of the Victory of Samothrace in favor of a
racing car. In point of fact, the "cheap" Venuses that populate liqueur ads
of the teens and twenties represent a stylistic current that continues to exist
alongside the bolder graphics of the neofuturists and other international
modernists.

A whole series of rules comes to govern the targeting of women in a
marketing campaign, based on this sort of "commonsense" sexism. Female
psychology assumes that women are ultimately pragmatists who prefer shorter
texts and direct language rather than superlatives, or — to use Mussolini's
well-worn phrase — "women are analytic, not synthetic." The notion that
women might be important targets of a *rational* campaign could be seen as
a sort of feminist victory over control, but this seems too optimistic. Perhaps
Mussolini ought to be taken literally at his words: women do consume, they
do form a part of the market, but their particular psychological makeup actually only enslaves them to this market:

> Today's woman is intelligent and well informed. A feminine text
> that is affected and *charmant* does not convince her at all. For the
> woman of today, silly poetry and the pseudointellectual babble
> that once might have elicited "oohs!" and "ahhhs!", to say noth-
> ing of "sures!", sighs, and so on, now appear ridiculous. All of those
> companies, those advertisers that turn to so-called D'Annunzian
> writing and graphics when they have some product to sell to women
> ought remember that ... it is better to be slippery with one's feet
> than with one's tongue.[6]

More proverbial wisdom from the pages of *L'ufficio moderno* for the modern
ad man to read on his way to work. But in fact, whereas the author of this
piece seems to echo Roggero's "innocent sexism," the reference to a D'An-
nunzian pictorial and verbal language offers concrete advice to avoid what
were considered traditional feminine styles (art nouveau, or Liberty, graphics). These very styles had been at the heart of a debate on the "woman
question" that positioned Mussolini on the side of marriage and traditional
morality, against Marinetti and the futurist "marriage as bourgeois slavery"
decrees, with their Leninist echoes.[7] "Modern" ads should thus avoid a

feminine *style* on the surface, but should also "work over" the female target through a subtle manipulation of psychological factors. This avoidance of older graphics allows the ad to appear in a fascist (male) marketplace without drawing attention to gender. The market, then, is beginning to grow up, and its modernization thrusts images into a fascist ethos, where they either sink or swim by winning broad consensus.

According to the new, modern science, then, women tend to buy products for a number of reasons linked with their primarily invidious nature: either the female consumer sees another woman with the product or she believes that if she acquires it, she will make another woman jealous.[8] The discourse of advertising excuses women for this character imperfection and almost finds it endearing in the way that any dominant discourse can make light of peccadillos of a subjugated group without seriously questioning internal contradictions. Men respond to brand names, whereas women are more economical and often will choose the item available at the most "rational" price, relates an article on gender difference and buying habits.[9] But the inherent rationality of the female raises an interesting question; namely, why shouldn't the woman, with her superior sense of saving, be an effective business executive, an effective fascist leader? The reason is that, although she is good at consumption within the domestic sphere, a woman loses her economic sense when it comes to durable goods like tools or machines. These products—the heavy-duty and "serious" goods of fascism—should therefore be sold through persuasive advertising, or that which the Americans call "reason why" advertising. In other words, the thrifty and rational female consumer ideally mirrors the larger mechanisms of the fascist market, but she is limited in some "intuitive" way to performing home economics. The science of advertising makes a perfect and supposedly "natural" equation between the psychology of the target group and the products to be pitched to this target.[10] This universal harmony exists within a capitalist economy whose laws have now, magically, become "natural" and "necessary."

But shifts in feminine consensus become irrelevant when all bodies are represented not as entities whose sexuality is knowable through a gendered division of labor (men as producers of goods for fascist industry, women as producers of soldiers for the fascist army), but rather, as beings whose very identity is protected from all sexual desire (which is, however, often assigned to the female, as Klaus Theweleit insists throughout his work). On the other hand, this discussion of the ways in which the irrational is confined and constricted cannot utterly do away with the scholarship that seeks to trace the relation between state apparatuses and individual behavior. My point, at least initially, is simply that the two sectors should be presumed as neither utterly intersecting nor absolutely incongruous. There should be no theory of sexuality without history, no history without theory.

The bodies that I consider in this chapter are not paragons of their gender or reflections of historical assignments of characteristics to gendered subjects as much as they are pathetic and vacuous representations stripped of identity altogether. The relation between a vacant equalizing tendency in certain images and the persuasion of the marketplace is not something one can find "rationalized" in the pages of *L'ufficio moderno* or other trade publications. At times, the body seems to erase any traces of its own gender—to masquerade or cross-dress—as a security measure, almost as if to escape the controls of the regime. I do not mean to suggest that the advertisers themselves resisted regime standards through a subversive manipulation of traditional gender roles. Rather, it seems as if the body takes control of its own boundaries and retreats within the protective, framed representations of certain products.

Male-Order Armor

During the 1930s, the Pirelli Tire Company of Milan, one of Italy's largest corporations and a key supplier of arms and other matériel to the war machine, ran a series of ads for their "modern" trench coats (figure 39). Pirelli dealt in rubber; they manufactured tents and canvas tarpaulins; they furnished parts for the trucks and tanks that navigated the harsh East African landscape. On the domestic front, however, they were carving out a piece of the water-repellent outerwear market—an area of significant potential, given the climate of northern Italy. Their ad campaign aimed to make the trench coat an essential item in every individual's closet; like other products encountered in this study, the trench coat was presented as classless, genderless, ageless, timeless, and free of ideological implications. Beige, waterproof, lined: there is not much difference between the tailoring of one coat and another. So the key was to promote a brand name as the most resistant, the most "classical"—in short, to strip the coat of any semiotic implications whatsoever, reducing it to a kind of body armor that, in turn, causes the body itself to disappear.

Like the armor of cartoon chases, the raincoats of these advertisements stiffen or follow the contours of a well-toned body that is itself eerily absent from the representation. The effect of such inflation suggests a kind of

39. Pirelli trench coats. (Salce Collection, 03810.)

sympathetic animation of garments, similar to the comicality of the inelastic body in Bergson's essay on laughter. As discussed in the context of the white homunculus (see chapter 3), clothing without a body takes on the qualities of a crust:

> Here we perceive how easy it is for a garment to become ridiculous. It might almost be said that every fashion is laughable in some respect. Only, when we are dealing with the fashion of the day, we are so accustomed to it that the garment seems, in our mind, to form one with the individual wearing it. We do not separate them in imagination. The idea no longer occurs to us to contrast the inert rigidity of the covering with the living suppleness of the object covered: consequently, the comic here remains in a latent condition.[11]

Bergson's animated garment has implications for a discussion of mechanization as inherently comic when viewed against the motility of "real human" behavior. "On Laughter" also opens a passage to a possible link between the mechanistic man of modern industrial production and his embarrassment in finding himself "trapped" in fashion. For once the trench coat is removed or becomes the object of a scrutinizing gaze, it ceases to fit "naturally" onto the bourgeois body, but reveals itself as fashion, that is, as something tied to specific socioeconomic conditions and as subject to change.

Images like the disappearing body of Bantam hats (figure 31) confirm the cultural discomfort with leisure wear, after the uniform garment is removed. So clothing that tries to pass off the body unnoticed only draws all the more attention to itself (as fashion) when the body is gone. The inflated and rigid shirt collars of Bergson's comedy represent a kind of bourgeois chain mail that functions in a complex economy of sexual energies.[12] In fact, the visual precedent, in Italy, for clothing without a body might be Dudovich's famous poster for Zenit brand hats, created in 1911 in full belle epoque style (figure 40). The poster shows an upholstered chair set in front of a curtain in what is obviously the waiting room of a feminine boudoir. On the chair, carefully arranged, are a gentleman's hat, gloves, and cane. The absence of the body and the highly suggestive unstated narrative originally provided grounds for the rejection of the poster by the Zenit firm; but after Dudovich won the prestigious Borsalino competition, the image was embraced. As in later versions of the absent body, there is a kind of latent sexual energy that circulates within the image that "puffs up" the clothing and gives it life. Dudovich seems to have understood this in his prophetic narration of the hat that awaits its master like a patient dog.

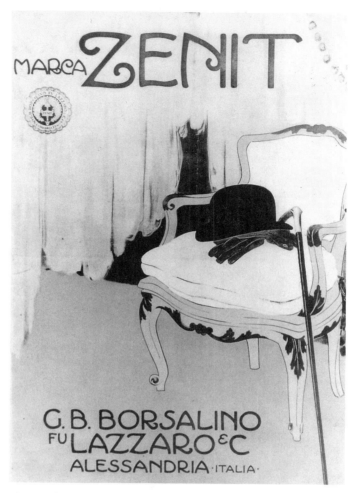

40. Zenit hats by Dudovich.

The history of the Noveltex shirt and collar campaign reveals that the artist Sepo was constantly working toward brand recognition that would also avoid any specific cultural connotations linked with a human image (figure 41). Noveltex was a French product, but Sepo's strategy could well have been applied to the Italian market. The artist could have chosen to vary the human physiognomy or corporeality associated with the shirts and collars in order to give a broader identification, but this would have been costly and inefficient. Gradually, he developed the "bodyless" shirt that not

41. Sepo Noveltex shirt collar.

only made a striking graphic design, but could be placed in the store windows that provide such an important visual matrix for marketing. The stiff and animated shirt, without any mannequin, became a well-known icon, and the goals of brand-name recognition and a broadened, almost "universal" address for the product were achieved. The many ads for Noveltex, which may have resolved a particular (and rational) marketing problem, also resonate with the "uncanny," that is, matter that literally comes to life when common sense dictates it ought to be inanimate. Beyond what I have described as a rather vague sense of "strangeness," these shirts may be linked with armor, like bourgeois uniforms (hence their putative "universality" and uniformity in terms of a marketing target) for the middle-class soldier. The shirts march along without human intervention through urban centers. Or better, the human body may slip in and out of them at will, but they retain their shape and rigidity. The waiting hat and gloves, the pert and prompt shirt, serve as bourgeois alibis at the scene of desire.

The clothing without a body also signals discipline, and in this sense, one could make a connection between civic attire and military attire. Sepo's stiffened shirts cannot be understood outside of a knowledge of the shaping of the male body through military training, even though they may appear to belong to the "white collar" sphere of bourgeois elegance. Sepo's Promethean undertaking in recreating a new (male) body of bourgeois culture as part of his ingenious ad campaign even parallels, in some way, the work of the (militarized) state. As Foucault wrote:

> By the late eighteenth century, the soldier has become something that can be made; out of a formless clay, an inapt body, the machine required can be constructed; posture is gradually corrected; a calculated constraint runs slowly through each part of the body, mastering it, making it pliable, ready at all times, turning silently into the automatism of habit.[13]

In the Noveltex ads, Sepo seems to make a visual pun on the now well-worn cultural topos of "mechanical man" that, for Foucault, is expanded in the eighteenth century when it becomes applied en masse to individual bodies at the level of "movements, gestures, attitudes, rapidity."[14] In the historical passage from the large-scale institutionalization of discipline of the eighteenth century to the witty play of Sepo's hollow shirts, the market witnesses the decadence of the "noble" body. But this does not mean that Sepo's bodies resist or critique the systems of repression that exploit their very docility. Instead, these systems are so ingrained in the fabric of everyday life under fascism that the bodies are themselves made to be the objects of a humor that takes discipline for granted and consents to it absolutely.[15]

The military body is comic in its attempt to pass itself off as a "natural" body. There is a tension, in the fascist state, between the preparedness for war and the preparedness for work:

> The most characteristic thing about a soldier is that he lives in a permanent state of expectation of commands, which is expressed in his bearing and his very shape. When he steps out of it he ceases

to be a soldier and his uniform becomes merely a facade. A real soldier is easily recognized; nothing could be more public than his state.[16]

In *Male Fantasies,* Theweleit deals extensively with the notion of "armor" for his soldier-males, and he is particularly indebted to the writings of Norbert Elias for this term. Elias, over a broad historical span, and Theweleit, within a more abbreviated one, both understand armor as it relates to the development of a particular type of ego formation or defensiveness that can be "explained" to some degree by the rise of the bourgeoisie and the triumph of a capitalist economy. Body armor suggests self-restraint against desire itself, against the libido, whether this is understood as a force coming from without or from within the body. Armor is considered absolutely necessary for adaptation to capitalism. Parallel to this formation of body armor is a shift in gender relations: both can be mapped in a diachronic axis along which fascism is merely one point, and not an aberration or break. One of Theweleit's strongest and most persuasive arguments concerns the gendered split of the subject as part of a historical process leading up to fascism:

> Men themselves were now split into a (female) interior and a (male) exterior—the body armor. As we know, the interior and exterior were mortal enemies. What we see being portrayed in the rituals are the armor's separation from, and superiority over the interior.... As a matter of course, fascism excluded women from the public arena and the realms of male production. But fascism added a further oppression to the oppression of women: When a fascist male went into combat against erotic, "flowing," nonsubjugated women, he was also fighting his own unconscious, his own desiring-production.[17]

In the images of the raincoats that I have collected in this chapter, I see a full-blown confirmation of this phenomenon.[18] Both men and women in Italian advertising wear the trench coat, and a number of companies seem compelled somehow to erase any signs of gender difference in their campaigns. Pirelli's advertising brochure from 1926 conforms to a pattern. The coats are worn by male bodies—always two identical bodies to a page, as if the whole campaign somehow hinged on representing the implicit conformity, the equalizing of identity, of this product. Like a military uniform, the trench coat lifts up the body to its full height and helps the wearer march forth into the bad weather, shoulder to shoulder with other comradesin-armor.[19] Umbrellas are also useful shields, but they can encumber the carrier and may bear an aura of "bourgeois comfort" or effeteness that would make them anathema during the 1930s. Mussolini went out in the rain with his head unprotected, and a whole generation of men followed. In his early speeches, the Duce referred to *himself* as the umbrella of Italy, as if fascism, as a political scheme, offered enough protection against the elements that a secondary, personal shield would only be redundant.[20] But what seems most interesting about the raincoat advertisements is not the antibourgeois bodily freedom implied by the rejection of the umbrella, *but the proximity of male bodies, one to another, under the protection of the armor.*

The male body — whether alone or engaged in a homosocial or homosexual position of self-reflection — must always remain in a state of protection because fascist language presupposes the inevitability of war. The body stripped of gender is an even better image, for all bodies must prepare themselves for war. A man and a woman walk side by side, both protected in their raingear (figure 42). The Ministry of War sees the umbrellas they carry as "bourgeois shields," preparatory for future battles. The accompanying text reads:

> When rain pours down from the sky, take an umbrella and you will be protected. If tomorrow something else should pour down from the sky, for example, gases, take your mask, and you will also be protected. Rain no longer bothers you when you have your umbrella. Gas no longer bothers you when you have your mask.[21]

Huddled together under the man's umbrella, the smiling couple are unaware of a silhouetted figure in identical impermeable wear just behind them.

Bourgeois armor is very easily transformed into military equipment, and there is a reciprocal interaction between these two spheres that influences what is considered normative, "civic" fashion. According to a handbook for young boys in a premilitary academy, the clothing worn by a soldier in training

> is a protective means against external influences. It must thus be in concordance with the climate, the season, the temperature, and with the type of work performed by the soldier.... Linens (undershirts and underpants) will be changed at least once a week. The wool doublet will be used as much as possible during cold or humid weather, in humid areas such as marshes, or whenever there is a threat of intestinal illness. It should be washed at least once during the season. The soldier should remove it before going to

MINISTERO DELLA GUERRA : SERVIZIO CHIMICO MILITARE

QUANDO PIOVE...SI PRENDE L'OMBRELLO....

Quando dal cielo vien giù la pioggia voi prendete l'ombrello e sie-
te tranquillo. Se domani dal cielo venisse giù dell' altro, per esempio
dei gas, prendete la maschera e sarete altrettanto tranquillo.
Con l'ombrello non vi fa più paura la pioggia.
Con la maschera non vi faranno più paura i gas.

42. Man and woman in coats from Ministry of War propaganda. (Courtesy of the Bertarelli Collection, Milan.)

bed, except if he is sleeping outdoors or in a tent. The waistcoat is indispensable for maintaining the most constant temperature possible of the organs of the lower belly. The use of flannels over the stomach is also quite useful, especially when there are extreme changes in temperature between day and night, and in the case of epidemics such as dysentery or cholera.... The care of the self, especially bodily cleanliness, is an absolute necessity for one's health. It is of the highest importance that we keep our skin clean in order for it to fulfill its normal function, and for this reason, the soldier, who is constrained to perform numerous exercises and must live with others in the barracks, is especially obligated to take the greatest care of himself, both for personal reasons and in order not to inconvenience in any way his companions or pose any threat to them with his unhealthy vapors.[22]

Bodily armor, as described here, not only protects the male body from the enemy in actual battle, but forms an intrinsic element in his daily routine, in his "care of the self," to paraphrase a Foucauldian formulation. The strips of fabric and layers of girdles that cover the body are to be peeled away and washed (but quite infrequently, compared to contemporary standards of hygiene), and then girded on again. Hygiene represents a set of personal acts that are performed as part of a larger group-management problem, and the thrust of this group is to "cleanse" (itself) through war.

"The history of all times and all nations proves that the strength of an army lies in discipline rather than in number. Discipline must be maintained during peacetime; it must be solidified during war," informs the boys' handbook.[23] The body carries itself in a state of constant readiness for death, and this has particular implications for the rules governing the social relations between men:

> Two or more men placed one next to the other constitute a row; two or more men placed one behind another constitute a line. The space between two men, placed one next to another, measured from the front, constitutes an interval; the space between two men, placed one behind another measured in terms of the depth from front to front constitutes distance.[24]

And sentinels, who often pass the night in groups of two, must never speak to one another and must never inadvertently touch as they pass one another while on guard. Older males do not mix with the boys in a form of tutelary or pederastic apprenticeship; they remain outside of the line formation, separating the bodies at precise intervals. "The instructor must intervene to correct the tendency of the men to clump close together, by teaching each one to choose two distant points ahead, and then to proceed in a forward march so that these points are always aligned."[25] In this way, (homosocial) contact between young men becomes a way of defying patronizing parental authority—the very same authority that "rains down" on Theweleit's paranoid soldiers, as I suggest in the following paragraphs. Likewise, homosexual practices seem to oppose the regulations of the military academy, but strangely, they preserve its generational and authoritative structure. All of these measurements ("management problems") are carefully controlled during training, during the imposition on the body of progressive stages of restriction by this front of fathers.

Theweleit's soldiers, who exist in a (narcissistic) state of being "not yet fully born"—that is, not substantially detached from their mothers, or "individuated"—only find their autonomy and fullness on the battlefield, at the moment of killing. The maternal overstimulator of the fascist savings campaign (figure 37) who exercises a perverse form of control in directing her gaze into the child's anus is a perfect example. Until the moment of full fascistization in battle, the soldier boys are constantly under the sway of their "parents" (even when the parental role is transferred to other figures such as the military instructor). These parents exist, for Theweleit, "up above," and they "rain down" their castigations on the infantalized soldier. *Male Fantasies* includes the following account:

> What possible defense could there be against rain that was being poured out of troughs up above? One was helpless, a child exposed to the whims of adults.... Not being recognized for what they are, or consider themselves to be, is one of the basic torments children experience at the hands of their parents and from the adult world as a whole. Adults are up "above"—more than this they look down on their children.... When does their patronizing start? Most often, when children begin to express an interest in the areas adults keep to themselves. These are the areas the children have learned to recognize as "dirty" places, the places where "dirty" things happen—especially the genitals.... These writers feel themselves being drenched "from above"; they experience themselves once again in the situation of children—a situation that reactivates feelings of hatred toward the "grown-ups" of their childhood. The associated affect is so overwhelming precisely because reactivation of that hatred simultaneously conjures up the old situation of helplessness; they couldn't fight their parents.... The most important thing to remember here is that the men in question were defenseless, and to make matters worse, innocent. (They were no longer children, so why treat them as such?) They were being subjected to the greatest injustices.[26]

Although Theweleit treats a specific group of writers, soldier males whose childhood experiences and class affiliations make for a relatively homogeneous "case study," his analyses can be applied, it seems to me, to the images of the raincoat that appear in Italian mass culture. What is significant is that the sense of defenseless innocence (the victimization of the soldier by his overbearing parents) leads him to develop armor, but also motivates him in battle, where his hatred of the enemy is a substitute or alibi for his anger over the patronizing cover-up of sexuality by the good, bourgeois family. The ultimate goal of military training is to build the body to a stage of absolute resistance whose "fundamental principle is that of handling arms calmly and with the firm proposition of not ceding; as well as the fact that any withdrawal, no matter how small, means having to reconquer lost terrain."[27] Resistance, then, is both a specific strategy for using weapons and an aphoristic ideal or slogan for the military body to follow in its effort to maintain resolve. It seems clear that the struggle of the generations in the military academy, and the bonds formed between men of the same age group in strict defiance of orders, also aid in the development of this resistance. Can it be that the homosociality of the academy is actually a necessary step in a process, even if this fact is contradicted by military discourse? Is it possible that the "protection" or "separation" of the drill, which purports to "make men of boys" through the formation of bodily armor, in some sense constitutes a highly rigid form of homosexual behavior—that is, a behavior involving men and their desires to the exclusion of women? Resistance (to desire), which is the goal of the military exercise, brings men together in a precise formation, but it nevertheless brings them together. The drill makes men into a disciplined esprit de corps in which the individual body maintains its own boundaries, while also forming a larger, common body with other men; the visual analogue to this appears in the advertisements for the raincoat.

Perhaps the relation goes even further than mere analogy, since resistance is also a key word both in fascist industry and in marketing itself.[28] Raincoats, the armor that men wear in groups, are advertised as being "resistant" to the elements. Autarchic dyes sold by the Indanthren corporation are resistant to sunlight, as well as to use itself, as I suggest again in chapter 5. In other words, a whole series of products use the term "resistance" not only to suggest "strength," but also to point to a state of alterity or existence beyond functionality where the product is literally untouched, unconsumed. The male body, moving along a trajectory toward death, becomes another of these products, and this is incorporated into the vocabulary of advertising psychology itself. Indanthren is the "most resistant" dye available, according to its campaign, and the company can be cited as exemplary in its demonstration that "any commercial resistance whatsoever can be overcome and any goal met when, with courage and a clear vision of our objectives, we are able to make effective use of propaganda."[29]

The proximity of men in the military leads to a certain disposition of the male body that undergoes reciprocal influences with civic culture, all turning around the term "resistance." Here is another fantasy, represented in an ad for Aquasol all-weather coats (figure 43): two men, one slightly taller than the other, have just gotten out of a small plane and are headed toward their waiting car. Pictures of elegance, they both wear caps, and both hold their left hand in their pocket. The shorter gentleman, escorted along by his more masculine partner, has his femininity encoded in the

43. Aquasol raincoat ad. (Salce Collection, 08023.)

binoculars case and gloves that swing freely from his right hand. His coat is more slimly cut than that of his friend, and it swings suggestively between his legs, revealing that the fabric is less rigid, less of a confining coat of ar-mor than one might expect. In fact, below this swinging coat one can see the gentleman's hose, disappearing at his slim ankles into a pair of delicate saddle shoes. There is no question that the model's body is feminine; yet his chiseled features, high cheekbones, and narrowed, dark eyes mirror those of his companion. This is not an entirely male world, because in the background, presumably about to step into the passenger seat of the plane, the viewer glimpses the curvy outline of an attenuated female. The plane seats two people, a pilot (active and male) and a passenger (passive), perfectly represented by the two gentlemen in their Aquasols. The poster reproduced here, like so many of the images in this book, bears the official stamp of the ministry, but one might almost be tempted to ask with a kind of puerile, morbid curiosity: How did they get away with it? How could this rather blatant picture of homosexual desire pass the censors? The ad suggests a whole narrative of flight, speed, erotic coupling, narcissism, freedom; but of course, this is not the way it would be read in the point-of-sale context of a fashionable men's boutique, for example. In fact, it is precisely because a viewer would tend *not to see* the details, but would simply register the styles of the coats themselves, perhaps coming away with a vague sense of the motility of the fabrics, that this image mitigates out-and-out subversion.

I am not suggesting that the Aquasol corporation encoded homosexual desire into an ad for their outerwear as a way of subtly evading the censors or even playfully outwitting the conservative consciousness of fascist corporate ideology like some Hollywood directors did in early films.[30] Such a reading would imply that a small group of initiated viewers could then recuperate this "hidden meaning" and find satisfaction in their (illicit) self-representation in mass culture. These hypothetical viewers, I argue, only came to be constituted with the larger recognition of a gay subculture that was not yet in place during the 1930s. Instead, what I see operating here is a totally conscious representation of certain bodies (the manifest form of the image) that may have a certain relation, although not a planned one, with broadly mapped unconscious desires (the latent content). Does this mean that, at least within the bourgeois condition represented here, the proximity of (feminized) male bodies actually offers something like "comfort," imputed to the feminine, as a positive selling point? Have we then come full circle, back to the truism that sex, here subtly encoded in feminized features of maleness rather than explicitly revealed in some more banal form, sells? Whether or not this reading is acceptable, it seems clear that the raincoats, which are the putative object of the advertisement, provide a form of protection from the very desire that emerges from a detailed reading of the image when stripped of its "persuasive" element.

I wish to turn now to some more obviously threatening or coercive representations of homosexual desire as contained in the worker-safety propaganda discussed in chapter 3: a worker stands on his ladder holding an oil can with its spout at crotch level (figure 44). He stares into the eyes of a

44. Worker-safety ad with man on ladder. (Salce Collection, 07437.)

coworker whose open mouth both utters the warning slogan "lubrification must be done with the machinery stopped!" and waits to receive a drop of fluid from the "erect" container. For a certain subset of viewers, this image holds a determinate homosexual charge. The body of the man about to incorrectly lubricate a large rubber belt is, through a subtle shading of color, incorporated into the machinery itself. He forms a vector with the band, and the *contrapposto* of his perch on the ladder parallels the twisting of the band around its wheel. The warning, which seems to come just in time, will have the effect of saving the inevitable waste of oil, its dispersion in a thousand different directions, should the inexperienced worker make the error of applying it directly to a gyrating wheel. And this "waste" is also the squandering of scattered seminal fluids condemned in classical oppositions to homosexual practices.

In *Modern Times,* the start of Chaplin's nervous breakdown at the steel mills is signaled by his ballet around the machinery, and it ends with his exhilarating play with just such an oil can. He begins to douse first his fellow workers, then the factory owner and police, all the while two-stepping and twitching his mustache flirtatiously. He even swings on a cable, holding the can at crotch level, as in the safety ad, then uses its long neck as a kind of swashbuckler sword. At the most basic level, the point of this scene is to show that, although such behavior is "insane," it is, of course, the most natural and cathartic for the viewer, who finds joy in the reckless inversion of the logic of productive rationalization. Chaplin's play is sexual, but not in a sense that implies a hidden subtext, since play itself, figured here in the scattering of oil on his fellow men, has the status of sexuality within the factory, where the "natural" must be suppressed. The category "natural" is constantly questioned in the film, however, and remains unresolved with the closing credits as the pair of innocents leave the metropolis and head toward an unpopulated, mountainous landscape.

Consider another example: "Danger of Infection!" warns the small poster to be hung in various worker congregation points or in a manufacturing plant (figure 45). Inside a framed space, a "bad act" is being committed. A worker wearing a cap pokes a small twig into the eye of his feminized coworker, whose powder-white complexion and cherry-red lips insert a small but determinate note of ambiguity into the proceedings. "Always turn to a doctor or nurse, never to your coworker," runs the slogan below.[31] The individual with something in his eye leans back ever so slightly, his lips parted and his facial muscles taut as if he were experiencing the start of an exquisite moment of passion.

Now, it could be argued that these two representations — one a flirtatious encounter between a machinelike "oil can" and his nervous partner, the other a gentle caress stimulating a moment of pure *jouissance* — bear no explicit or implicit relation to same-sex desire or "homosexual practices," if that term can be said to have historical or empirical meaning. What is most interesting, however, is not the reading of a coded message "behind" or "into" these pictures, but the question of how and why they came to be hortatory emblems or negative exemplars for a rhetorical discourse that employs both pictures and words, and that is specifically addressed to manual or agricultural workers. The positive, "high" version of this discourse

45. Worker-safety ad: Danger of Infection! (Salce Collection, 07414.)

emerged in the Aquasol image, and the codings of the feminine body there are very similar to those used in the sketches for the worker-safety propaganda. At the "lower" level, however, the images form the first part of a two-part persuasion—the "before" of a "before and after" advertisement. The pictures of male bodies pressed together or merely brought together, in a *tableau vivant* of "bad" behavior, are meant to repel the viewer, who will associate the disgust of such contact with the "bad" act depicted.

All of the ambiguity that was associated with "resistance" within the military academy and the raincoat advertisements is here replaced with a banal form of antihomosexual propaganda that also seems to acknowledge the real possibility of such "bad" behavior. In the sphere of the working classes, the act of rhetorically bringing together homosexual desire and erroneous social or work-related practices makes a clear message whose reception can be assumed to be rather direct, even if carried out at a subconscious level. But the raincoat advertisements, which seek to associate their products with positive rhetoric, are much more difficult to unravel, and suggest a highly ambivalent cultural relation with sexuality in general. One might see the worker-safety images as almost patronizing in their attempt to represent sexuality in black and white terms. If the raincoat tries to pass itself off as a classless commodity, this is belied by the repeated emergence of the body in armor that is associated, over time, with a particular style of depiction and narrative. As becomes clear in various ads, the "body" (more specifically, the bourgeois body) needs protection, especially when desire makes a particularly threatening assault. Where the worker-safety ads play on prevalent cultural *fears* about homosexuality (and thereby acknowledge the reality of homoerotic acts), the military-bourgeois encodings of homosexuality, and the denial of gender difference in advertisements for protective gear, suggest an unresolved and inarticulable fear of all desire.

All of the elements gathered together under the sign of the raincoat emerge in an earlier narrative episode that has been of great importance for psychoanalysis, namely, the case of Daniel Paul Schreber. His *Memoirs of My Nervous Illness* was published in 1900, and Freud's analysis of this text in "Psychoanalytic Notes on an Autobiographical Account of a Case of Paranoia" followed in 1911. (In the next chapter I treat Schreber's persecution by "divine rays" in greater depth, but the discussion here would not be complete without a mention of his symptoms.) For Freud, Schreber suffered from paranoia that was essentially reducible to a reversal of his own homosexual libidinal impulses. He repressed his feelings for his doctor, Flechsig, and these, in turn, were transformed into a feeling of being persecuted by

the object of his libidinal attention, as an alibi. The initial psychic formation "I (a man) love him (a man)" undergoes a turn to become "I do not
love him — I hate him." A second turn, through the distorting mechanisms
of the unconscious, results in "he hates (persecutes) me, which will justify
me in hating him."[32] Like the men in raincoats, then, Schreber feels himself
assaulted, a symptom of the desire (which must be repressed by all accounts)
for the "other man" in the picture.

Another common thread between the case of Schreber and fascist men
in raincoats is the eschatological scenario against which they are also in a
position of defending themselves. Schreber wrote extensively about a rupture in the natural Order of Things that either had left him alone on the face
of the earth, or, as in another phase of his delusion, had killed off everyone,
including himself. Again, for Freud, the end-of-the-world fantasy in paranoia
is a projection of the internal (homosexual) catastrophe within the ego:[33]

> Schreber's [creating and destroying] "rays of God," which are made
> up of a condensation of the sun's rays, of nerve-fibres, and of sper-
> matozoa, are in reality nothing else than a concrete representation
> and projection outward of libidinal cathexes; and they thus lend
> his delusions a striking conformity with our theory [of the homo-
> sexual-resistance component in all cases of paranoia]. His belief
> that the world must come to an end because his ego was attracting
> all the rays to itself, his anxious concern at a later period, during
> the process of reconstruction, lest God should sever His ray-con-
> nection with him — these and many other details of Schreber's
> delusional structure sound almost like endopsychic perceptions of
> the processes whose existence I have assumed in these pages as the
> basis of our explanations of paranoia.[34]

As various recent studies have pointed out, Freud's interpretation of
the *Memoirs* was really a very single-minded one.[35] He read the case as a
priori confirmation of his theory of paranoia, and refused to treat what
have since been regarded as the psychotic or schizophrenic aspects of Schreber's illness. At this point I choose not to take sides in the debate, or even
to defend Freudian doctrine, which ultimately rationalizes the case as a
conflict between the patient and his father (and thus serves as further confirmation for homosexuality as a result of problems in the Oedipal stage).
What I do wish to emphasize are certain points of commonality between
the case of Schreber and the fascist-in-armor: persecution by rays; paranoia; end-of-the-world feelings; so-called passive homosexuality as a social

disqualification (Schreber's voices tormented him: "Fancy a person who was a *Senatspräsident* allowing himself to be fucked"[36]) against the morality of exercise and corporeal discipline (Schreber's father was the celebrated author of textbooks such as *Medical Indoor Gymnastics* and an early proponent of German physical culture); and fears about reproduction (for the analysts Macalpine and Hunter, the fact that Schreber had not been able to father any children is the precipitating element in his illness, not repressed homosexuality).

Schreber's father also invented the *Geradehalter,* one of a series of orthopedic devices that constrain children's bodies and force them into unnaturally stiff positions. A recent trend in critical literature on the case has made much of these inventions, linking them with specific physiological symptoms that surface as bodily "miracles" in the *Memoirs.* Clearly, both Schreber and the fascist soldier grow up under conditions of extreme discipline. Here is a passage from one of the writings of Schreber *père* on his child-rearing philosophy:

> Our entire effect on the direction of the child's will at this time will consist in accustoming it to absolute obedience, which has been in great part prepared for already by the applications of the principles laid down previously.... The thought should never even occur to the child that his will could be in control, rather should the habit of subordinating his will to the will of his parents or teachers be immutably implanted in him.... There is then joined to the feeling of law a feeling of impossibility of struggling against the law; a child's obedience, the basic condition for all further education, is thus solidly founded for the time to come.[37]

The parallels between this text and the one quoted by Theweleit (in which rain becomes a figure for parental overstimulation) should be quite evident. Schreber *père* surrounds his punishments with a humanizing discourse. Although the child *believes* he is acting freely, this is only because the parental will is buried in a false illusion that sees the child as "naturally" good. Indeed, when Schreber is grown and the "parental role" has been taken up by divine rays, he perceives himself as both persecuted and chosen, a duplicity that exists in paranoia in general. This treatment is effected by a parent who *categorically* refuses to satisfy any of the child's desires, even those that involve basic necessities. The child will, of course, be "satisfied," but only when he has ceased to ask for things; that is, when he has ceased to perceive the desired object as desirable:

> Each forbidden desire — whether or not it is to the child's disadvantage — must be consistently and unfailingly opposed by an unconditional refusal. The refusal of a desire alone is not enough though; one has to see to it that the child receives this refusal calmly and if necessary, one has to make this calm acceptance a firm habit by using a stern word or threat, etc.... This is the only way to make it easy for the child to attain the salutary and indispensable habit of subordination and control of his will.[38]

One might attempt to understand the parallels between the case of Schreber and the raincoats in, precisely, the relation between the paramilitaristic father of Schreber/the fascist state, and the male subject whose body is formed under the father's gaze, performing these disciplining exercises. In this sense, I am extending Freud's analysis of a *particular* case of repressed homosexuality to a class of men whose *sexuality,* without regard for object, is subjected to severe forms of restriction and who then, as Theweleit would say, exhibit symptoms of psychosis. I address this issue again in chapter 5, because I believe the rays that assault Schreber (and other subjects in the fascist state) have a specific significance related to technological–industrial developments under the regime. Ultimately, it may turn out that neither a purely psychosexual account of Schreber's case nor a contextual, cultural one is adequate by itself to "explain" the specificity of his cosmological doctrine, but that together they begin to achieve a certain degree of coherence.

The Baths

Another locus of degendering, self-protective stances is the institutional space of the public bath.[39] The curative bath has a very important place in the culture of Italy during fascism. Like the rays I will treat in chapter 5, water comes to be invested with tremendous ambivalence, for it both heals the body and drains it of energy, transporting it to a realm of pure pleasure where it is no longer productive. During the pre–World War I years, advertisements for the baths followed a prevailing formula: a full-body portrait of an attractive woman — sometimes nude or bathed in white light to appear like a classical sculpture, sometimes dressed in feminine "leisure wear" — would stare out at the viewer underneath the name of the particular spa.

This formula of equating the bath with a promise of the availability of the female will shift during the fascist period, for a number of important reasons. During the 1930s the bath is always sold as "hygienic," and this word too conveys a contradiction between its connotation as "clean," "curative," "free of disease," and a place of "bourgeois pleasure," and its connotation as "antiseptic" or "antithetical to life," obliterating the complacency of bourgeois values, in the sense that for Marinetti, "war is the only hygiene." A key to the range of meanings of the term lies in the degree of class consciousness. In many images of the bath, the body loses its gender along with its status as producer within the fascist economy. In one sense, this is explained by the fact that the baths are a place to shed one's "outer skin," to strip off the mask of sexuality (figure 46). The bodies of workers, taking the waters at Montecatini, like the "real" body of the mother in *A Special Day,* shed their fascist rigidity. Trips to the baths would include ingesting mineral water, wearing mud packs and steam wraps, and so on, and were associated with the putrid stench of sulfur or the uncomfortable feeling of iodine in the nostrils; and so they would be invested with the same double meaning attached to the notion of hygiene. Hygienic outings, whether sponsored by one of the fascist organizations such as the Dopolavoro, or promoted for the family vacation, saw individuals take on uniforms that putatively served to level class, gender, and even regional differences. Until very recently, the curative bath was legislated as a right for Italian workers as part of the national health insurance. The paid trip to "take the waters" that had originated with state-sponsored antituberculosis campaigns, seen as an economic necessity for the nation's corps of workers, only recently was repealed because of a national deficit crisis of baffling proportions.

The fascist regime contributed to promoting the bath as a hygienic and recreational vacation for entire families, whether at a spa with particular curative waters, or at the seaside. But at the same time, the bath was associated with cultural anxiety because it is a site of unmediated social relations, leisure, and the exposure of the (female) body. This anxiety can be traced through a history of the bathing suit and the "sexualization" of the body as part of the postwar revolution in women's fashion. By the early 1920s, women had begun to wear a crude version of a two-piece suit, and, increasingly, clinging fabrics were used.[40] There is a cultural conflation made between curative waters and swimming in general. One need only flip through the women's magazines of the period to understand the centrality of water to the entire cult of the body: water was a purgative, a leveler of emotions; it was thought to drive aggression (and desire) from the body.

The exposure of skin to sunlight also brought the healthy effects of swimming into contact with another long-standing, ambivalent discourse focused on the suntan and the problematic of racial purity. Like bathing itself, the suntan was promoted in the 1930s as a healthy and protective armor

Monsummano Terme - Interno della Grotta Giusti

46. Montecatini sulfur bath postcard.

for the body against various diseases, but it was also associated with a whole series of racial and class issues that could not be wiped out in a single generation (figure 47). This ad for Coty skin cream tries to preserve older notions of (bourgeois) protection from the elements along with newer ideals of healthful exposure. Coty "allows you to tan" while "avoiding the rays of the sun." The sea was promoted as a national resource in Italy, but there was clearly a class of individuals for whom the suntan equaled agricultural labor and for whom paleness continued to signify nobility, even if it was simultaneously associated with tuberculosis and other diseases.

In the 1930s, suntanning was itself a category of vacation, an "activity" that resulted in the marking of the (classless) body as "healthy." But it seems clear that the bath/suntan was also a kind of compulsory "vacation" subject to overdetermination and overorganization by the regime to the point that, as one cultural historian has suggested, diversion was made to equal consensus, and "being in agreement" was synonymous with "enjoying oneself."[41]

The genderless bodies one finds in advertisements for the baths seem to embody this larger cultural ambivalence toward the forced nature of recreation. The conformity of the bodies under the steaming cave in Montecatini not only attests to the cross-class, cross-gender marketing of the bath, it also suggests a dead end, an evacuation of the self that parallels the slipping away

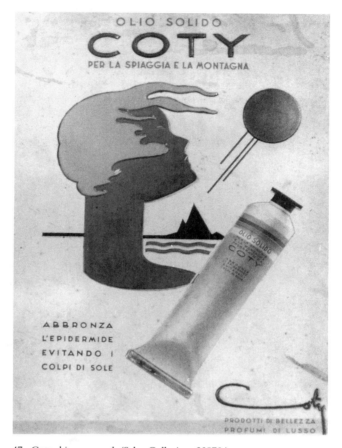

47. Coty skin cream ad. (Salce Collecion, 23870.)

of the corporeal "stuffing" in the Noveltex shirt collars. Perhaps too much hygiene—overexposure to the curative waters, to the sun, to desire itself—leads the body to form another sort of "armor" and to erase any signs of its own sexuality. Desire, like the germs that threaten fascist productivity, is steamed out in the bath. But as I suggest later, the sea always threatens to engulf the body and flood it anew.

The Radio

A man and woman, stripped of anything but the most essential gender characteristics, sit in trench coats listening to a live radio broadcast from La

48. La Scala radio ad. (Salce Collection, 03570.)

Scala (figure 48). Like the martial, masculine couples marching under a rain-
storm, this heterosexual couple is mesmerized and vacuous, their eyes drawn
by the artist Nizzoli like empty sockets. If these figures captivate the viewer,
it is only through the graphic starkness of their pose and the strong forms
of the image, but not through any sort of traditional identification techniques. The man smokes. Both individuals, bathed in eerie green light,
exhibit extreme outward symptoms of depression. Why would the radio
industry represent itself as a site for the girding of the body into armor,
into the trench coat that wipes out gender and protects the self from the

evil gases sent down "from the enemy"? (In chapter 5 I explore implications of the etymological, hence radical, link between radio, radium, and "evil rays," so for the moment I will limit the discussion to the radio image by Nizzoli.

As an advertising medium itself, the fascist radio enjoyed only limited success. Throughout most of the *ventennio,* listeners were forced to pay a tax to hear transmissions. On one hand, the radio reached consumers in small towns and villages who might otherwise not be exposed to the enormous posters or other advertising forms that flooded the urban landscape.[42] On the other hand, the regime itself did not initially exploit the radio as it might have (Mussolini was strictly a newspaper man, as many scholars of fascism and mass media have pointed out), and the fact that they paid for the privilege of receiving sounds into the home made listeners less open to the "tricks" of invasive aural advertising.

Evening radio broadcasts in Italy consisted almost entirely of orchestral music or opera (as in the Nizzoli ad featuring La Scala). An article in *L'ufficio moderno* points out that given the inherently "high" tone of the medium, listeners might tend to be disturbed by the "violence" of an advertisement directly after a concert broadcast.[43] Thus, the most successful radio advertising during the 1930s consisted of some form of sponsorship of a weekly program: companies such as Perugina or Cirio linked their brand names with a repeatable, mass cultural experience and literally became part of the daily vocabulary as "household words."[44] Linked with the "dignity and seriousness" of classical music, these companies enjoyed a "large moral and material remuneration." The real danger of radio advertising seems to be that listeners would "tune out" or lose interest, forgetting the brand name. Radio texts were thought to be "evanescent," and as such, not nearly as effective as visual media. In effect, one might say that a central problem in radio advertisement is precisely the lack of a "body" through which to mediate persuasion. The sort of tactile control in the raincoat ads, say, was not possible with the radio, which was most effective when transmitting music, the most abstract form of art.

Nevertheless, radio transmission was in the hands of a state-run monopoly that began in 1924. Although radio *manufacturing* was never completely turned over to the state, the regime began to place certain controls on its production during the 1930s. In particular, Mussolini's policies encouraged the middle and working classes to buy radios, which had been a luxury good with few subscribers prior to the mid-1920s.[45] In other words, the industry was effectively split into two separate groups: the laborers who created individual radio units covered by a range of decorative boxes that signified their real market value, and those who controlled the broadcasting of programs to a fixed group of subscribers. Both groups, however, were absolutely interdependent, and both functioned under the state agency EIAR (Ente Italiano per le Audizioni Radiofoniche), the sponsor of the "La Scala" advertisement with which I began this discussion. The radio ad campaigns did not focus on the potential propagandistic value of radio for the regime, or even on its value as a transmitter of news during a time of crisis (music, not news, continued to be the primary program format throughout the 1930s). Instead, radio broadcasters focused on the pacifying or relaxing quality of the listening experience.

The Turin-based advertising concessioner of the state radio, SIPRA (Società Italiana Pubblicitá Radiofonica Anonima), printed a brochure beginning with the following statement: "When we have finished with a hard day of work we all feel a great need for quiet and joy. Radio is a great relaxer. For only twenty cents a day, RADIO in every home makes life better and more comfortable."[46] This text provides an excellent example of the industrial and market confusion associated with the radio. What is the product being sold in this brochure: an actual brand or style of radio, or the subscription itself? But the question is complicated further by the introduction of the image on another page of the brochure (figure 49). A screaming head over the city scatters nervous workers toward home like a strong west wind. This Medusa–head signals mass hysteria in the manner of a grotesquely gigantic body marching through urban spaces in a horror film. In fact, the gap between the text and image of this particular *dépliant* is highly significant precisely because the former begins by explaining the value of radio for the listeners themselves (as pacification), and then explores radio as a means of "yelling," or powerful diffusion, for advertisers. In essence, the radio industry had not sorted itself out into targetable components by the early 1930s; it was still grappling with its troubled image in a large and vaguely defined cultural milieu.

To return to the "La Scala" image, then, how is it possible that radio, and especially a broadcast of the finest lyric opera performed in Italy, corresponds in this culture with the trench coat/defensive armor and a depressive outer shell, rather than the "joy" suggested by the text of the SIPRA *dépliant*? At the center of my response lies a class contradiction: although the radio would seek to be a powerful ("screaming") form of mass communication, it was simply not within the grasp of a large mass of consumers. Acknowledging this fact, the regime, through organizations such as the

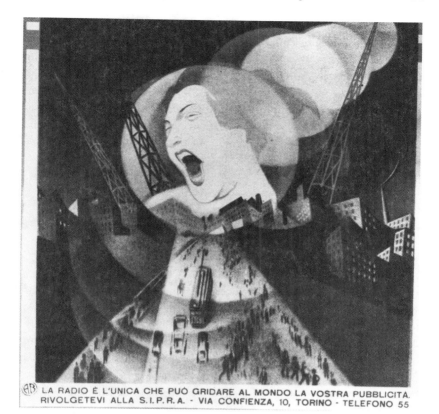

LA RADIO È L'UNICA CHE PUÒ GRIDARE AL MONDO LA VOSTRA PUBBLICITA.
RIVOLGETEVI ALLA S.I.P.R.A. - VIA CONFIENZA, 10, TORINO - TELEFONO 55

49. Screaming-head radio ad. (Courtesy of the Bertarelli Collection, Milan.)

Dopolavoro, promoted "group listening."[47] Another ad for radios from the period follows the expected conventions for this phenomenon: three peasants drawn in novecento style sit "transfixed" before a glowing box. The mother with enormous breasts does not hide her gender, but like other forms of propaganda for the working classes, this image entails a traditional scenario of pacification and unity that is certainly much less ambiguous than Nizzoli's bourgeois couple. In fact, it is precisely this economic contradiction that is carefully effaced in the propinquity of the elite La Scala with the domestic interior of a young couple. Could it be possible to read the image of listening in protective gear as a sort of shield against the controlling aspects of radio as it pretended to level all class distinctions in some ideal, fascist sense? In other words, does Nizzoli's couple represent a (bourgeois) ideal of self-insulation, shelter, and privacy that would also have addressed rural or working-class consumers whose own experiences with the radio were linked with regime-imposed standards of group camaraderie?[48]

In some sense, Nizzoli's "La Scala" advertisement represents a significant departure from the normative rhetoric of mass leisure and mass communication. The radio was a family affair, for the most part, and so it was associated with another sort of forced camaraderie under fascism, that particular brand of control exercised over the nuclear family and its leisure time. Here is a description of the prototypical (Oedipal) group listening to the radio during the 1930s:

> Whereas in the past the husband took refuge in his study to smoke his pipe and read his newspaper, while his wife received her friends in her drawing room and the children made a din in the corridor or in an unfurnished room, there is now one room for all, which the English, masters of home comfort, call the "living room." And it is indeed in this room that they all now live their hours of rest, of relaxation or study.... A "radio," then, cannot be situated elsewhere than in the "room for everyone," of which it forms, as it were, the nucleus.[49]

In this context, the degendered couple of the EIAR ad, listening to the radio without the "joy" of children or the comfort of the Oedipal nucleus, might be seen as resisting just such a scenario. In their death masks and outdoor raingear, they specifically position themselves outside of the "living room," the room of sexual and family organization where the gender division of leisure (the study for men, the drawing room for women) is compacted, economized into a single, nodal space. In 1939—several years after the images under consideration in this section—the prestigious Cremona prize for painting was awarded to a work depicting the following theme: "Listening to a speech of Mussolini on the radio." Significantly, the vast majority of entries were rendered in novecento style, or at least depicted peasants huddled around a radio box, either in a somber shack or in a field. Several works in the competition focused on a mother and child (a listening "pietà"); others presented a small nuclear family unit. A winning work, by Luciano Richetti, depicted an extended peasant family in which gender divisions and the interdependence of family relations are very clearly demarcated (figure 50). A massive woman holding her child sits next to her muscular and thoroughly masculine husband, who places his arm, in turn, around the rigid shoulders of another son in his Balilla uniform. Various neighbors, also grouped into family units, listen in. The room is bare except for an image of Mussolini, saluting in the background. In other words,

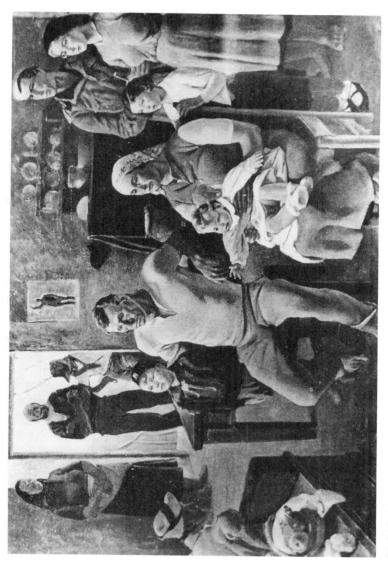

50. Richetti's painting, *Listening to the Duce on the Radio.* (Reprinted from the *Catalogo del Premio Cremona,* 1939.)

this "prize winning" work is an impeccable identification of fascist ideals of the radio, where the transmission of a message is perfectly received. What may have clinched the prize for Richetti was that, instead of signing his name and thereby particularizing this highly generic work, he simply wrote the fascist credo — "believe, obey, fight" — in the lower corner of the canvas. The painting anticipates fascist critical judgment absolutely. There are thus no contradictions to be read into the work at the level of its iconography, as may be the case with Nizzoli's EIAR couple.

In addition to the class contradiction and the resistance to the Oedipal situation that might be read in Nizzoli's image, it is clear that the radio presents an irreconcilable and very basic contradiction between its purported value as pacifying recreation, and the kinds of cultural tensions associated with the technology of the transmission of sounds from a central station into the domestic sphere. Marconi was celebrated in fascist Italy as the inventor of the radio, but a popular association was quickly made between this "good" form of transmission and the transmission of evil death rays. In fact, during the early thirties it was rumored that Marconi had harnessed microwaves into a gun that was believed capable of stopping cars or planes in motion and even killing human beings with silent, untraceable rays. At the same time that the regime promoted radio as a classless mass consumer good and as a means of expressing autarchic, nationalist sentiment, Mussolini also helped maintain the "death ray" rumor. It is difficult for those of us who have grown up with the radio as innocuous "background" or white noise to imagine the putative power of this medium to penetrate the private sphere in the form of "rays" and subsequently to transform general conditions of daily life. Yet like so many forms of machinery, the radio was received by the public with tremendous ambivalence. The futurists, as might be expected, seized on radio as a thoroughly modern *form* that, if divested of bourgeois *content,* might boost autarchic production and help the savings plan of the fascist economists by broadcasting condensed food:

> After all, the notion is not so extraordinary. Since the radio can diffuse asphyxiating and sleep-inducing waves (lectures, jazz, poetry readings, to-conclude-ladies-and-gentlemen, etc.) it surely should be able to diffuse some extracts from our best dinners and luncheons. Then what abundance there would be![50]

This passage elevates the radio as a popular medium, but also manages to preserve its sacred mystery. The physics of such a transmission remain elusive; like so many elements of the futurist aesthetic this alimentary radio is inevitably projected into the future and constitutes part of a joke in the present tense, one played out at the expense of passé, bourgeois ideals. Following marketing conventions of the industry itself, Marinetti finds it quite obvious to separate the production of the radio from broadcasting. The former is a clearly positive, autarchic field of modern machinery. The latter represents a more troubling area in fascist control that has been subjected to leaden, bourgeois ideology. Marinetti displays an incisive understanding of the difference between the two spheres (a difference that is elided in advertising itself). What is clear is that the radio occupies a space in the culture as an offensive "ray gun" that spurs a series of defensive postures.

The anxiety generated by the fear of "death rays" from a radar gun seems to emerge uncannily in the "radio" advertisement where a couple in armor joylessly attend a concert in their own home. Their protection, which involves both an effacement of gender and the trench coat as armor, shields them from the evil rays of the radio that penetrate their home and bounce from wall to wall, controlling relations within the domestic sphere (particularly sexual relations).

The Psychopathology of Sport

In my research I have encountered a whole series of androgynous bodies engaged in various precipitous dives. A female, girded in a bathing suit and cap, leans backward in space with no apparent support (figure 51). A lean and feminized male, also armored in a sports suit, remains suspended in midair (figure 52). In my classification of bodies, this particular subgroup of the body without gender in a *salto mortale,* or mortal dive, seemed to deserve a special place, and the question of a death instinct came to be of the utmost urgency in this context. This connection between the death leap and the death drive may at first seem odd, given that the diving bodies almost all appear, on first glance, to represent a form of freedom from restriction, a sudden unbound burst of energy and vitality.[51] In fact, this is probably how the artists who initially sketched these bodies were thinking. Clearly, their strategy was to affiliate the freedom of motion with the freedom of leisure time, since the dive appears to be associated on many occasions with resort wear, beaches, sporting facilities, and other holiday activities or products.[52] As a purely formal element, a design "solution," the diving body is a way of elongating especially the female body, of extending its lines without insinuating a "*crisi*" waist. The body in the dive seems to refer to the 1920s style of fashion that was anathema for the cultural institutions

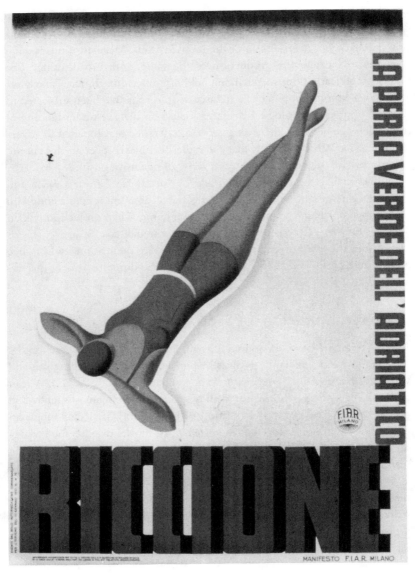

51. *Salto mortale* leap, female. (Salce Collection, 12748.)

52. *Salto mortale* leap, male. (Salce Collection, 13260.)

controlled by Mussolini's aesthetics of reproduction.[53] Not that the diving body represents a consciously conceived, subversive strategy, but the association of freedom — whether taken in a leisure/temporal context or in a body-image/spatial one — with a product is completely within the logic of the market.[54] The practice of sport could be said to be a primarily economic problem that, under "normal" circumstances, follows the law of the pleasure principle, a "lowering of tension" in the body. But just as Freud's critics wondered how dreams that repeat the experience of a traumatic neurosis or some other disturbing event can satisfy the law of wish fulfillment and not contradict the economics of the pleasure principle, one could ask why it is that bodies repeat fearful experiences like the dive, or why such a frightening event would come to be represented in advertising. After all, advertising, a form of public discourse that seeks to persuade readers to consume products, would seem bound to embrace the pleasure principle. The issue bears some discussion.

It might be suggested, in accordance with Freud's initial findings in *Beyond the Pleasure Principle,* that the representation of the dive is a form of mastery of the instincts, or a rational and conscious way of overcoming fear, an example of what Gaston Bachelard called a *défi cosmique.*[55] The possibility that a series of quasi-dangerous acts may serve to strengthen existing psychic structures remains quite compelling — all the more so, because repetition would not necessarily threaten the primacy of the pleasure principle as a dominant force governing all instinctual activity. In fact, Freud never seems to satisfactorily dismiss this "mastery" explanation for repetition, except to say that the *Fort-da* game would *seem* to "go beyond" or "override" the model of the pleasure principle.[56]

While fascist sports policy maintained that man (I leave this in deliberately sexist terms) instinctively strives for perfection, and that this process is aided by (dangerous or mortal) sports, *Beyond the Pleasure Principle* holds this affirmation untenable. "I cannot see how this benevolent illusion is to be preserved," Freud wrote.[57] Of course, for the fascists this sort of reasoning can be explained away as Jewish pessimism, and disproven by the excellence of the Italian (Aryan) race in physical culture.

Traditionally, studies of fascism imply that masochistic types (feminine personalities) are said to respond well to the authoritarian structures inherent in fascist organized physical culture.[58] Corporeal alienation, like the kind of anomie associated with mechanistic labor, is related to a sense that the subject is no longer playing a game or engaging in healthy competition, but has somehow lent his or her body to the state for exhibition. Deprived of any cathartic or ludic power, movement becomes a "dehumanizing," repetitive function more closely associated with Taylorization than with either competition or the moral superiority attributed to the athlete in fascist physical-education policy. What I am talking about here is an extreme consequence of control that seems to correspond to the corporeal alienation of an out-of-body experience. A humanist view would be that, under normal circumstances, the process of posing oneself a challenge and then overcoming a physical obstacle leads to a release of energy and a renewed sense of well-being; but when the individual is pushed into a dangerous position — the high dive, or *salto mortale,* for example — the death instinct is excited, and the individual can no longer be seen as being involved in something positive or uplifting, but as plunging toward self-extinction. A fine line separates the positive challenge of sports from the negation of the mortal dive, and in examining the boundaries of this distinction, questions of gender become paramount.

Physical culture, whether in a humanist context or a fascist one, involves an implicit assumption about gender: a masculine nucleus within the body is what motivates it toward sport. This "scientific truth" lies at the basis of many contemporary textbooks on the subject and should in no way be thought of as a historical, outmoded notion.[59] The impulse to engage in sport, understood as a healthy set of kinetic practices that may involve a challenge, is controlled by a kind of internal masculine homunculus.[60] Like certain ego models based on a similar notion of a controlling homunculus, the "sport-man" is actually a convenient metaphor for understanding the psychological disposition of the athlete, and it is not a biological (or hormonal) ontology. The sport-man belongs to that tradition of ego psychology that would also promote sport as a way of strengthening the little man inside, and that locates a center of control inside the body.

In theory, then, this tiny sport-man of the physical-culture textbook might well inhabit the bodies of biological males and females without any particular statistical privileging of one or the other. And, again, *in the theory of physical culture,* this animus, this little man at the control panel, is generally encouraged in fascist males and females because both sexes gain self-confidence or strength through athletic performance; ultimately, sports are positive for any nation. Inasmuch as this training threatens female reproductivity, however, it is demonized. For the fascist era, the question of the female body and sports was extremely troubling, especially because for men, sport was definitely linked with pre- or paramilitary activity. Male bodies that are pushed beyond their own limits, bodies that are on the verge of *jouissance,* are comprehensible in the cultural context of fascism. The inevitable homosocial and homosexual bonding that form part of these group exertions make "situational homosexuals" (to use the Nazi terminology) of men, whose collective orgasm along the trajectory of the death drive brings them to a "higher plane" of experience, an exalted state where, freed from desire itself (figured in woman), they believe themselves pure and noble. Clearly, this is the "aim" of some collective drives of fascism in the German context, but also in Italy, where men can exploit their group interactions to rise above the mutilated victory of the First World War and to overcome the national inferiority complex that many historians have attributed to late unification, retarded industrial development, and general notions of "backwardness."

But what of women in this scheme of sport as collective nirvana? The regime bureaucracy tried to ignore gender differences in various organizations such as the Balilla, divided as it was into military battalions. The kind of delirium that followed mass demonstrations in the stadiums of Italy were, at times, all-inclusive, wiping out individual identity (including sexual identity) and replacing it with the uniformity of the new man, an "indivisible physiopsychical unity, a microcosm of the larger world."[61] But what if this new man, this classical figure of the body as microcosm, were to be interpreted as a gendered subject, as specifically male? The Academy of Orvieto, created specifically for the physical and moral education of young girls, contained all of these contradictions within its institutional frame, without necessarily reconciling any of them. Physical education as taught at the academy allowed young women to "resolve the problem of life" and to perfect themselves as "companions for men, by deferring the sad ripening of old age."[62] In other words, the female-body-made-male dispels desire (resolves the problem of life), and, rather than working along the model of the death drive, the female reproduces and maintains herself in a youthful (bound) state of economic equilibrium. So the girls of the academy do not "go beyond" the pleasure principle in their sporting activities; they do not reach collective *jouissance*; they do not fall into the *salto mortale*.

In addition to physical culture, the girls of the elite Orvieto academy also undertook academic study (within bounds). A photograph from the academy shows three high-spirited and identical girls holding their textbooks in one of the courtyards outside a rationalist building. On the back of a notebook are scribbled the words, "I've had it up to here with Psychology, but I've still got a smile on my lips."[63] This innocent line, in no way part of any official presentation of the regime, seems to sum up a whole ideological moment: the girls of the academy, highly trained and disciplined, would prefer not to have to work on their minds (and the fact that they are studying psychology is a kind of double bind). The notebook implies that the girls have a "healthy" dislike of the sedentary, academic world, or better, that they are "full of life." It is extremely ironic to view the image of these exemplary and indistinguishable females displaying their joking, ingenuous critique of psychology for a camera lens, since the foundation of such a critique resides precisely in the putative universalizing tendency of this science, according to popular and fascist thinking. Psychology, for fascism, tends to reduce humans to a set of uniform instincts and so represents a clear debasement—the opposite of what physical culture is supposed to accomplish.

The fascist critique of psychology, expressed by these perfect premothers, has implications for the culture of publicity as well. Even in the context of the progressive science of advertising, "psychology" is a term to be used with extreme caution:

> Is objective psychology, if it exists, always a constant norm of action, or better, can it be a law fixed in time and space? The response is negative.... Certainly, in moments of crisis or difficulties in the general economy, the denouncement of evils and the correction of defects, the prevention of disastrous effects and the attainment of a better life requires both therapy and a study of etiology. Not every single case can be examined, nor is there a single remedy or generic antidote for every illness.

The humanist voice speaking here is not a doctor of medicine, but a scientist of publicity who moves from his general critique of psychology as fixed law (psychoanalysis) to conclude:

> So I am in agreement with those who believe that a single form that would be rational for all psychomercantile uses is inconceivable.... I was speaking about therapy for individual cases; this is impossible without consultation of all single and special cases.... Let us focus, then, on subjective psychology, on individual psychology, on filling up the lacunas, curing defects, attaining a better life ... this ... plows and cultivates the field of concordance between producer and consumer, and, this is to say, it represents one of the major variables in avoiding the waste of wealth. Moreover, it will help avoid fruitless stages between production and distribution.[64]

In essence, this passage from *L'ufficio moderno* suggests that psychology (and decidedly not psychoanalysis understood as a set of normative or binding precepts), or better, its commonsense application to marketing practices, performs the same sort of feminine, economizing function as the ideal fascist woman. Just as home economy is something practically innate in women (although it can be coaxed along and strengthened by the discourse of comportment books and pamphlets), advertising is ultimately a sort of positive, female, "wives' tale" form of cognition that carefully distances itself from the pathological model implied by the "therapy and etiology" of "objective psychology." The language of this critique does not diverge substantially from that of periodicals such as *La difesa della razza,* where psychoanalysis often is linked with degenerate, Jewish aesthetics.

The assignment of "subjective psychology" (which I have related to feminine economics) to form a bridge between fascist production and fascist distribution is very suggestive in terms of reading the Orvieto female bodies. They spurn psychology as an academic discipline precisely because they already *know* how to perform healing acts on a case-by-case basis; because in their cheerful personae, they already contain the seeds of an internal disposition that will be applied to their conjugal and maternal psychologizing. There is an important link between this popular critique of psychology and psychoanalysis, and the strategies of advertising itself. The female body represents a site where the two meet and enter into a sort of perfect thematization.

The extreme and degraded form of this mass psychology as chipper, feminine "therapy" may lie in the body of the athlete who has plunged into a *salto mortale,* the mortal dive.[65] A whole series of advertisements for products and services associated with leisure time (the Venice Lido, bathing wear, various resorts) exploit the *salto mortale* and the acrobatic body as a symbol of escape and freedom. But the simple association of diving with nonproductive, free time will have to be interrogated, especially given the problematic of fascist control of leisure. If the body is always under the gaze of the regime, this is particularly true during the highly structured vacations of the working class, and at the institutionalized resorts for the middle and upper classes. Because of the special anxiety posed to fascism by the very concept of "free time," it would be misleading to consider the diving body as a beautiful image of perfect human form; rather, the body suspended in midair, often diving backward or fixed in a contortionist pose, represents a form of bondage, the kind of pathological "damming up" of energy that a physical-culture textbook might associate with negation lived out in sports. In psychoanalysis, "negation" means, essentially, the denial of a dangerous or threatening reality, and applied to the advertising images, it seems a perfect term for understanding the diving body that defies gravity and that should be distinguished from, say, a more strictly futurist representation of exhilarating motion.

The centrality of water (even where it is invisible, lying somewhere underneath the stiffened, diving body) cannot be merely casual, but must be read in the light of Theweleit's work on the "interior states" of the body as related to flowing, streaming, the feminine abject, and so on. In fact, streaming, the oceanic feeling that Freud "could not recognize in himself," is normally described as the libido (the drive). Freud's metaphor for the imposition of the ego in the formation "where id was, there ego shall be" is linked with the "civilizing process" of draining the Zuider Zee.[66] The diving body represents a similar impulse to split, drain, and dry up the water, but it also suggests the danger of the failure of such an enterprise: the risk that the body/ego may not master the water, but may sink down and find itself overcome. The water is femininity, whether this is understood as a traditional symbolic equation or an economic one. The diving body, however, has no gender. It not only rehearses death as a way of strengthening its ego, it also defies desire, accumulated in or symbolized by the feminine. These two psychic exercises reinforce one another and ought to be understood as part of a single, economic "plan."

The images grouped together here do not share anything like a common matrix within advertising strategies or campaigns. My own iconography of degendered fascist subjects reflects a particular interest in coming to terms with the relation between the individual body and the state. Over and over one is told how the politics of fascism preys on or oppresses women through the over-emphasis on reproduction. For Deleuze and Guattari, fascist body-coercion represents only a more extreme version of the politics of any democratic state with its formation of "molar" individuals.[67]

I do not believe that the various advertisements in this chapter bear witness to strategies of active resistance against the molarization of subjects, nor even to celebratory forms of subversive cross-dressing. Rather, I see an uncanny and perhaps unconscious adaptation to the overdetermination of gender difference under fascism. These subjects, from the two Aquasol men to the diving bodies, develop a hard outer shell; they withdraw like turtles into their own "homes," where they are still battered by the projectile-voices emanating from the radio. They pull their caps down over their eyes in winter.

In summer, they cultivate a full-body suntan; their thickened hides repulse the missiles that are sent toward them by the god *amor*. Then they tighten up their muscles and make *themselves* into missiles, splintering the morass of desire that swarms around in the water beneath. These images figure the effacement of gender as part of a strategy of defense by both males and females, but they also presuppose the assignment of desire to a feminine other that must be resisted and repelled.

The following chapter examines how the body boundaries of both men and women are threatened by evil rays. The bodies depicted do not necessarily develop a hard shell through drills and exercises. Instead, they disappear into thin air, gassed and vaporized.

5 / The Body Disappears: Negation, Toxicity, Annihilation

Disavowal of the Body

In a significant group of advertisements from the 1930s, the human body seems to slip away, vanishing into thin air. Design discourse has found a vocabulary for praising the elegance of this graphic design "solution"—the silhouettes and shadowy forms; the wispy, haunting outlines—but this language eclipses a more disturbing discourse about the disappearance of the self. Under what conditions does the body leave behind its own materiality? Does it reconstitute itself elsewhere, in some more congenial realm? And if corporeality is to be nullified or denied, why does the body always leave behind traces of its presence? Why is disappearance represented as a work in progress whose potential reversibility is constantly posed, perhaps even desired?

In many of the representations I have considered here, the body is subjected not to negation (it does not become not-body in any kind of absolute sense), but rather to disavowal. Both negation *(Verneinung)* and disavowal *(Verleugnung)* are, quite obviously, Freudian terms whose theoretical matrix is an experience of infantile perception. Negation arises out of the child's cognition of objects—those taken into the body (good objects, affirmed objects), and those rejected (bad objects, negated objects). Disavowal

195

arises out of the child's experience in perceiving the genitalia of both males and females, and concerns a feeling of incredulity over the theoretical possibility of castration.[1] Both terms are problematic within the Freudian corpus and become so even more when they are applied to an aesthetic product. Later in this chapter I again address this question, but for now I wish only to suggest the second term—a dual, simultaneous affirmation and denial—as more closely related to the phenomenon of bodily disappearance.

An exemplary image for this entire discussion is an advertisement by Cavadini for "Rayon" brand men's shirts (figure 53). Against a black background, a body makes itself out of a bolt of cloth, surging upward, stiffened like Sepo's Noveltex shirt collars. Below it, the brand name, also a generic name for artificial silk, seems to emit a soft glow of radiated light. The "shirt-man" is sleek and well groomed with his tie perfectly nestled underneath his collar. He sports a half-formed nose and a perfectly circular mouth that seems to gape in amazement, almost as if, in the viewer, this man has suddenly recognized his own prototype; the legibility of this moment of "recognition" or epiphany constitutes the central organizing principle of the composition. The face is all the more curious, however, because it lacks the sensory organs that might, in fact, allow it to see the viewer. The material forming the face of "shirt-man" is still raw, still too undifferentiated to allow for the formation of eyes, of punctiform hollows that might reveal the absence of any light behind. As a subject, the man simultaneously affirms and denies the possibility for intersubjective communication.

The Rayon shirt-man, whose contours literally materialize (that is, arise from raw material) before our eyes, turns out to be nothing but a puppet, wearing the pathos of its own inanimation like a tragic mask.[2] This doll who would come to life, but whose vitality is just out of reach, dangled above it in a tantalizing scene of torment, seems an odd figure to sell men's ready-to-wear shirts. In fact, all of the elements described here belong inextricably to a cultural discourse about the body as it is subjected to assaults—from within and without—that ultimately threaten a sense of boundaries. Unable to fashion proper armor, the body regresses to a state of indecision that may best be described as that preceding the mirror stage.[3] But it would seem that rather than experiencing some enchanted return to Imaginary bliss, the Rayon shirt-man finds itself trapped in its pretense to humanity, caught under a gaze that reveals it for the puppet it is.

How, then, does the Rayon-man come to be named spokesman for a commodity, his picture hanging in various stores and on billboards? How does he find his own ethos in the world of retail clothing? By the 1930s,

53. Cavadini Rayon shirt-man. (Salce Collection, 09499.)

window shopping was a crucial social ritual in Europe, carried out along major urban arteries and in the spaces of highly ornate covered galleries. These shopping arcades—described by Benjamin in his *Passagen-Werk*—were built primarily in the later part of the nineteenth century in Italy. They reflected the habits of the growing urban bourgeoisie at that time, and they utterly transformed social life. The decorative complexity of their Liberty facades, dripping with foliage, with light filtered through muted glass ceilings, was the setting for new forms of exchange; and, more significantly in the case of Italy, for the evening *giro nel centro,* a crucial ritual in Mediterranean cultures. As the sun sets, the middle-class family dresses up and parades—literally makes a turn—around the central piazza of the town. The Oedipal family makes a spectacle of itself for others. Pushing the unmarried girls to the front, it prepares for kinship exchange with members of its own class. But if at one time this ritual was carried out in the context of food and drink, or around public monuments that stand for the glory of regional culture or courage during the unification of Italy, by the early part of the new century the logo-center of the stroll—the radial point of the circle—is the central cluster of shops, the arcade or galleria.

Following Benjamin, one must continue to understand these arcades, the now archaic bedrock of the city, within a very particular historical context. By the 1930s, when Benjamin was involved in the research for his project in Paris, arcades were decidedly "historical," the "first consumer dream worlds," now "commodity graveyards, containing the refuse of a discarded past."[4] And although they hold a place of particular importance in the megalopolis of Paris, arcades are fundamental also to modernization in cities such as Milan, Turin, Bologna, and Padua. Perhaps in the particular case of Italian cities, the layout of the arcades could be considered less labyrinthine and, instead, as conforming to an older model of urban planning in which streets open up to a single central circle or square. The galleria of Milan, for example, expands like a tunnel into the Piazza del Duomo, which still has the feel of a focal point, in spite of the complexity of the city and its surrounding residential sprawl. Indeed, the piazza is still the unique and obvious rallying point for public demonstrations in the city.

For Benjamin it was essential to understand the history of class relations and modern consumerism through the *transformation* of the arcades along a modern time line. Benjamin read Paris as caught up in a drama that resembled a kind of family romance such that the "old-fashioned effect" of arcades on people in the 1930s is like the "antiquarian effect of the father on his son."[5] More importantly, for the present discussion, these airy, ethereal strolling spaces also served as the galleries for the first mass-produced advertisements. But by the time the Rayon shirt-man makes his appearance on the scene, there is nothing new about the colored images of little men and women, the trademarks of hundreds of different products lining the walls of the shopping enclosures within the city. Rayon-man enters a world of exchange that was constructed several generations earlier, and he is imposed on it like a decal sticker that will eventually be covered up with ever more layers of mass cultural sediment. The short shelf life of Rayon-man should be measured against the background of the "eternal" structures of modern consumerism. The elegant specialty shops that predate the department and ready-to-wear retail stores were built to attract the bourgeois consumer with the illusion of nobility: chandeliers; smooth, luxurious wood surfaces; masked courtiers discreetly bringing out the merchandise (figure 54).[6] Within the arcade shop, then, the consumer transcends labor and enters into a world where money is dirty. And the figure of Rayon-man remains trapped in a no-man's-land between this world and the squalid reality outside. Rayon, after all, is cheap artificial silk; a perfect product for the "classless" fascist market; an inexpensive imitation of haute couture styles. At times, Rayon-man's art deco lines and geometrical elegance serve him well, as he dangles over the goods in the shop; but at other times, he fails his masters, and the whole charade of the *mass* consumer market is revealed. He is then trampled over by other posters.

Rayon-man emerges from a perfectly folded bolt. He sits on the shelf and waits for an impeccably dressed salesman to remove him for the client's inspection. (Even today, high-end shopping in Italy often discourages browsing; one must enter a store with an idea already in mind.) Clothing is folded with absolute precision on shelves that are off-limits to the consumer. Fabrics on the bolt, or even ready-to-wear shirts, are organized by color and are pulled from their display by the salesclerk. The consumer is kept at a distance from the literal "material" of the consumer goods. And this is reflected later, when the consumer actually puts on the stiff garment, the shirt-without-a-body that never really seems to "fit" (it is not tailor-made), but that retains *its* proper shape around the body contours.

How, then, does Rayon-man find himself at home in such a cold and forbidding environment, or what role does he come to play in a world of exchange where distance, alienation, and deferral confer value on commodities, as long as advertising is understood at the level of a psychology of identification,

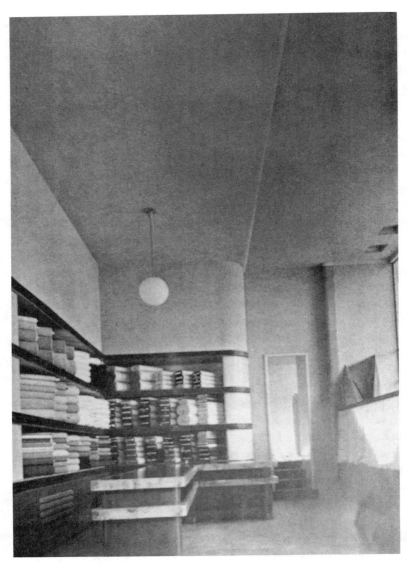

54. Interior of an elegant fabric store.

a humanism? In fact, this Rayon-man's image does make sense within the context of the fascist economy, and its gaping mouth reflects the gaze of a particular subject whose particular psychology can be posited.

Ready-to-wear clothing, in Italy, develops out of the same impulse to autarchy that has placed its imprint on the bodies appearing throughout this book. The turn-of-the-century boutiques, which reflect an outmoded, local economy, begin to be replaced under fascism with department stores that are themselves historically linked to modernization in textile production. If *tailleur,* like everything French, is to be superseded by a national signifier, it is precisely Rayon-man who marches into the empty space. But once ensconced in the galleries of mass culture, he finds himself oddly out of sync, strangely uncomfortable. In following his sad trajectory in the next section, one begins to understand the philosophical parameters of the disappearance of the body.

Rays and Radiation

As historians of the relations between science and the popular imagination have attested, the term "ray" maintains a place of tremendous ambivalence in the modern cultural imagination. Positing future wars, science fiction writers in the nineteenth century like H. G. Wells invented "heat rays" and choking black clouds. These technological nightmares multiplied in the years after World War I. Spencer Weart's book *Nuclear Fear* documents the unresolved contradiction between positive and negative aspects of rays as a dominant paradigm in various *epistemes,* even before the actual discovery of radiation.[7] The *idea* of an atomic bomb entered popular culture long before its invention, and military theorists such as Giulio Douhet in Italy foresaw the possibility of large-scale annihilation. His predictions had an effect on the strategy for and reaction to the Ethiopian campaigns, where the bombers displayed such immense power that it was believed the indigenous peoples would surrender almost immediately.

On the other hand, beginning in the 1930s, "radium" was primarily associated with social utopias, societies that would harness power from a tiny source, live free of disease, and dispense with the need for manual labor. Cultural reaction to radiation has been so heterogeneous that it is impossible to assign a particular political ideology to any position within the debate. Needless to say, a general equivocal relation with rays holds within fascism as well. The futurists, for example, embraced a "hidden technology"

of transformative powers. In the writings on food that made pasta anathema, Marinetti called for food preparation to be subjected to

> ozonizers to give liquids and foods the perfume of ozone, ultra-
> violet ray lamps (since many foods when irradiated with ultra-
> violet rays acquire active properties, become more assimilable, pre-
> venting rickets in young children, etc.), electrolyzers to decompose
> juices and extracts, etc., in such a way as to obtain from a known
> product a new product with new properties; colloidal mills to pul-
> verize flours, dried fruits, drugs, etc.; atmospheric and vacuum
> stills, centrifugal autoclaves, dialyzers.[8]

This celebration of alchemical transmutation clearly places Marinetti on
the side of the "good rays" that travel an unmitigated path toward progress,
and in this he echoes many of his compatriots. Popular novels by Brun-
ngraber and Carrel, translated into Italian during the 1930s, captured the
cultural fascination with rays, atoms, radium, and radiation. Women's magazines of the period promoted "radiation" therapy for the home. An essential aspect of maternal care included subjecting the child's skin to artificial
rays during winter; and in summer, the obligatory visit to the beach for a
prolonged exposure to the sun. These new technologies of the body imply faith in the institutions of scientific research, and an acceptance of a
new discourse of pragmatism. The presence of rays in any form guarantees
the efficacy and seriousness of any product or procedure that previously
might have been marketed in the classified section, the "fourth page" of
Italian newspapers. Fascist science managed to elevate the status of a whole
pseudomystical discourse that once would have aroused skepticism among
the educated classes. Even though the ray is invisible, it is often *represented*
in advertising and other popular imagery; these ads thus reflect the in-
congruity between faith in the existence of the ray and the lack of any objective verification of this existence. On one level it was understood that
the formation of a strong outer shell—the body armor discussed in the
previous chapter—was a superficial *sign* of health (and of the absence of
tuberculosis, more specifically) worn for another subject. On another level,
the rays were thought to transform something within the body, something
intrasubjective or "interceptory," to use the terminology of physiology. Paradoxically, these inner changes can be perceived only through the intervention of a technology such as X-ray photography, the dispatching of rays
into the body's viscera to record "hidden secrets."[9] The ray annihilates the

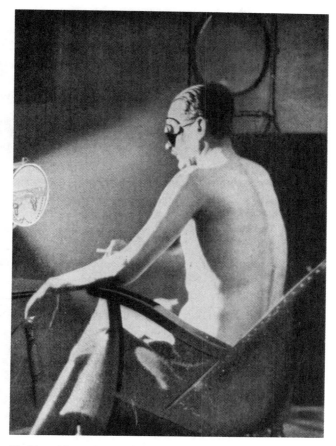

55. Man with goggles at sunlamp. (Reproduced from *Gente nostra*, November 17, 1935, inside front cover.)

self and breaks down the very body boundaries deemed essential for the fascist soldier.

Artificial sunlamps, sold in Italy in the back pages of magazines and small black-and-white inserts, became central to a commonsense language of the daily regime. A man sits at home without his shirt, in clear imitation of the Duce, who often had himself photographed in this way (figure 55). Strapped to his head are protective rubber goggles. A dusty light emanates from the lamp and forms an eerie glow that caresses the man's entire body and makes it seem to disappear at various points. His left hand is bathed in such a strong blaze that it is nearly invisible. In his right hand, he holds a cigarette. This ad is a perfect picture of the sterilizing, self-annihilating aspect of what I have called the hygiene of fascist culture. The body draws in smoke, leans back, and relaxes into a trancelike state of vaporization. But just as the steam baths were promoted as part of a healthful, (hygienic) periodic regime, this moment of nirvana is also interrupted by ambivalence, fear, and denial.

In the popular imagination, there is an equation made between the rays emanating from the lamp or the sun, and those mythical "death rays" believed to be in the final stages of development by the "national" scientists Marconi and Fermi (the "traitor," who emigrated to America, bringing his evil black box). The immense potential of radioactivity to induce hygienic purgations was recognized by a variety of manufacturers of *personal* hygiene products. Soaps were marketed as "radioactive" or "radio-curative" and were associated with a graphic style that made use of bright, glowing colors; luminous, opaque whites; and rays flowing from an incandescent source. To-Radia Facial Soap featured an image of a woman's face that appears to have been bathed recently with a form of radiation, exuding a holy aura that transcends simple cleanliness (figure 56). The proximity of this "modern" face to *the* emblem of classical beauty—the Venus de Milo— suggests a reverse-Pygmalion narrative of frozen perfection. After an application of rays, beauty turns to stone and becomes ungraspable. Saponetta Radioattiva (radioactive soap) was marketed with an explosion of bright colors emanating from a nucleus; streams of radiation mirror the joyful, youthful energy of the target consumers. Feminine beauty is linked with "radiance," which could be considered as much a (narcissistic) reflection of male attention as a physiological phenomenon. Pregnant women are often described as "radiating happiness," as if this outer patina signified a hidden regeneration and vitality; and of course, in Western art the golden ray has long been a symbol of impregnation, sent down to penetrate the wombs of Danaë and the kneeling Madonna, the expectant virgins locked in their gardens and cages.

But while various manufacturers celebrated the positive, transformational, and "progressive" powers of rays, the body went into hiding or provided its own protective armor against just such forms of assault. Cultural fears about rays were bred early in young children, related to the certainty of war that is contained within fascist ideology, and prior to the intervention of any specific enemy. Consider, then, an example of the intrusion of rays into the fascist daily regime: a pamphlet for the Gioventù Fascista del Littorio, the

Metodo scientifico

To-Radia

per la cura della bellezza

(Creme, Cipria, Belletti, Latte detergente)

SOC. ITAL. PRODOTTI PROFUMERIA E IGIENE - FIRENZE - VIA JACOPO NARDI, 44

56. To–Radia facial soap. (Salce Collection, 06010.)

national fascist youth organization, instructs its readers how to pass their summer vacations. In addition to giving information about sports, nature walks,
premilitary drills, and "character formation" exercises, the brochure,
adorned with colored sketches of the shining sun and azure waters of the
Mediterranean, suggests that each Littorio member ought to practice anti–air
raid drills:

> At any given moment we could be attacked by foreign airplanes.
> An attack consists of the launching of incendiary bombs, explosive
> bombs, that is, demolition bombs, asphyxiating gas, tear gases, etc.,
> and also germs, that is, microbes that cause disease, placed in choco-
> lates and candies. Against the threat of bombs, we have first aid
> and fire squads, but every citizen also has the duty to put out ex-
> plosions with sand and to collaborate in any way possible against
> the spread of fire. Against demolition bombs, there is nothing to
> be done; we can only administer first aid to those hit. Against
> germs, we can defend ourselves by never eating food or sweets
> found on the ground. We defend ourselves against gas by using a
> mask of which every citizen ought to be in possession, and by go-
> ing into subterranean shelters. In any case, maintain calm, discipline,
> and a sense of duty toward the injured and toward the Nation.[10]

The Littorio brochure, which is also a sort of calendar to mark the time
during vacations, offers this paranoid account on the page reserved for the
last day of summer. To counteract the harmful effects of rays, the child
must learn to construct armor, linking duty (work) with self-protection
and *national* discipline. In particular, after a long period of summer repose,
of letting down "body-guards," the child must be reminded of threats to
the interior of the body, whether evil rays emanating from the sky or germ-
laced candies that penetrate through the blood.

The infiltration of diabolic bacteria in the raw materials of Italian
autarchy is a moral problem. In response to threats of germ warfare such as
the one just described, dessert industry scientists developed methods for
"cleansing" their materials, but ultimately, it is overproduction and the con-
sequent need to leave materials in storage for long periods of time that is
problematic. However, as I suggested in chapter 3, the regime could not afford to condemn overproduction, which was now built inextricably into the
system of autarchic, fascist production. And so the bacteria themselves become the culprits. Human intervention is effaced from yet another narrative of production and distribution. And just as X rays may cause mutations
but are also "good" penetrators of the body,

we should note that vapors of carbonic sulfur [used to purge mi-
crobes from chocolate] are dangerous to the human organism and
are even lethal if breathed in high doses. Consequently, we should
take precautions when using it. Similar effects have been noted
for the various ammonia-based gases and asphyxiating elements
of which we now have expert descriptions, given their uses in
warfare.[11]

The link between the economic battles against the effects of over-
productivity and the gassing of an undefined enemy is made explicit. "Attacks" — whether on raw materials or on human bodies — are inevitable in
fascist discourse, hence the importance of developing a "thick skin" or a
coat of armor. And as I have suggested, periods of legislated but unsuper-
vised vacation (at the beach or the baths, on a cruise, under the glare of the
sun) were dangerous because individual bodies might neglect to take proper
care of their armor; one is tempted to "let oneself go."

Coty skin cream was marketed in a fascist context as "allowing the
skin to tan" while "avoiding the rays of the sun" (figure 47). The brown
head in the advertisement wears a shield that paradoxically seems to deflect
the rays, while at the same time permitting them to perform some curative
action. The artist who created this ad went to great lengths to avoid any of
the codes that might link this physiognomy with blackness: it is most definitely a white body that has undergone a mutation into an ambivalent anti-
body.

The same linguistic contradiction emerges in the ads of Indanthren
dye, which promoted its own resistance not only against rays from above,
but against "use" itself. Indanthren's corporate headquarters in Milan were
housed in a rationalist building, another perfect shield for the body of the
impiegato.[12] At street level was a brightly lit display window holding the latest fabrics and colors to have emerged from the factories. The company's
logo — the sun and moon — were emblazoned in neon on the facade, break-
ing up the monotonously spaced apertures and plain gray voids. The building was thus imbued with a kind of incandescent glow emanating from the
celestial bodies, the two alchemical icons. In the ad, the body wrapped in
Indanthren cloth walks boldly through the elements, assaulted by rain from
clouds and rays from the sun, using the company name as a shield (figure
57). Rays, both "good" and "bad," are thus incorporated as an unresolved
duality within the language of visual culture.

Between the children's Littorio manual and the Coty skin cream advertisement, nationhood and technology, harmful and helpful rays, and racial

57. Indanthren body takes on rays. (Salce Collection, 03804.)

identity all intersect in the body and try to coexist there under the sign of "protection." The nation is strengthened through the physical buildup of its individual members, but if (evil) rays come showering down, these bodies will suddenly become indelible signs of their nation, *Italian* victims that lose any *particular* identity. Ironically, the *nation* promotes a darkening of the skin (the accretion of armor) as part of a daily hygiene routine, but it simultaneously identifies its *citizens* as Aryan within the justification for colonial expansion. In short, rays are equalizers. Inasmuch as it is construed as a positive element of mass consensus, such "equality" also obliterates individual, heroic bodies that are promoted by the war machine through physical culture. The image of a mass grave of (national) subjects stricken by enemy rays stands in absolute contrast to the phallic body of the ideal fascist male posited in much advertising. Yet the piling up of bodies could be imagined as the exhilarating moment when the dream of national identity is finally achieved—finally, that is, after so many fits and starts, delays, and episodes of cultural "backwardness."

Soul Murder

The heroic body, then, constructs a shield. In fact, it may be precisely the lack of such a shield that accounts for the illness of the infamous Daniel Paul Schreber. His case bears some mention here as a cultural paradigm for the new century. He is, essentially, an embodiment of the cultural fears conveyed in the ray. His paranoia derived from an idiosyncratic cosmology that involved the discharge of rays from God (who is himself formed from nerves or rays). These rays are capable of affecting *every* aspect of human existence. Rays speak (utilizing a "basic language" of incomplete sentences); they commit "soul murder," reducing Schreber's existence to a gray state of boredom; they torment their victim by penetrating the body's viscera; and they are responsible for Schreber's *unmanning*.

It is essential to examine, then, some of the structural and instrumental properties of these rays. First, they are able to effect transformations over spatial separation, much like the radio with its putative hypnotic powers. In the asylum, Schreber explains to his doctor:

> One might even raise the question of whether perhaps all the talk of voices about somebody having committed soul murder can be explained by the souls (rays) deeming it impermissible that a person's nervous system should be influenced by another's to the extent of imprisoning his will power, such as occurs during hypnosis.[13]

This cognitive penetration of the "other" not only disturbs the victim, but also gives pleasure to the penetrators, the souls of dead men,

> whose greatest happiness lies in continual revelling in pleasure combined with recollections of their human past. They were able to exchange their recollections and by means of divine rays ... obtain knowledge about the conditions of persons still living on earth in whom they were interested.[14]

Like radiation, this secret access to thoughts can be harnessed for good or evil purposes:

For one distinguished "searing" and "blessing" rays; the former
were laden with the poison of corpses or some other putrid matter, and therefore carried some germ of disease into the body or
brought about some other destructive effect in it. The blessing
(pure) rays in turn healed this damage.[15]

Schreber believes that his doctor, Flechsig, tried to "cure [my] nervous illness alternated with efforts to annihilate [me] as a human being who, because
of his ever-increasing nervousness, had become a danger to God himself" (pp.
55–56). The controlling master, the evil scientist who ends up abusing his
power, encompasses familiar figures as diverse as Simon Magus, Dr. Faust,
Dr. Franz Mesmer, the chemists on Anatole France's *Penguin Island* (1908),
and the "Professor Radium" of early-twentieth-century comic strips.[16] In
general, the scientist is a male who exercises a fascination over his passive
(often female) subjects. This gender division is certainly in place, for example, in the history of "mesmerism," as I discuss later. In any case, the fact
that Schreber's doctors/rays *unman* him is very important. Schreber's rays
often exhibit an annihilating power:

> My head was frequently surrounded by a shimmer of light owing
> to the massive concentration of rays, like the halo of christ is pic-
> tured.... The reflection of this crown of rays was so strong that
> one day when Professor Flechsig appeared at my bed with his as-
> sistant Dr. Quentin, the latter disappeared from my seeing eyes.[17]

This description parallels the visual annihilation of the subject before the
sunlamp (figure 55). While some rays are projected inside of Schreber's
body (into his "mind's eye"), others fall on the exterior, where they seem
to make of him a sort of public spectacle. For example:

> I saw the upper God (Ormuzd), this time not with my mind's eye
> but with my bodily eye. It was the sun, although not the sun in
> her usual appearance as known to every human being, but sur-
> rounded by a silver sea of rays which covered a 6th or 8th part of
> the sky.... However that may be, the sight was of such overwhelm-
> ing splendor and magnificence that I did not dare look at it con-
> tinually, but tried to avert my gaze from the phenomenon. One of
> the many things incomprehensible to me is that other human be-
> ings should have existed at that time apart from myself.[18]

Finally, Schreber imagines that this assault, which makes him "the only
being on earth," is ultimately intended to save the race (which at one point
in his *Memoirs* is clearly marked as Aryan), and so:

Nothing was left to [me] but to reconcile [myself] to the thought of being transformed into a woman. Nothing of course could be envisaged as a further consequence of unmanning but fertilization by divine rays for the purpose of creating new human beings.[19]

As mentioned in chapter 4, for Macalpine and Hunter this particular fantasy is the key to understanding Schreber's mental illness. The precipitating cause of the unmanning fantasy lies in Schreber's inability to father a child by his wife.

In another key, however, Elias Canetti has taken Schreber as emblematic, not of the "new everyman" who would mother a race, but of the paranoid ruler, a cipher for Hitler himself. Canetti understands the rays and the cosmology of Schreber to be elements of a particular power structure that is inherently political before it is psychopathological. In fact, the rays, for Canetti, exhibit symptoms of the "crowd" that is attracted by the figure of the despot or charismatic leader. Ironically, then, Schreber is placed at the center of this crowd formation, in spite of the fact that he feels himself "powerless" and emasculated. Canetti cites

the strong and lasting attraction exercised over the individuals [i.e., the rays] who are to form the crowd; the ambiguous attitude of these individuals; their subjection through being reduced in size; the way they are taken into the man who in his own person, in his *body,* represents political power; the fact that his greatness must continually *renew* itself in this way; and finally, a very important point not so far mentioned, the sense of catastrophe which is linked with it, of danger to the world order arising from its sudden and rapid increase and unexpected magnetism.[20]

An inherent part of Schreber's delusion is his wish to be the last man alive (even though he claims to dread this). And although some psychoanalysts have painstakingly linked Schreber's *physical* ailments with particular events in his childhood or with the orthopedic devices invented by his father, Canetti disregards any personal etiology. Instead, he sees a coherence to the ailments based on the fact that they all involve penetration of the body:

The principle of the impenetrability of matter no longer applies. Just as he himself [Schreber] wants to extend and penetrate everywhere, even right through the earth, so, in the same way, everything penetrates through him and plays tricks *in* him as well as on him.... For him *greatness* and *persecution* are intimately connected and both are expressed through his body.[21]

Canetti's remarkable seizure of Schreber to represent the type of the paranoid despot does not necessarily negate other psychoanalytic readings of the case. But Canetti's reading does displace causality in paranoia from (Freud's) repressed homosexuality to almost any precipitating event. Or rather, Canetti is not particularly interested in cause (that which provides the basis for therapy of the case); he focuses instead on "the structure of the delusional world and the way it is peopled." Implicitly, his analysis removes Schreber from the scene of pathology and cure, and recasts him into a political drama where his tragic flaw exercises a deterministic effect on the plot.

In fact, Canetti understands Schreber in a particular position at the center of power. To what degree, though, is this "centrality" a metaphor for family relations? Does Canetti understand the center strictly in terms of state power? Although it is not impossible to fathom the paranoia model of power in the context of multiple, nuclear units (families), Canetti does not insist on its application to either the family or the state. In the final analysis, Canetti is interested in the peculiar attraction and repulsion exercised by the center of the unit over the "populus" (of whatever dimension) surrounding it. Canetti makes an equation between rays and "people" that respects the structure of Schreber's cosmology. In essence, nevertheless, it is not important to locate Schreber at either the center or the periphery of this circle, because paranoia seems to be a rhyzomatic illness that implicates its victims as both subject and object (see my comments in chapter 3).

Without taking sides in the Schreber debate (is the text primarily about paranoia, homosexuality, psychosis, or pregnancy fantasy? Is it a metaphor for power or an unfulfilled wish that must, of necessity, have been subjected to some form of distortion or condensation?), I now want to shift the focus away from Schreber (as a particular psychological entity) and onto the rays themselves. To summarize, they embody the following structural principles: they transform (gender); they can be either curative or destructive; they have the power to "light up" the subject from the outside or penetrate the inside; they are life-bearing and can cause impregnation; they threaten bodily boundaries; and they coerce subjects into "compulsive thinking." These properties combine to form an elaborate cosmos that is not so much overridden by the reality principle, but that dominates an imaginary space that has become the (psychotic) source of verification for Schreber's reality testing. Later I will address the specific relation between these symptoms and "nuclear fear," the condition of living with weapons of mass destruction. But for now I turn to another site that is penetrated by both good and evil rays, where nationality, gender, and reproductivity all are elevated to the highest, yet most precarious plane.

Rayon

Artificial fibers constituted one of the most important industries in fascist Italy. Since cotton could not be grown on the peninsula, and the dreams of finding obedient and wooly sheep in East Africa were not borne out, the possibility of manufacturing fibers from synthetic, chemical compounds became a central obsession for the regime, particularly during the autarchic period after sanctions were put in place by the League of Nations. As I discussed in chapter 3, the term "autarchy," borrowed by fascist economic policy from political theory and invested with all the authority of a supernatural or mystical sacrament, referred to a very specific ideological goal. Even before the sanctions were declared, Mussolini sought to increase Italian exports and decrease imports toward a zero-degree utopia of independence. On a practical level, however, "autarchy" had come to be synonymous with higher prices and lower quality for a number of essential and luxury goods. The textile industry had seen several failures, including the difficult "Lanital," a form of synthetic wool extracted from milk compounds.[22] Rayon, on the other hand, was a remarkable exception to the inferiority complex of autarchic production, and it contributed substantially to the growth of the entire textile industry, both domestic sales and exports. The price of autarchic success, however, was an increased participation of state agencies in various sectors of the marketplace, and the strengthening of favoritism and payoffs between government officials and capitalists.[23] (Repressed in the name of normalization, these ties have emerged with a pathological vengeance to haunt industries and elected officials alike at the time of this writing.)

As a synecdoche for fascism itself, autarchy was also a politics of war in the way it formed necessary alliances between the state and its free-market industries. As in a cover image from *La difesa della razza* (figure 18), autarchy makes an absolute cut or wound in order to delimit Italian nationhood from forces that would threaten its absolute boundaries. In the autarchy campaigns, the inevitability of the destruction of the national enemy, and hence, the marking of bodies with the dual sign of nationhood and death, is inscribed onto the consumer products themselves. In the cultural imagination, rayon is thus a variant of the ray, charged with ambivalence. Since cloth production could not be redeemed through the natural world, it would have its own revenge in the artificial one. The logic that bound artificial fibers with nationhood is quite simple,

> because the problem of autarchy is the same everywhere: to emancipate oneself from slavery; on the one hand, from the technical superiority of more advanced industrialized nations, and on the other hand, from the scarcity of available fibers.[24]

In colonialist language, the scarcity of natural resources in AOI was part of a moral and racist problematic.[25] But in Italy, the industrialists set about solving the dilemma through a campaign that promoted national products—and rayon in particular—as a classless commodity, within the reach of every individual in the body politic. If, as some psychoanalytic theories suggest, war is based on the paranoiac projection of persecutory motives onto a phantasmagoric enemy, then autarchic production—with its basis in the attribution of evil intent to the sanctionist nations—is an inevitable preparation for war.[26] Thus I have located in rayon the coincidence of paranoia, persecution, and annihilation inscribed in the disappearing body.

Cloth manufacturing in a great many societies works as a distinguished metaphor for the course of human life. Because it has often been assigned to women under an enormous variety of situations, cloth production remains linked in figurative and literal terms with human reproduction.[27] This connection is strongly maintained by the anthropologist Jane Schneider in her reading of the Rumpelstiltskin tale from folklore. Various forms of the tale have circulated: the central plot involves a young girl who spins straw into cloth (or straw into gold). Spinning will result in a reward (the girl can marry a prince), or it is considered a duty (she must spin to support her family and protect them from ruin). In the Rumpelstiltskin variant analyzed by Schneider, the girl is unable to produce cloth quickly enough, and therefore must resort to a pact with the devil whereby she agrees to relinquish her firstborn son (that is, sacrifice reproduction for productivity). This pact is read by Schneider as a sign of an ambivalence within the culture of nineteenth-century Europe toward the transformation to large-scale capitalist enterprise in the cloth-making industry, an industry that had long been associated with both the feminine and the "home." In the tale, spinning, once a domestic, feminine activity, is seen to be incompatible with reproduction. In the modern world, cloth production begins to interfere with the course of life, with "natural" female behavior; in the tale, this

problem can be "resolved" only by the intervention of a (male) figure whom
Schneider identifies with a demonized "brownie" or "fairy" type:

> The demonized spirits of the spinning tales did not seek to elimi-
> nate linen manufacture. On the contrary, Rumpelstiltskin and the
> witch-like crones contributed to its development, magically pro-
> ducing yarn and facilitating the status mobility through marriage
> that the linen schemes promised as the reward for diligent spin-
> ning. The spirits did, however, claim a piece of the action through
> their malicious sabotage of human reproduction. As such they splen-
> didly dramatized the core dilemma of the linen "protoindustry."[28]

The core anxiety of spinning tales (which might also include that of Snow
White, whose "normal sexual development," symbolized in her spinning,
is interrupted by a witch) lies in the disruption of female status mobility by
the new industrialization of the cloth industry. In the preindustrial world,
women were responsible for producing cloth for the trousseau; the "value"
of a woman was also gauged by potential suitors based on her spinning
abilities. Customs of courtship, preparation for marriage, and female development are thus all disrupted by mass production in the textile industry.
The shock waves are felt long after, even into the 1930s, when good fascist
women are supposed to uphold antiquated, traditional relationships with
cloth as a sign of their submission to male authority.

Cultural anxiety about the female body may be displaced if one focuses
on another aspect of the Rumpelstiltskin tale. In many versions of Rumpelstiltskin, the girl is asked not to produce cloth at a rate beyond her normal
capacity, but actually to spin straw or flax into *gold*. I do not believe that
the introduction of this variant weakens Schneider's argument, since the
activity of *spinning* is clearly the central element of the *fabula*, in all its mutations. Nevertheless, it seems important to invoke the *alchemical* narrative
line — the production of gold from a base material — because this morpho-
logical variant emerges also in the fascist textile industry. The brownie/
sprite/witch not only disrupts the normal process by which a girl learns to
be industrious and "sell" herself to potential suitors along with her cloth.
The "demon" also, in a parallel manner, disrupts the labor theory of value
in which a piece of work made from raw material and transformed into a
commodity is exchanged for commodity-capital in the market. The capitalist dream of bypassing the investment in labor and arriving immediately
at a phase of surplus value — the dream of freeing capital from the leaden

chains of transformation and commodification—seems to be embodied in the unfulfilled wish of the Rumpelstiltskin tale. The alchemical roots of this story are ancient: they predate both the transition from feudalism to capitalism and the institutionalization of female piecework in the cloth industry. In the modern telling of the tale, however, alchemy surfaces at this historical juncture in a particular relation with both cloth manufacture and the construction of the feminine.

In Italy, the textile industry underwent extensive rationalization during fascism. Modernization involved the creation of formulas for standardization that saw a "constant" factor in the mathematical relation between preparing, carding, and threading fibers. The human body was elided in these formulas and substituted with the "hand" in handwork *(mano d'opera)*. And as I have suggested, it is precisely this hand, in a severed form, that stands for the fixed rate of (over)production brought about by rationalizing processes. But ultimately, for the cloth industry, the most constant factor that can be calculated is the machine hour, not handwork. An industry analyst wrote:

> If the factory has been constructed on sound criteria, everything should be adjusted to the productive potentiality of this [machine hours].... Once the standard cost has been established for all work done and once the relative control we spoke of earlier has been put into place, which in substance comes to represent nothing more or less than the thermometer of costs, we will initiate a file for the standard cost of the threaders.... We admit that only rarely, especially in our first attempts, will we find a perfect response, and so it will be our duty to establish the various differences and to study them in order to prepare the way for our future search for standards that are ever closer to reality.[29]

This passage describes a process of arriving at a perfect kernel of truth embodied in the atomic reduction of human motion to a single numerical equivalent.

But there is more to the modernization of textiles than simply rationalizing (male) production. Not only was the textile industry (and particularly the introduction of artificial fibers) key to the fascist economy, but it was one of only a small number of fields in which women were heavily employed during and after World War I. The scientific management teams that concerned themselves with modernizing textile production under fascism were thus forced to confront issues of sexual reproduction. The industry was extremely dangerous, involving long hours in cramped, unventilated spaces and the use of toxic chemicals, especially during the so-called preparation phase of extracting the fibers. Clearly, a life spent under these conditions threatened to undermine the fascist birthrate campaigns. Textile plants had to be kept very hot and humid for the sake of the fibers' "docility," a technical term that could also be applied metaphorically to the workers themselves. Textile workers suffered from such severe dehydration that they had to be administered doses of a special saline liquid, as if their own bodies were also undergoing alchemical change.[30] Obviously, such conditions were understood to be utterly incompatible with the healthy, abundantly fertile fascist female. Ironically, then, artificial-fiber production was the single industry in which protective measures taken for the sake of maternity served to displace women.[31]

Nevertheless, the industry relied on low-paid, passive workers to co-exist in perfect harmony with the machinery, and the cultural relation of femininity to textile production was rooted in long-standing traditions. So women were kept on as both producers and consumers of artificial fibers. The cultural ambivalence toward this industry was repressed, but emerges in the symptoms of the disappearing body. An illustration from an industry publication of "modern" threading machinery makes this ambivalence utterly clear: threads would be treated in a series of baths and dyes, and then forced through the pin-sized holes of a threader that, here, is the visual analogue of the hymen (figure 58).

The process of manufacturing rayon (artificial silk) resembles a form of alchemical transmutation, and this is reflected in the language of production itself. One begins with the primary material, cellulose, which in Italy's case was derived from wood subjected to a series of baths (also called the "nobilization" process) in order to achieve a pure, homogeneous ("noble") product.[32] The "product," or secondary material, then undergoes a series of (al)chemical processes that soften and coagulate it until it emerges as a subtle fiber, usually viscose. Large vats used in the factories were called "hermetic vessels." These stages of the production process were primarily off-limits to female workers. The "female" stage begins when the fibers are carded, threaded, dyed, and woven; bolts of fabric are manipulated, cut, and folded for shipment—like the bolt that produces Rayon-man. Before the rationalization of Italy's factories, women were responsible for threading the fibers onto a bobbin by hand. But under fascism the industry underwent a highly significant transformation: the introduction of

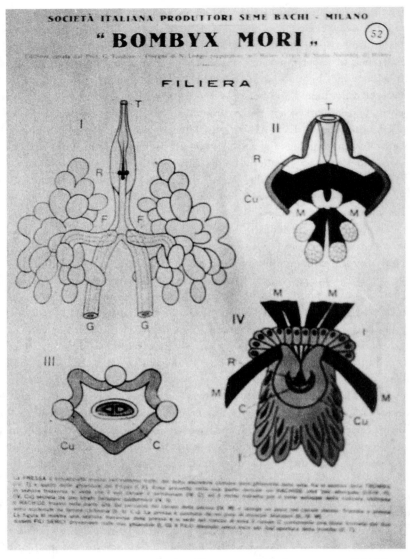

58. "Hymen" fiber-threaders. (Reproduced from "Sapere" brochure, courtesy of the Museo della Storia del Tessuto, Venice.)

threader machines that were composed of thousands of tiny holes (the hymen figure).

Thanks to the new machinery, Italy became the top exporter of rayon in the world, but the joy to be had from this fact was, as usual, not unmediated. The fact that women continued to work the mechanical threader-hymens and were primarily responsible for the postbath stages of rayon production raised deep cultural anxieties that seem to emerge in the advertising for the product.

Descriptions of the transmutation of rayon sound very much like the extraction of radium, which Marie Curie characterized in her autobiography:

> I had to work with as much as twenty kilograms of material at a time, so that the hangar was filled with great vessels full of precipitates and of liquids. It was exhausting work to move the containers about, to transfer the liquids, and to stir for hours at a time, with an iron bar, the boiling material in the cast-iron basin. I extracted from the mineral the radium-bearing barium and this, in the state of chloride, I submitted to a fractional crystallization.[33]

The image of a woman undertaking such an enormously dangerous operation (like the "male" stages of rayon production) must have aroused extraordinary cultural fears. (Does this explain why such a vast proportion of the rest of Curie's book is taken up with narrative about her marriage and children?)

The conjoinment of male and female "stages," the mixture of (sexed) materials in hermetic vessels, the closed spaces of the workshops, the attainment of a noble material—all of these terms derive from a long-standing discourse of alchemy in Western thought. My invocation of alchemy here may of course appear metaphorical, as if I wished to elevate textile production to the level of narrative coherence. But alchemy itself is taken metaphorically in the context of Western thought. The attainment of gold from base materials has been split into a hermetic-philosophical tradition and a set of questionable, equivocal practices. The theory of alchemy has retained a certain prestige in the West through its links with Renaissance Neoplatonism and the hermeneutics of a metaphorical "hermetic tradition." The practice of alchemy, on the other hand, has been so debased that it is excluded a priori from academic discourse. In essence, then, the fate of alchemy parallels the situation in the textile industry where a "philosophical" language comes to displace actual practices. In turn, these practices are charged with apprehension and are cloaked in secrecy.

Although the early (male-dominated) stages of production were primarily responsible for toxic fumes released by sulfur and carbon, it is clear that (female) workers connected with the later stages of threading and shaping were routinely exposed to highly dangerous amounts of chemicals. The effects of inhalation of sulfuric compounds are cumulative, so it was possible to continue laboring under noxious conditions for significant periods of time before symptoms would be evident. The industry was thus able to retain individuals (particularly women) on provisional contracts, after which they would be admitted to state hospitals or mental institutions if, as was common, they exhibited behavior consistent with neurosis, hysteria, or forms of dementia or psychosis. Until 1934 Italy provided no indemnity for "intoxication" and so the textile industry expediently discharged itself of any responsibility. Eventually, some compensation was granted to workers in the early (male) processes, but the state medical establishment did not recognize illnesses related to the "handwork" phases of threading, carding, and weaving.

In other words, the industry, in collusion with the medical community and the state insurance agencies, reinforced a gendered division of labor that allowed for a total negation of the toxicity that threatened female reproductivity and feminine "hygiene." Yet it was precisely the danger that work posed to fertility that had inspired the various fascist measures taken against female employment.[34] The industry had its cake and ate it too: women were denied any legal recognition, but at a more metaphorical level, they were denied their very existence. Women labored in closed spaces, hovering over vats of chemicals that were given euphemistic labels to hide their true content. Workers were stricken with physical and psychological symptoms that were then attributed to innate weakness and hysterical tendencies; they were incarcerated in state institutions and subjected to purging "cures." They literally disappear, annihilated by the fumes they breathe, or, better, they are transmuted into new subjects.

There is a strict link, then, between the discourse of rayon production, with all its allusions to the alchemical process, and the presence of women in the industry. Alchemy not only produces a noble substance from the combination of base metals through a "secret" and inexpressible process, but it has long been associated with a ritual marriage or sexual union. In the case of rayon, then, the process of production binds the industrialist/alchemist with the Duce/king under the sign of a royal wedding; but instead of hoarding the gold in his treasury, the king now makes it available to the masses in the form of cheap fashion, made in Italy (and most importantly, not in the capital of haute couture, namely, Paris). When Mussolini visited the factories and watched girls pulling bolts of fabric from the machines, he participated actively in the formation of this totalizing parable. Female identity is obliterated, figured in the vapid stare of a worker who finalizes the "female" stage of cloth production (figure 59).

At the same time, however, women's magazines contributed to the cult of rayon through numerous articles and countless fashion spreads of comfortable, loose-fitting fabrics whose style approximated French "fashion" in a kind of synecdochal relation. Rayon prizes were awarded, and at a national fashion show in 1938 Marinetti read his poetic encomium to the Torre Viscosa, the central factory producing artificial fibers. This reading was part of an evening "celebration" organized by the Snia Viscosa Corporation during which the high society of northern Italy paraded around in their rayon dresses. On the microtextual level, Marinetti's language seems to exalt autarchic production as "the new constellation" in the fascist firmament. The corporate headquarters, Torre Viscosa, is described as a utopian industrial community of theaters, dining halls, swimming pools, and soccer fields for the workers, divided by majestic avenues named after Vittorio Veneto and Arnaldo Mussolini (Il Duce's trusted brother).[35] Nevertheless, at the macrotextual, narrative level, the poem laments the castrating effects of this female, demonic technology, this "Goddess Geometry" on the futurist male. Buried within the virulent rhetoric of the poem is a subtle fear that the futurist "aeropilot" who has valiantly conquered Ethiopia will become engulfed by the hymen of the rayon factories.

The regime sponsored a rayon train, which toured the country distributing "rayon propaganda" and blaring a rayon anthem from mounted speakers. In part, the campaign focused on the process of production itself, for unlike advertising in general, autarchic advertising was grounded in an appreciation of the enormity of industrial machinery and the accelerated development involved. In an effort to demonstrate that artificial-fiber production had utterly wiped out the feminine cottage industries associated with textiles in an earlier phase of Italy's history, propaganda actually focused on the very alienation of the worker from the process that, elsewhere, the market nostalgically sought to restore. The magazine *Vita femminile* included a multipage layout of glistening threaders and weavers from the Snia Viscosa factory — the image captures the eye precisely because of the lack of any human figures. And the photo caption reads: "Perhaps these illustra-

59. Annihilation of the feminine in the textile industry. (Reproduced from "Sapere" brochure, courtesy of the Museo della Storia del Tessuto, Venice.)

tions, even though they are very technical, will contribute to your overall appreciation of rayon."[36] For the first time, the means of production had become the message; the machines, redeemed from the grasp of femininity, remasculinized and standing alone, symbolize a shift in the Italian economy, and particularly in habits of consumption. Women of all classes will now buy mass-produced dresses made from pressed cellulose in recognizable and repeated patterns. The introduction of ready-to-wear coincides with the regime's wresting the industry away from the hands of its female workers; at the same time, however, the consumer is defined in terms of a gender division that is so powerful it wipes out class distinctions. The perfect fascist chemical equilibrium had been achieved in the alchemical transmutation of raw materials into consensus.

But there is more: the propaganda developed by the regime's autarchy program was quite conscious of the etymological link between "rayon" (at first spelled *raion* in Italian, but then changed, ironically, to the French spelling for "ray" — "rayon"), "ray," and "radio."[37] Rayon was sold in a variety of campaigns, some "collective" and regime-sponsored, others bearing a particular brand name; many campaigns made an explicit connection between technological progress and "fashion" progress, the kind of seasonal acquisitions that characterize modern buying habits, but that were not part of the older mentality of couture that treated fabrics as durable, lifelong possessions. Like "ray" and "radio," then, "rayon" is charged with a dialectical ambivalence.

Cultural fears embodied in rayon are related to changing social roles that are mediated through fabric, one of the essential material elements of life. White linens *(biancheria)* are not merely the sign of an unmarried woman's commodity value; they are the actual currency exchanged by the matrilineal side for the protection of the father/husband. The introduction of cheap, low-maintenance fabrics into this carefully balanced equation means a certain loss or confusion. According to the traditional knowledge sustained by fascism and even published in a manual for women, all linens are divided into two groups: house linen and personal linen.[38] Linens must be mended as soon as any tear is made evident, and in cases of extreme overuse, a replacement may be made by the woman for some item originally in her trousseau. Clearly, however, this kind of indiscriminate waste is a moral flaw. As every woman knows, "It is better to have one less dress, and one more sheet."[39] Personal linens should be hand sewn and should be washed by the woman of the house with great care — this is what defines them, precisely, as personal. Moreover,

Limited resources and the difficulty of finding trustworthy domestic help must be kept in mind, just as the woman must recall that no action pertaining to the home is ever too low, no task will seem too difficult, when you are serving the needs of your own family. This is the true and useful collaboration that the woman can bring to the sphere of the home, and it is obtained by intensifying the feminine gifts of goodness and perspicuity in such a way as to achieve a high degree of economy in everything you do. *Buy the least amount possible. Produce. In the home all of this is possible.*[40]

In defiance of this form of commonsense knowledge, however, women of the 1920s and 1930s began to replace the traditional white linens with black ones — "blacks" — which required less frequent cleaning. After all, remarks the social columnist Irene Brin, women are essentially dirty creatures, but "blacks" allow them to feel more mobile; they can wash their undergarments "every so often," on a train or in a hotel washbasin. In addition, the departure from the particular forms of femininity encoded in the white linens meant that black immediately represented liberation to the female eye, a subtle kind of rebellion, private and unseen. Black linens must be purchased — they belong to the new ready-to-wear industry — rather than patiently crafted by the female "sewing circle" as part of the preparations for marriage. They are disposable, not eternal like the linens of the trousseau, and as such they are also signs of the new female buying power. They imply a whole series of social and cultural shifts away from traditional roles in the family and toward female suffrage and employment, at least from the perspective of the consumer herself. "Blacks" also represent a compromise between female desires for self-determination and male desires for tradition. Because men both uphold the subjugation of women and desire them as sexual objects, the resexualizing of the female body (as long as it remains hidden in the bedroom) allows fascist males to possess women in this dual sense.

But if black undergarments struck some male viewers as too "vampiresque," women might at the very least take advantage of the new artificial knits that could be hung out on a hotel balcony to dry in a matter of hours.[41] It is clear, then, that personal linens, but also those associated with the house, are a highly determined site for negotiating the relative freedom granted to the female body at any given time, and during the fascist era they are invested with tremendous doses of cultural paranoia.

Domestic economy implies a form of atomic autarchy whose obsessive object is, above all, the linens a woman brings into the marriage. Collected and embroidered, familiar to the female and alien to the male, these linens are to be stored in the *armadio,* the large wooden cabinet that symbolizes the containment of exchange, the absolute self-sufficiency of the family unit.

But the introduction of artificial fibers threatens this structure. In one advertisement, an elegant signora draws away the curtain of the linen closet and finds her perplexed servant standing before the empty shelves (figure 60). They perform the following dialogue:

SERVANT: And now how are we going to replenish the *armadio?*

SIGNORA: Don't worry. All we have to do is pass by the CASA DEL BIANCO at Corso Magenta number 2 so that I can conveniently purchase every-thing I need with total confidence in both price and quality.

The scene is part of an urban panorama, one that would certainly not translate well into rural life. But the ad raises one very significant question, which it purposefully refuses to answer; namely, where have the linens gone? Have they simply been consumed, their resistance worn down? In effect, haven't these linens disobeyed a fundamental tenet of fascist (male) produc-tion and (female) consumption, by wasting themselves needlessly? And the very subversive merchants who run a "home" of linens beckon the con-sumer in a gesture that overtly spits in the face of fascist domestic economy. Paradoxically, however, the low-price, high-quality store-bought linens ad-vertised here celebrate fascist industry. And so the seductive gesture of this ad is one in which morality becomes slippery. Given the perturbation that this mistress–servant dialogue represents in a pattern of female relations and identities, it is now clear why the face of the domestic is wiped out, her contours merely suggested by the tone contrast of apron and dress. Neither she nor her mistress can afford specific representation: they are like the vic-tims of violent crime who currently appear in the mass media with their faces blotted out or scrambled, their voices fed through a distortion box. Such subjects ask to remain silhouetted or semirepresented, because on one hand they have something to say, but on the other hand, they are uncom-fortable with their agency in the utterance. So this urban consumer finds herself in the vanguard: she defies convention (and she can do this only through the power of her class, whereas the servant remains rooted in tra-ditional anxieties), but she also consumes a new, autarchic product that the

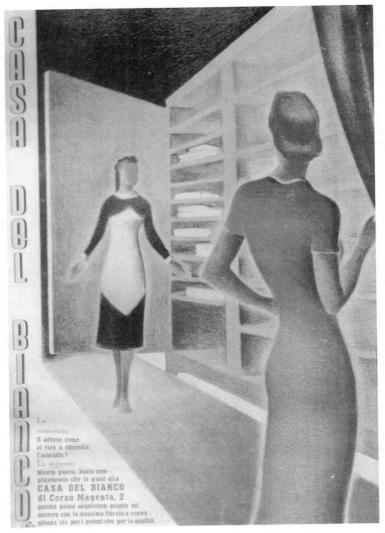

La
camericra:
E adesso come
si farà a ritornire
l'armadio?
La signora:
Niente paura: basta sem-
plicemente che io passi alla
CASA DEL BIANCO
di Corso Magenta, 2
perché possa acquistare quanto mi
occorre con la massima fiducia e conve .
nienza sia per i prezzi che per la qualità.

60. Casa del Bianco dialogue. (Courtesy of the Bertarelli Collection, Milan.)

regime is promoting with all its energy. In her discussion of customs and habits during the fascist *ventennio,* Irene Brin reflects on the increasing murkiness surrounding the position of the domestic:

> If, in very refined homes, one continued to distinguish the duties of the cook and the servant, our bourgeoisie tended to blur and

limit the role of the single domestic, the mistress always allowing herself the pride she had in whipping up certain dishes and the pleasure she had in mortifying the rough and inexperienced girl: in any case, the relation was usually quite cordial.[42]

Writing during the Second World War, Brin already could foresee the end of such practices and relations as the genteel, feminized form of domination and submission was replaced by the figure of the middle-class "housewife," who would be solely responsible for every aspect of housekeeping and would therefore have little time for the mundanity so dear to women of the early fascist generation. With a nostalgic glance backward, Brin chronicles the winding down of bourgeois pleasure in the incessant imitation of an aristocratic ideal (mortifying the servant) and in small accomplishments ("whipping up certain dishes") whereby the middle class expresses its superiority and conformity.

During the *biancheria* dialogue, the mistress and servant are nearly indistinguishable in their silhouetted forms, and this is essentially a problem brought on by the introduction of cheap, artificial silk. In other words, the very manufacturing process that elevates fascist Italy (with its productive working class) also threatens to equalize class distinction, and so signals a danger for the bourgeois consumer. The problem emerges, like a repressed and unfulfilled wish, again and again in images from mass culture. During the thirties, the Ente Nazionale della Moda (National Fashion Bureau), the same fascist organization that promoted artificial fibers, also sponsored a collective campaign for hats. One advertisement showed two women drawn in rudimentary fashion, with identical silhouettes. Both figures wear the same high-waisted, simple dress and block heels. "Which is the mistress and which is the servant?" the ad asks. "The habit of not wearing a hat produces an apparent leveling among women that leads to confusion that is often embarrassing if not downright displeasing. The hat is indispensable in female dress, even as an element of distinction and prestige. Hats are as necessary as shoes."[43] The putative problem here — the loss of the hat as a signifier between subjects of different classes — is really only a symptom of the larger problem of the introduction of ready-to-wear and the scrambling of class codes under fascist production. During the 1920s, flapper women threw off their hats as a liberating gesture, as part of a movement in fashion that also saw the streamlining and masculinization of the female body.[44] In this context, the hat is a highly conservative way to counteract the insecurity generated by cross-class dressing. When women take off their hats and put on their rayon dresses or stockings — their autarchic clothing — they disappear (figure 61).

61. Rayon stockings.

Smoke without Restrictions

The generation of women who threw off their hats would wake up from their postwar reverie to find their liberation severely curtailed, only a decade later. Smoking, which became acceptable for women of "high principles" just around 1920, was thus also a de rigueur symbol of a woman's freedom; a symbol of the "new" generation, like black linens. Nonsmokers were known to spread a brown substance on their hands to resemble nicotine stains.[45] Once the "bad girl" image of the 1920s had lost its innocence and charm, the fascist conduct books warned against the hygienic and social effects of smoking. But for the generation that came of age before Mussolini seized power, their addiction had taken hold. Women rarely appear in cigarette ads from the 1930s for reasons related, precisely, to this shift in accepted feminine behavior. What emerges instead is a tension between the power of the physical addiction and the power of the economic addiction of the cigarette monopolies.

In Sepo's ad for the French ANIC cigarettes, a mask whose hollow back is revealed in a sideways view puffs on a lit cigarette while a pool of dark-stained nicotine forms underneath (figure 62). Although scientists had not yet gathered statistical evidence linking smoke with cancer or other lung ailments, the addictive nature of nicotine was well documented, so the chronic smoker (male or female) was tainted with an aura of immorality. At the same time, occasional smoking—or the use of a filter—was generally considered harmless, since it was, precisely, the psychological nature of the compulsion rather than any physical danger that placed the subject at risk. Sepo's mask represents a "filter" that in theory is meant to keep the nicotine from ever reaching the lungs of a smoker. Here, however, the human body is absent, and the charade of "safe smoking" goes on with puppets filling in for humans.

"Smoke without restrictions" reads another popular slogan for Abadie brand filters (figure 63). A zephyr figure, his chiseled features drawn into death-mask determinacy, has become decapitated. His disembodied face occupies a geometrically limited space, a triangle with a cutout hole to accommodate the jutting tube of his cigarette. From his nostrils billow forth two powerful, "toxic" clouds of smoke. The very concept of a filter that removes any harmful effects of smoking belongs to the register of "personal hygiene" technologies that is diffused in the popular press. The paradox between consumption of a patriotic product (in Italy a national brand was produced and distributed by a state monopoly) and the self-annihilation of inhaling the cigarette smoke emerges in the images of the mask. Smoking,

62. Sepo's ANIC cigarettes.

63. Abadie cigarette filters. (Salce Collection, 07737.)

the act of taking a dangerous and toxic chemical into the lungs, is figured as a moment of pure pleasure, a withdrawal into private spheres of relaxation. This moment is traditional in the marketing of cigarettes and involves a form of cultural disavowal. Like Sepo's work for Noveltex, his ANIC ad makes absence present through the nonrepresentation of the human body.

In oil painting, smoke and smoking paraphernalia were traditional icons of *vanitas* compositions. By the turn of the century, however, they are evacuated of their earlier moral charge, transformed into the instruments of decadent, poetic, masculine expression. Baudelaire, for example, reflects a nineteenth-century mythology of the aesthetics of addiction that replaced the female sexual object with the gratification of the pipe. For his generation smoking could be understood as a solitary, highly erotic experience, to be carried out in the privacy of a study, as a way of stimulating the poet.[46] In his "Poème du haschisch," Baudelaire perfectly expressed the disappearing act of the cigarette-smoking body: "Par une équivoque singulière, par une espèce de transportation ou de quiproquo intellectuel, vous vous sentirez vous évaporant, et vous attribuerez à votre pipe (dans laquelle vous vous sentirez accroupi et ramassé comme le tabac) l'étrange faculté de *vous fumer*" (emphasis added). ("Through a singular equivocation, through a sort of transportation or intellectual quid pro quo, you will feel yourself evaporate, and you will attribute to your pipe [in which you will feel yourself tamped down like tabacco] the strange capacity to smoke you.") This last line — "you will attribute to your pipe the strange capacity to *smoke you*" — was particularly linked to a problem in poetics that saw the disappearance of the author and his subservience to a language that writes him, just as the pipe smokes him. Increasingly, the poet abdicates responsibility for his words; he submits to them like the addict to his drug. And although this specific problem may not intrude on the marketing of the tobacco-related products, it is clear that smoking, although not yet linked with cancer or other physical ailments, hinged on a poetics of illness. This illness is both desired and feared; or better, it is disavowed. Like the evil rays, the evanescent vanity of smoke transforms the human body itself into an invisible entity.

Rays from the Eye

"Rays" of smoke emerge from the mouth and nostrils and return to "smoke" the body away. A similar self-annihilation can be attributed to rays from the eye. The X ray was discovered in 1895, the same year that Svengali became widely known in the popular press. But much earlier, throughout the nineteenth century, magnetism and hypnosis were presented as public spectacles, first in the context of upper-class salon life, and then in middle- and working-class forums such as fairs, circuses, and town squares. Mesmerization techniques were believed to work by the eyes of a subject in power sending rays to another individual, who would then lose control, like Schreber when he is unmanned.[47] As Spencer Weart maintains in *Nuclear Fear,* the early-twentieth-century cultural imagination was highly preoccupied with the implications of these powers: "Stern eyes could also seem threatening when they saw 'into things,' for example into a child's misdeeds or forbidden sexual matters. The discovery of X rays called forth nervous jokes about people using gadgets to peep through closed doors. A brash London firm offered X-ray proof underclothes for sale."[48]

Whether in spectacles or private therapy sessions, magnetism and hypnosis took many forms, but the one unifying aspect of these practices seems to be the interaction between a male (magnetizer) and a female (magnetized). Again, this gendered split parallels the experience of Schreber under the power of his rays. Magnetism attracted a considerable number of intellectuals, including Alessandro Manzoni. Treatises on the subject suggested that women were incapable of magnetizing, and in any case, they were universally considered much more effective "patients" because of a biological tendency toward a more "porous nervous system," whose fibers were more conveniently penetrated.[49]

Once under the influence, however, the "patients" were themselves able to penetrate opaque masses with their eyes and to make extrasensory observations of various sorts. Contrary to initial appearances, therefore, the male "doctor" comes to express a state of "masochistic, passive, defense receptivity" against "the eccentric authoritarianism, the sadism of the patients who allow themselves to be magnetized for hours upon hours by prostrated magnetizers."[50] There is an immediate link, then, between female sexuality and danger that also serves as a "justification" for the whole process of pacifying the patient. In any case, for the anthropologist Clara Gallini, the magnetism phenomenon is essentially construed as the relation of a fixed, monogamous couple (often the "performers" of magnetic spectacles were actually married). The "electromagnetic sympathy" posited between the two subjects had obvious sexual overtones, and the "science" is based on affirming new bourgeois family models and controlling women's (dangerous) bodies.

Of course, advertising itself was often viewed in conservative Italy as conforming to the paradigm of hypnotic subliminality or mind control. The cultural imagination clearly related the receptivity mechanism of ads with magnetism, but without the element of marvel that would redeem the early experiments and spectacles for a mass audience. Some ads did make use of the "rays from the eye" image, but in a context that overtly acknowledges and plays on fears of "suggestion" (figure 64). At the level of

64. Calze Santagostino rays from the eye. (Salce Collection, 06488.)

design, the ray makes a compositional link between the body in the image and the body that views the image, through eye contact. Santagostino was a large manufacturer of socks and stockings whose management had embraced rationalization in production and the application of "modern" psychology to advertising campaigns. The firm recognized the special challenge of creating desire for a product that was traditionally linked purely with need or obligation, and for which consumption was considered limited.[51] The company's long-standing logo, pictured in the triangle above the gentleman's head, shows Saint Augustine (*Santagostino*) holding up his hand in a gesture of faith. It is clear that this orthodox mark of fidelity would not work in the modern marketplace for a company that had made a serious investment in the rationalization of its factories and its marketing techniques. Without eliminating the older image entirely, the artist managed to incorporate Saint Augustine into a composition of triangles that radiate from the eyes — one upward, one downward. The creator of the Santagostino ad wanted to provide a dual focus to his composition — one on the brand name, and one on the specific, new product, "super socks," which were being promoted through the more modern and compelling graphics. The ad not only softens the public fear about hypnotic, subliminal advertising through a kind of visual pun, it also mitigates the ambivalence toward brand names in fascist economics — the unresolved, contradictory promotion and destruction of competitive private enterprise.[52]

This strategy of splitting the eyes and focusing their rays in different directions is not unique. Depero also used it in a figure for the Campari Company. "With one eye he sees a Campari Bitter, with the other a Campari Soda," Depero suggested when he was commissioned to create something that would encompass both products (figure 65). The slogan–image combination brings the campaign strategy to the fore; Depero thematizes the task of promoting two different and potentially competing items under the same brand name. Rather than disguise his strategy, in other words, Depero celebrates it within the campaign, linking the products with salesmanship.

A malevolent aura lurks behind Depero's jubilant picture of the eyes split into two separate gazes. The images perceived by the subject represented are distinct, not fused into a single depth of field as they ought to be according to conventional optics. A viewer might find the experience of gazing at the visible and nonparallel rays rather uncanny. One might, for example, compare the split gaze to the mysterious diagrams of vision offered by phenomenology. In fact, it is precisely the function of envy, or *invidia* (from *videre*, "to see"), that is exercised by the lure of advertising. For

65. Depero's split gaze for Campari.

Lacan, following a tradition of research into perception developed primarily by Merleau-Ponty, the "evil eye"—the eye that is seen seeing, the eye that emits rays—acts out of *invidia*. In its visual function, *invidia* plays a specific role that should not be confused with jealousy:

> What the small child, or whoever, *envies* is not at all necessarily what he might want—*avoir envie,* as one improperly puts it.... Everyone knows that envy is usually aroused by the possession of goods which would be of no use to the person who is envious of

them, and about the true nature of which he does not have the least idea.

Such is true envy—the envy that makes the subject pale before the image of a completeness closed upon itself, before the idea that the *petit a,* the separated *a* from which he is hanging, may be for another the possession that gives satisfaction, *Befriedigung.*[53]

Lacan's formulation makes explicit the relation between advertising (as a visual form, generally speaking) and the scopic drive, as they intersect in *invidia*. In the images of ray-emitting eyes, the materiality of vision and the link between seeing and possessing are literalized, but in a context that seems almost friendly, cartoonish, playful. Nevertheless, vision is structured like a powerful harness between subjects and objects that ultimately threatens the isolation and sovereignty of the body. Beholding the compelling advertisements, the consumer is transfixed, perhaps annihilated, by the mesmerizing rays that return the gaze.

The Body Disappears (Not a Conclusion)

This chapter began with a focus on Cavadini's Rayon shirt-man, a figure who juts upward like a fetish, a form of disavowal, a visual alibi (against the threat of castration?). I questioned how this erect homunculus fit within the glittery world of consumer goods in the city center, and what his relation might be to real bodies engaged in exchange there. I traced his lineage to visual topoi of disappearance and annihilation that reflect a cultural crisis of unfathomable depth, taking him as a paradigm for certain symptoms or, better, as a paragon of an unnamed disease. If there is a unifying pathos to these images of disappearance, it may be said to lie in the body's own inability to maintain its materiality, to maintain a necessary level of tension or, rather, "attention."[54] Lack of attention—the psychic equivalent of the body fading in and out—was seen by Italian psychology as a phrenaesthetic problem. And a heightened "attention quotient" is precisely the goal of any modern, rational advertising campaign, as discussed in chapter 1. In a landscape that is becoming increasingly crowded with images and subject to greater forms of interference, the ad struggles to be noticed. And as a function of the rationalization of the market, attention is dispersed, more difficult to contain. In advertising, the body figures its own disappearance or lapses in attention, almost as if it wishes to slip away from the grasp of fascist/market control. In other words, it is not coincidental that just when the regime achieves an apotheosis of control (in the production of rayon) the body vanishes.

Disappearance, then, could be understood as a strategy for escape from a political and moral arena of such overmanagement that the body cannot possibly suffer. As I suggested in the beginning of this chapter, however, the disappearing body may best be described by the term "disavowal." To some degree, this term has a metaphoric rather than a heuristic value in this context. In living out a relation to fascism, the body both adapts to control and, at the same time, absents itself. Similarly, the infant adapts to the reality that certain subjects (mother, sister) do in fact lack a penis. But the infant also creates a dreamworld in which either all subjects possess a penis or, better, the theoretical possibility of lack simply is never raised. The fetish is thought to be a compensatory object in this dreamworld; and in the dreamworld of the disappearing body, it is the commodity (fetish) that takes on a positive, redemptive role.[55] A "good consumer," one who has adapted well to capitalism in a fascist context, will make ample use of such compensatory objects; a "bad consumer" will tend to disappear more readily, hence disappearance becomes a moral problem.

An analogy from popular culture may help to explain the moral dimension inherent in disappearance: the fictitious "transporter" of the *Star Trek* universe enacts disappearance. Bodies are "read" by a scanner, decomposed, and then reconstituted at some designated set of spatial coordinates, with almost no temporal delay. When all functions normally, the bodies travel through space as their particles are "beamed up" as totalities; but in certain episodes, the characters reappear on the transporter pads as ghostly outlines, as if the infinitesimal parts were trying desperately to find one another. The image wavers at its borders, but then it bursts apart; the body has been lost as a result of interference with the flow of the particles. Sometimes the engineers manage to isolate the body parts and reconstruct them after considerable effort. Sometimes the parts are left floating in space, unable to meet each other and retrieve their form—a true tragedy of annihilation.

In the narrative logic of science fiction, it is never a major protagonist, never a life worth saving that ends this way, but someone shady, someone with whom the audience has never fully identified, someone whose boundaries are, literally, obscure. "Can there be a less honorable way to die?" the warrior Klingon asks. "Not in battle, but dispersed in the air?" And of course his voice is the voice of the epic hero on whose ashes "civilization" has been built. Disappearance immediately becomes a moral question for the warrior, while the technician struggles to put together the atomic bits that have split apart in the transport.

In fact, the disappearing body is disturbing because of its centrality in the debate about fascism and morality. To what degree are the fascists — the dictator and the consenters — really present, really "attentive" in their actions?

The disappearing body shares many symptoms with the psychotic, who, in Karl Jaspers's definition, often comes equipped with his own personal philosophy of negation. Like Schreber, the subjects represented in this popular imagery seem to be the victims of assault. The world is coming to an end, but the apocalypse may be diagnosed as a symbolic objectification of the radical destruction of the ego. It is difficult to know whether these fantasies originate in a brutal relationship with the father (Freud), or in some "basic fault" relation with the mother (Melanie Klein, Franco Fornari, and Michael Balint), but, many of these "end-of-the-world" complexes seem to follow a determined sequence of phases: first, the destruction and negation of the body; next, a sense of guilt for having destroyed. This secondary moment, emphasized by Fornari in particular, initiates a depressive phase that may be followed by the subject's attempt to rebuild the world according to a utopic, reintegrative plan.[56] The subject attempts to defend against the destructive catastrophe represented by conflicts in the ego, sometimes regressing into a narcissistic, infantile phase and exaggerating his or her role in the creation of the world or even misapprehending the "confines of [one's] body."[57]

In a very influential article of the early 1930s based on case studies of individuals suffering from schizophrenia, Victor Tausk made a connection between specific forms of persecution suffered by his patients and the peculiar case of Schreber's assault.[58] People with schizophrenia, he argued, display a remarkable homogeneity in their descriptions of "influencing machines" they perceive to be attached to their bodies and forming a kind of shell around them. The machines often consist of the boxes, cranks, levers, and wheels of modern industry, an externalized factory of production, a functioning member of capitalism. As in the case of Schreber, soul-robbing rays often are attributed to these machines; as in the case of Schreber, again, the machines have the capacity to deprive (male) patients of their sexual potency. And like the radios emitting influencing rays (see chapter 4), these machines are capable of harnessing invisible currents to either drain the victims or subject them to forms of "suggestion." According to Tausk's reading, these machines represent forms of self-projection or accommodations that the individual exhibiting schizophrenic symptoms makes with the outside world. The patient does not utterly withdraw, but makes himself or herself "available" to other subjects in this distorted, unrecognizable form as a defense in much the same way as the Freudian paranoiac "in-

vents" persecution as a defense against homosexual desire. The moment of
rupture or pathology in the development of these schizophrenic subjects
lies in the infantile stage of ego development, something akin to the mirror
stage in Lacan's terminology. Something goes wrong, and, as a result, the
subject feels threatened by his or her own sexuality and so hallucinates this
horrifying machine to justify the sense of threat. As Joan Copjek has remarked, Tausk's essay falls into a contradiction in that it defines this machine as a projection first of the body ego and then, later, of the genitalia.[59]
Tausk justifies this slippage by his statement that in the narcissistic (mirror)
stage, the child's ego is cathected by free-floating libido, and the entire
body becomes an erogenous zone. It is only a small step from self-erotization
to the equation of a body projection with a genital projection. For Lacan
and Copjek, what is really most important about the Schreber case and its
place in the Freudian corpus is the fact that the rays retain the property of
speech. Where some readers understand the constant jabbering of the rays
as just one among a series of modes of persecution that the rays enact, the
Lacanian position takes the speech persecution as central. Tausk himself,
however, acknowledges an experiential basis for this delusion (the infant
has language "imposed on him" by parental figures; he learns to reason
through language, and so he logically assumes that he also has thoughts imposed on him). The "influencing machines" article emphasizes the way in
which the machine represents a certain relation to sexuality that is *not necessarily* linguistic before it is visual. The key to Tausk's model of persecution
lies in the relations among libido, ego, and body ego. For the (male) subject, it is a visual experience — the erection — that communicates desire for
another subject. Once constructed as a defense, the influencing machine is
"no longer subordinated to the will of the ego, but dominates it. And the
fact that the erection is shortly conceived as an exceptional and mysterious
feat, supports the assumption that erection is felt to be a thing independent
of the ego, a part of the outer world not completely mastered."[60]

Once again, Tausk describes a situation in which invisible rays exercise
some power over a "defenseless" subject. But from the perspective of the
rational observer, outside the body, these rays (indeed invisible) are merely
hallucinatory projections from inside the body. The scientist — the doctor —
who knows better, explains that the imagined rays are a defense against sexuality, and although this may be the case *from the outside perspective,* rays really do exist *from the inside perspective.* The (evil) scientist who tells the patient
that it is all in his imagination seems suspiciously like the physicist splitting
atoms in his secret laboratory, like Marconi with his ray gun. Tausk's case

studies of individuals diagnosed with a specific pathological disorder, in which body boundaries are broken down and the body ego is made abject by what he terms the "psychic ego," mirror a larger cultural topos of the power invested in the scientist as the controller of weapons of mass destruction.

The possibility of mass destruction — nuclear fear, rather than the specific formation of the state at a given moment — becomes a common denominator in many modern theories of war. Such a conception affirms that "at the level of the psychic entity, the themes of destruction and the necessity for reparation constitute two fundamental modalities of human essence."[61] Again, though, in such a construction, the body has been elided. Of course, the psychosis/schizophrenia paradigm could be taken at the metaphoric level, but as a paradigm, it does not negate the power of the "scientific/nuclear fear" hypothesis of which it is a kind of derivative. Any attempt to privilege one explanation over another would weaken the correlative links that bind them together at a particular moment in history. In fact, it is precisely *not* my aim to arrive at *a* theory of fascism through a combination of these various, highly suggestive theorems, but merely to propose a framework in which to view the disappearing body. It is fitting that psychoanalysis has chosen the term "borderline" to describe cases that do not fall easily into the fields known as neurosis and psychosis. For whether one locates the source of the "problem" inside the body (inasmuch as the ego can be said to be "inside"), or outside of the body (the state and its arsenal of destructive weapons), it is nevertheless at its very borders that the body mediates problems, and reacts to assault by absenting itself. As Dean and Massumi have written:

> The "individual" in a despotic state is a working part in a mega-machine — or rather, a megaorganism. The people of the empire are organs of the emperor's body. The organicity of the system is supra-individual. In other words, body parts have been abstracted from individual bodies and recast as social functions. One of those functions, the dialectic of unity and dismemberment (presence and absence, transcendence and becoming-immanent) so fundamental to the erection of the Empire, is attached to the penis abstracted as phallus. In the despotic state, *the phallus is the emperor's whole body.* Since that body is coextensive with the realm, which is coextensive with the law, all three are struck by strange convulsions and multiple disappearances — not the least of which is the disappearance of women from official existence in any other capacity than that of reproducers of man.[62]

Because of the boundedness of any state to the body, the despotic/phallic state in particular experiences embarrassing moments of disappearance, and sometimes uncanny reappearances. In contemporary Italy, then, the extremes of the fascist state—particularly in its relation to gender, race, and class—have been tempered, but the mechanisms that trigger disappearance are still very much in place.

At the time of this writing, for example, the "crisis" of Somalia is literally history, of the past. Italian and other troops have withdrawn from that country, not because of any precipitating event resulting in closure, but simply because, as one official put it, "nothing is being done."[63] Undeniably, time is moving at a more rapid pace than during the period of colonization, which is viewed with inevitable nostalgia by a certain generation of Italians. In the span of approximately one year, Somalis have been "rematerialized," we are told. They have found their proper bodies, thanks to Western aid.

Meanwhile, though, as many as ten thousand Somalis have "disappeared" during this period of "nothingness." The United Nations has been unable to determine what percentage of these "disappearances" was due to the intervention of its own forces, and what percentage to clan (in)fighting. Perhaps two-thirds of the casualties of this non-war were women and children, used by the Somali militia as human shields. What is clear, in any case, is the inability of the United Nations forces to become proper despots, for that role presupposes the state's ability to count bodies. The state-media apparatus has affected what may be the most insidious sort of disappearance through its disavowal of Somalia in favor of other "hot spots" of crisis.

On Italian soil, bodies drift in and out of states of density. The corpse of a businessman is found days before his scheduled arrest for participation in "normal business life." The prime minister of Italy asks for bodies to be released from prison in what would be a decidedly noncorporeal flood. In August, while Italians soaked up the rays of the obliterating sun on the beaches, Berlusconi had his body decomposed into millions of pixels, and transported, radiating out from the center of government. He would distance himself from his investments, he said in what was deemed a powerfully successful teleconfession. He would make his body into a shadowy figure that hovers behind the Fininvest Corporation like the "Cervo" man who slips his green hat into his pocket and disappears (figure 31).

After his arrest in conjunction with illegal payoffs, leading industrialist Carlo de Benedetti remarked that the relative "attentiveness" of actors in the bribe scandals can be directly compared with consensus under fascism.

But unlike the bodies subjected to disavowal in this chapter, the bodies of the mythical land of Tangentopolis continue to be tallied. In fact, there is something very disturbing for the public in the image of businessmen reduced to their corporeal states as they wallow in prison. Incarcerated, they achieve a bodily fullness; their outlines are etched with ever greater precision. "We must stop the handcuffing!" cried the public. As if to say that by locking up the felonious organ, the member that exchanges dirty cash (and the spectacular title for the whole operation, we should recall, is "*mani pulite*"), the prosecutors only draw attention to the materiality of the bodies involved. The synecdochal arrangement by which the body is made bodily reminds us of the hand-as-body motif of fascist autarchy.

Meanwhile, on a stark highway outside of Palermo, a car explodes, and the bodies inside are so utterly fragmented, so completely mixed with metal shards, that a full disappearance is achieved. The visual traces of Mafia terror lie in the deep pit left by the bomb, the structural damage suffered by buildings.

Mogadishu, Milan, and Palermo are only three points in a possible modern geography of the Italian body. Bodies exist in various stages of materiality; disavowal serves as a convenient metaphor for a state in between the extremes of total embodiment and utter annihilation. Perhaps some critics would like to retrieve the body from its shaded, negated "crisis" under the fascist regime, but I can offer no definite conclusion, only the vague suspicion that such a rematerialization or closure remains impossible.

Notes

1 / The Body and the Market

1. Much has been written of the relation between humanist emblems and the *brevitas* topos in aesthetics. The standard Renaissance treatise calls for a perfect relation between the emblematic *inscriptio* (motto), *pictura* (image), and *subscriptio* (a text, usually poetry, but sometimes prose) such that a "right reading" of the emblem can be achieved only through a consideration of these three elements. In the translation of this theory to modern advertising, the tripartite scheme could be made to conform to the brand name or logo, the image, and the explanatory or persuasive text.

2. In fact, any particular style came to be seen as antithetical to the smooth functioning of the ad in the marketplace. For example, Federico Seneca, an artist whose work figures prominently in this book, served during the late 1920s as the art director for the Perugina-Buitoni corporation. Although Seneca created some of the most arrestingly brilliant images of the period for Perugina, he was criticized in the pages of *L'ufficio moderno* for imposing his recognizable style on the communicative function of advertising campaigns. For Seneca's affiliation with Perugina-Buitoni, see Giampaolo Gallo, ed., *Sulla bocca di tutti: Buitoni e Perugina, una storia in breve* (Perugia: Electa, 1990). For Seneca's own interest in issues relating to artistic copyright and notions of "authorship," see "Il diritto d'autore dei cartellonisti nelle dichiarazioni del pittore Seneca," *L'ufficio moderno* (October 1930). (Most of the articles from this publication were printed without the writer's name. I indicate exceptions in subsequent notes.)

3. For theoretical issues involved in iconography and iconology, see Norman Bryson, "Semiology and Visual Interpretation," in *Visual Theory: Painting and Interpretation,* ed. Norman Bryson, Michael Ann Holly, and Keith Moxey (London: Polity, 1991), pp. 61–73; Keith Moxey, "Panofsky's Concept of 'Iconology' and the Problem of Interpretation in the History of Art," *New Literary History,* 17 (Winter 1986); Michael Ann Holly, *Panofsky and the Foundations of Art History* (Ithaca, N.Y.: Cornell University Press, 1984). Each of these texts responds to the methodological limitations of Erwin Panofsky's canonical essay on iconology in his *Studies in Iconology: Humanistic Themes in the Art of the Renaissance* (New York: Harper & Row, 1962).

4. Panofsky, *Studies in Iconology,* p. 11.

5. Ellen Lupton, "Reading Isotype," in *Design Discourse,* ed. Victor Margolin (Chicago: University of Chicago Press, 1989), p. 152.

6. In *Theory of the Avant-Garde,* trans. Michael Shaw (Minneapolis: University of Minnesota Press, 1984), Peter Bürger links his exemplar of the "inorganic" artwork, John Heartfield, with the "old" form of the emblem.

7. From the *Passagen-Werk,* quoted in Susan Buck-Morss, *The Dialectics of Seeing: Walter Benjamin and the Arcades Project* (Cambridge, Mass.: MIT Press, 1989), p. 181.

8. See, in particular, Depero's manifesto on advertising art, "Il futurismo e l'arte pubblicitaria," in *Numero unico futurista* (a give-away book sponsored by the Campari Company, Milan, 1931). "Patronage" is also discussed with acutely interesting results in Roland Marchand, *Advertising the American Dream* (Berkeley: University of California Press, 1985).

9. A. G. Bragaglia, "Lo psicoanalista," *Critica fascista,* no. 22 (1932): 437–39.

10. For this, see, for example, Vittorio Guerriero, "Il dottor Freud," *Il regime fascista* (June 22, 1934); also, A. Petrucci, "Il demone della sessualità," *La difesa della razza,* no. 24 (1939): 27–31. For Petrucci, Freud's thought reduces all men to automata, passing "from the bordello to the insane asylum, with a stop at the stock market." This is labeled as purely Jewish doctrine after 1938, but the resistance to psychoanalysis predates Hitler's intervention into the Italian juridical system. For the cultural conflation of psychoanalytic methods with the abject black and Jew, also see Sander Gilman, *Freud, Race, and Gender* (Princeton, N.J.: Princeton University Press, 1992).

11. "L'umorismo," in *L'ufficio moderno* (November 1935): 513.

12. Adolfo Pellegrini, "Analisi psicologica della pubblicità," *Rivista di psicologia* 20 (1925): 97.

13. For advertising strategies of the 1930s as an "overcoming of backwardness," see Giulio Sapelli, "La razionalizzazione della vendita: Alle origini 'del marketing e della pubblicità in Italia," *Quaderni di sociologia* 27, 2-3-4 (1978): 136.

14. Pellegrini, "Analisi psicologica," 103.

15. See an ad for "pubblicità tramviaria," *L'ufficio moderno* (January 1938), inside front cover. The ad shows a male figure engaged in various physical activities and suggests that it is useless to speak with him when he is busy. "But when he is constrained to remain seated or standing, for ten minutes or a half hour; when he cannot read the paper or even think seriously about his own business; when he tries to kill time by studying the faces or the legs of his fellow travelers; when he reads with great attention all that falls before his eyes . . . then is the moment with a capital M, then is the moment for tram advertising that enters the eyes and fixes itself in the memory by suggesting and recalling a name and the necessity to make a certan acquisition."

16. Althusser's forceful presumption of the later Marx's antihumanism is crucial here. In "Marxism and Humanism," the French theorist wrote that "in philosophy, man is theoretically affirmed; in the proletariat he is practically negated." *For Marx,* trans. Ben Brewster (London: NLB, 1977), p. 226. We might paraphrase this maxim to read that in the philosophy of advertising, man is theoretically affirmed; in the praxis of consumption he is practically negated. It is precisely such a notion that is mystified in the "humanism" that opposes the powerful advertisements of the 1930s and that actually is appropriated by Mussolini at times. It also underlies his mistrust of high-technology advertising groups such as GAR (the Friends of Rationalism) and their work in *L'ufficio moderno,* as we will see.

17. Quoted in Buck-Morss, *The Dialectics of Seeing,* p. 184.

18. "La fisionomia umana come mezzo pubblicitario," *L'ufficio moderno* (July 1931): 442–43.

19. For the use of mannequins as part of store display, see "Manichino, che significa?" *L'ufficio moderno* (September 1931): 563.

20. Marco Helin, "La suggestione in pubblicità," *L'ufficio moderno* (May 1933): 301. Also see Virginia Smith, *The Funny Little Man: The Biography of a Graphic Image* (New York: Van Nostrand Reinhold, 1993).

21. On metaphysical painting, see Massimo Carrà, Ewald Rathke, and Patrick Waldberg, *Metaphysical Art,* trans. Caroline Tisdall (New York and Washington, D.C.: Praeger, 1971); Paolo Fossati, *La "pittura metafisica"* (Turin: Einaudi, 1988); Francesco Poli, *La metafisica* (Rome-Bari: Laterza, 1989); and the very useful exhibition catalog *La pittura metafisica,* ed. Giuliano Briganti and E. Coen (Venice: Neri Pozza Editore, 1979). From a detailed study of the Ferrara climate of metaphysical painting, the mannequin emerges as an artist's model come to life, the animation of the most banal and everyday object that the painter faces in his or her encounter with human forms in a studio context. Ferrara was understood by the meta-

physical painters as a melancholy, isolated, provincial setting in which to wait out the horrors of the war. The mannequin gains its life at the hallucinatory noon hour, but its season is brief, poetic.

22. Irene Brin, *Usi e costumi, 1920–1940* (Palermo: Sellerio, 1981), pp. 124–26.

23. From the *Passagen-Werk,* quoted in Buck-Morss, *The Dialectics of Seeing,* p. 101.

24. "Il manichino moderno," *L'ufficio moderno* (October 1935): 438.

25. Wolfgang Haug, *Critique of Commodity Aesthetics: Appearance, Sexuality and Advertising in Capitalist Society,* trans. Robert Bock (Cambridge, Mass.: Polity Press, 1971), pp. 60–61.

26. Ibid., p. 61.

27. For the "family" photo album of the Duce, see Mario Cervi, *Mussolini: Album di una vita* (Milan: Rizzoli, 1992).

28. Kenneth Dean and Brian Massumi, *First and Last Emperors: The Absolute State and the Body of the Despot* (New York: Autonomedia, 1992), p. 138.

29. Elias Canetti, *Crowds and Power,* trans. Carol Stewart (New York: Continuum, 1981), p. 417.

30. See Gallo, *Sulla bocca di tutti,* and Dino Biondi, *La fabbrica del duce* (Florence: Vallecchi, 1973).

31. For the campaign, see Gian Luigi Falabrino, *Effimera e bella: Storia della pubblicità in Italia* (Turin: Gutenberg 2000, 1990), pp. 151–68; and Gallo, *Sulla bocca di tutti.* Various articles from *L'ufficio moderno* treated the figurine phenomenon, including Luigi Dalmonte, "Discorso sulla pubblicità radiofonica" (February 1931); "Figurine e propaganda collettiva" (March 1937); "Spiegazione di un fenomeno" (October 1938); and in *L'industria dolciaria,* the sweets industry monthly, "Pubblicità a premio," no. 4 (April 1937); "Concorsi a premio," no. 5 (May 1937). Mussolini's law against the distribution of figurines and prizes was enacted in 1937, and the industries involved tried both to defend their previous actions and to conform to the regime's moralistic discourse with statements affirming the producer's goal to sell a "well-made" and "traditional" product rather than to increase sales through the chimera of the plastic collectible.

32. Indeed, this state of "indifference" might be said to resemble the "soul murder" of Daniel Paul Schreber, as I will discuss in chapters 4 and 5. For this "front," and its relation to general market conditions under fascism, see Gallo, *Sulla bocca di tutti,* p. 26.

33. See Falabrino, *Effimera e bella,* p. 165.

34. The following works are particularly important for the futurism-fascism debates: Enrico Crispolti, ed., *Arte e fascismo in Italia e in Germania* (Milan: Feltrinelli, 1974), and also his very influential book, *Il mito della macchina e altri temi del futurismo* (Trapani: Celebes, 1969); Laura Malvano, *Fascismo e politica dell'immagine* (Turin: Bollati Boringhieri, 1988); Giuseppe Carlo Marino, *L'autarchia della cultura: Intellettuali e fascismo negli anni trenta* (Rome: Ruinti, 1983); Maurizio Calvesi, *Le due avanguardie* (Rome: Laterza, 1981); Claudia Salaris, *Artecrazia: L'avanguardia futurista negli anni del fascismo* (Florence: La Nuova Italia, 1992). It seems to me that the scholarship of these works ought to be supplemented with the approach to a politics of form in the relations of a molecular and molar text suggested by Fredric Jameson (after Deleuze and Guattari) in *Fables of Aggression: Wyndham Lewis, the Modernist as Fascist* (Berkeley: University of California Press, 1979). For Jameson, first and foremost, the choice between a micro- and macrolevel (i.e., between style and narrative) of any text is unsatisfactory. The discontinuity between these two spheres should not be understood as a methodological inconsistency, but as an objective reality that "requires us radically to historicize the gap between style and narrative, which then may be seen as [a historically specific] event in the history of form.... In this use [i.e., Deleuze and Guattari], the molecular level designates the here-and-now of immediate perception or of local desire.... To this microscopic, fragmentary life of the psyche in the immediate a counterforce is opposed in the molar ... which designates all those large, abstract,

mediate, and perhaps even empty and imaginary forms by which we seek to recontain the molecular: the mirage of the continuity of personal identity, the organizing unity of the psyche or the personality, the concept of society itself, and, not least, the notion of the organic unity of the work of art. *This distinction allows us to respect the specificity of the narrative level, while grasping its function to recontain the molecular proliferation of sentences on the stylistic level*" (pp. 7–8; emphasis mine). This approach might allow for a formalist analysis of protofascist (futurist) works that seem to defy narrative totality, but that actually exhibit some kind of molar coherence.

35. Giacomo Balla and Fortunato Depero, *Ricostruzione futurista dell'universo*, ed. Enrico Crispolti and Maurizio Scudiero (Modena: Fonte d'abisso, 1989).

36. See Guido Armellini, *Le immagini del fascismo nelle arti figurative* (Milan: Fabbri, 1980), pp. 81–82.

37. For this general impression, see Biondi, *La fabbrica del duce*.

38. Mario Sironi et al., "Il manifesto della pittura murale," in *La colonna*, no. 1 (December 1933).

2 / Selling the Black Body: Advertising and the African Campaigns

1. Lessona is quoted in Renzo De Felice, *Mussolini il duce: Gli anni di consenso, 1929–1936* (Turin: Einaudi, 1974), p. 604.

2. The most important history of Italian colonialism, Angelo Del Boca's three-volume *Gli italiani in Africa Orientale* (Bari: Laterza, 1976), begins with this premise of a fundamental "lack of interest."

3. Antonio Gramsci, *Quaderni del carcere*, vol. 2 ed. Valentino Gerratana (Turin: Einaudi, 1975), pp. 710–11.

4. Of course, the black body was also part of advertising imagery in other countries. For the situation in France, the exhibition catalog *Negripub: L'image des noirs dans la publicité depuis un siècle* (Paris: Société des Amis de la Bibliothèque Forney, 1987) is quite helpful. Also see Michael-Scholz Hänsel, *Das exotische Plakat* (Stuttgart: Institut für Auslandsbeziehungen, 1987). For general questions of the representation of blackness in Western art, see Ladislas Bugner, ed., *The Image of the Black in Western Art* (New York: Morrow; Fribourg: Office du Livre, 1976–1989).

5. "Interest" (in German, *Interesse*) initially was used by Freud to indicate the psychic energy of the instincts of self-preservation, as opposed to the libido (energy of sexual instincts). But "interest" has been taken also in a broader sense to mean roughly the same thing as "cathexis." See Jean Laplanche and J.-B. Pontalis, *The Language of Psychoanalysis*, trans. Donald Nicholson-Smith (New York: W. W. Norton, 1973), p. 226.

6. See Dyer's very provocative essay "White," *Screen*, 20, no. 4 (Fall 1988): 44–64.

7. For a recent cultural studies–oriented reading of the ideology behind the English-language equivalent of *Le vie d'Italia*, see Catherine Lutz and Jane Collins, *Reading National Geographic* (Chicago: University of Chicago Press, 1993).

8. For the French associations of blackness with perceivable shapes, and with a particular geographical situation, see Léon Hoffman, *Le negre romantique* (Paris: Payot, 1973), p. 148.

9. The issue of food "surrogates" became culturally and economically overdetermined during the 1930s, when the global depression and the economic sanctions against Italy made certain raw materials extremely scarce. Brazil did not participate in the sanctions and provided Italy with most of its coffee and cocoa beans. Italian brand names would, however, be affixed to the products made from a variety of substitute sources, and so the whole issue of additives was problematic for the politics of autarchy. See, for example, "Cacao," *L'industria dolciaria*, no. 1 (April 1936): 3–4. Even earlier, however, during the late nineteenth century, the problem of surrogates was raised in the context of a utopian vision of colonial abundance. The very word

"surrogate" stamped on an alimentary product was a constant sign of Italy's inferiority, its defeats, and the projection of its hopes for an empire.

10. There is a fascinating correlation between leisure time and racial consciousness as mediated through societal attitudes toward the sun and skin tone. For this, see Giorgio Triani, *Pelle di luna, pelle di sole: Nascita e storia della civiltà balneare, 1700–1946* (Venice: Marsilio, 1988).

11. Quoted in *Storia d'Italia: Dall'Unità a oggi,* vol. 4 (Turin: Einaudi, 1975), pp. 2242–43. The "previous events" mentioned by Mussolini obviously refers to the defeat at Adua, an event that would become associated with the inadequacy of the liberal state, but that also served as a springboard from which the fascists would launch their virulent campaign. Adua, emblazoned on the collective memory for decades, also provided a justification for the use of chemical warfare.

12. Cited in Luigi Preti, *I miti dell'impero e della razza italiana negli anni '30* (Rome: Opere Nuove, 1965), p. 115.

13. Ibid., p. 49.

14. Frantz Fanon, *Peau noire, masques blancs* (Paris: Editions du Seuil, 1952), p. 148.

15. Filippo Tommaso Marinetti, "Processo per Mafarka il futurista," in *Distruzione* (Milan: Edizioni Futuriste di Poesia, 1911), p. 8.

16. Ibid.

17. Ibid., p. 9.

18. Ibid., p. 84.

19. F. T. Marinetti, *Mafarka il futurista* (Italian edition) (Milan: Edizioni Futuriste di Poesia, 1910), p. 75.

20. Ibid., p. 77.

21. Marinetti, "Processo," p. 9.

22. Jean-Paul Aron, *Le pénis et la démoralisation de l'occident* (Paris: Grasset, 1978), p. 196.

23. Marinetti, *Mafarka,* pp. 12–13.

24. F. T. Marinetti, *La battaglia di Tripoli* (Milan: Edizioni Futuriste di Poesia, 1912).

25. Mary Douglas, *Purity and Danger: An Analysis of the Concepts of Pollution and Taboo,* 2d ed. (London: Ark Paperbacks, 1984), p. 91.

26. Paul Radin, *The Trickster: A Study in American Indian Mythology* (London: Routledge and Kegan Paul, 1956), pp. 18–19.

27. Marinetti, "Processo," p. 94.

28. For more on the exposure of breasts and the covering of the penis, see the photographic essays in Christian Maurel, *L'exotisme colonial* (Paris: Laffont, 1980), and Malek Alloula, *The Colonial Harem,* trans. Myrna Godzich and Wlad Godzich (Minneapolis: University of Minnesota Press, 1986). Both are collections of photographic postcards taken by colonizers that reveal the uncanny theatricality of "natural" exposure to the lens of the camera.

29. For this see Alice Yaeger Kaplan, *Reproductions of Banality: Fascism, Literature, and French Intellectual Life* (Minneapolis: University of Minnesota Press, 1986), pp. 81–90. Also see Barbara Spackman, "Fascist Rhetoric of Virility," in *Fascism and Culture,* ed. Jeffrey Schnapp and Barbara Spackman, *Stanford Italian Review,* 8 (1990): 81–101.

30. Aron, *Le pénis,* pp. 226–29.

31. For this contradiction in Nazi aesthetics, see Jost Hermand, "Artificial Atavism: German Expressionism and Blacks," in *Blacks and German Culture,* ed. Reinhold Grimm and Jost Hermand (Madison: University of Wisconsin Press, 1986), p. 83.

32. In Fortunato Depero, *Fortunato Depero nelle opere e nella vita* (Trent: Legione Trentina, 1940), pp. 271–72.

33. For the Falasha, see Emanuela Trevisan Semi, *Allo specchio dei falascia* (Florence: Giuntina, 1987). For the conflation of black and Jew, also see Sander Gilman, *Freud, Race, and Gender* (Princeton, N.J.: Princeton University Press, 1992).

34. "Il pansessualismo di Freud," *La difesa della razza* (October 5, 1938): 43.

35. The perspective offered by this montage corresponds very closely to something we would expect to find in cinematic manipulations of camera angles as a sign of confusion. In fact, when Chaplin's tramp in *Modern Times* is released from the comfortable prison where he has found security, a view of his bewildered face is spliced with just such oblique-angle shots of a metropolis (presumably New York, although other scenes in the film apparently represent Los Angeles with its single-story houses and palm trees). It is clear that these intercuts stand for the hallucinatory world of capital and poverty. Chaplin never enters the urban panorama but remains oddly cut out from it, like the nursing grandmother in the *Difesa* montage.

36. L. Robecchi Brichetti, *Somalia e Benadir* (Milan: Aliprandi, 1899), pp. 43–46.

37. Freud's troubling 1917 essay "The Taboo of Virginity," *The Standard Edition of the Complete Psychological Works*, vol. 11, ed. and trans. James Strachey (London: Hogarth Press, 1953–1974), presupposes a society much like that of bourgeois, fascist Italy, that is, a *modern* one in which modern neurotics act out the archaic affect of the horror of rupturing the hymen. Subsequent references to the *Standard Edition* of Freud's works will employ the abbreviation *S.E.*

38. During the 1920s and 1930s, Italy got most of its cocoa from West Africa or Brazil. After the imposition of sanctions, various experiments were attempted in East Africa to determine whether or not it would be possible to cultivate cocoa there. Of course, this research was of primary importance to the regime. See "Cacao," *L'industria dolciaria*, no. 1 (1936), and A. Cagliano, "La coltivazione del cacao sull'altopiano etiopico," *L'industria dolciaria*, no. 3 (1936).

39. See Sauder Gilman, "The Hottentot and the Prostitute: Towards an Iconography of Female Sexuality," in *Difference and Pathology* (Ithaca, N.Y., and London: Cornell University Press, 1985).

40. Let me stress, however, that this "smoothness" is indeed a fantasy because Somali women do not, in fact, correspond to the body descriptions given in the media; they do not lack the buttocks of other African women.

41. Quoted in Del Boca, *Gli italiani in Africa,* vol. 2, p. 90.

42. *Lei* (February 1, 1935): 19.

43. Quoted in Del Boca, *Gli italiani in Africa,* vol. 2, p. 287.

44. Ibid., p. 686.

45. For an example of this positive nostalgia, see Luciano de Crescenzo, "Faccetta nera," *Il Venerdì di Repubblica* (Friday, August 21, 1992): 21.

46. For this term in Italian thought, see Gianni Sofri, *Il modo di produzione asiatico: Storia di una controversia marxista*, 2d ed. (Turin: Einaudi, 1974). The "controversy" concerns the question of "Asiatic despotism," and whether or not the "Orient" (but here we could just as well speak of Africa) can be conceived as a series of political systems in which all the people were slaves of the emperor and none held any private property. Of course, this was, in part, a justification for the Europeans to take their own slaves or to replace the particular despot through expansion, only to enjoy his very same rights of absolute sovereignty over the subjects. I am using the term "Asiatic" here in the sense that one might use "Orientalism," from the Eurocentric position. In fact, I have noticed the same iconographic themes of the multiple, identical bodies in poster art from other European nations, and depicting Asian, or even Middle Eastern bodies, rather than black bodies. For several examples, see Hänsel, *Das exotische Plakat.*

47. This is a case of seeing what one wanted to see. While the vast majority of the Italian public was not well informed about the slave issue, a subtle but persistent cultural anxiety can be documented. Gramsci, for example, was acutely knowledgeable about the situation. See *Quaderni del carcere*, vol. 1, p. 205.

48. Quoted in G. Rochat, *Militari e politici nella preparazione della campagna d'Etiopia: Studio e documenti, 1932–1936* (Milan: Franco Angeli, 1971), p. 26.

49. As I discuss in greater detail in chapter 3, the question of a "national" chocolate was very much on the minds of the regime hierarchy. Perugina-Buitoni did its best to conform to

the fascist ideals of production, and it was one of the first companies to undergo extensive "rationalization."

50. Quoted in Del Boca, *Gli italiani in Africa,* vol. 1, p. 123.

51. Pietro Badoglio, perhaps Mussolini's most "conservative" military leader, used to say during the preparation for the Ethiopian advance that Italy was not primarily intent on aggressing, but on carving out for itself a "premio di assicurazione" (an insurance premium). Speech of October 21, 1926, of the interministerial council for military-colonialist questions. See Rochat, *Militari e politici,* p. 22. In Badoglio's biography it is possible to read a desire for self-insurance coupled with a military instinct. This duality is perfectly legible in the image of black bodies laboring behind the figure of the paternal "insurer." For more on this cautious and yet bellicose individual, see Piero Pieri and Giorgio Rochat, *Badoglio* (Turin: UTET, 1974).

52. Del Boca, *Gli italiani in Africa,* vol. 2, p. 410.

53. For example, both Shell Oil and Fiat used images of the Arab in their advertising. By the thirties, General de Bono was one of many voices proclaiming the absolute inadequacy of Fiat vehicles in AOI. The regime had to import Fords and Caterpillar trucks for navigating the rough terrain there. See Del Boca, *Gli italiani in Africa,* vol. 2, p. 307.

54. Quoted in Del Boca, *Gli italiani in Africa,* vol. 1, p. 3.

55. Alloula, *The Colonial Harem,* p. 7.

56. The topos of the knife is very important in Klaus Theweleit's account of boundaries. See his *Male Fantasies,* vol. 1, trans. Stephen Conway (Minneapolis: University of Minnesota Press, 1987). For the "nomadic" body condition in its relation to the despotic state, see Kenneth Dean and Brian Massumi, *First and Last Emperors: The Absolute State and the Body of the Despot.*

57. Carlo Enrico Rava, *La mostra dell'attrezzatura coloniale alla triennale di Milano* (Milan: VII Triennale di Milano, 1940), p. 10.

58. For one example, see a spread on new trends in garden furniture in *Domus,* 16, no. 129 (September 1938): 48–49.

59. Although the color black obviously makes its periodic appearance in fashion, when Italian postpunk youths of the mid-eighties began to wear black clothing and makeup, they were termed *i dark* by the media, which appropriated the English word as if to defer even further the question of blackness as a cultural sign. Even these "cultural others," the *dark* who looked to London for their visual vocabulary, did not take up the issue of race. For more on this see Gianfranco Manfredi, "Arrivano i dark: Canti che ti passa," *Panorama* (December 15, 1985): 168–70.

60. For an interesting discussion of Benetton's role in the politics of multiculturalism (specifically, its market presence in Cuba), see Vernon Silver, "All Cash Is Not Created Equal," *New York Times* (Sunday, February 7, 1993): sec. 9, p. 3.

3 / The Fascist Body as Producer and Consumer

1. For the whole question of a justification of fascist economic policy, see *L'economia italiana tra le due guerre: 1919–1939.* (Rome: IPSOA, 1984.) This excellent exhibition catalog includes advertisements for various industries and services under the regime.

2. This supports the notion that the fascist economists were particularly concerned about reshaping the nature of distribution by eliminating the chains of independent wholesalers and retailers and replacing them with a new strategy—the brand name. See Giulio Sapelli, "La razionalizzazione della vendita: Alle origini del marketing e della pubblicità in Italia," *Quaderni di sociologia* 27, 2-3-4 (1978): 134–51.

3. Judith Williamson, *Decoding Advertisements* (London: Marion Boyars, 1978), p. 47.

4. Gilles Deleuze and Félix Guattari, *Anti-Oedipus: Capitalism and Schizophrenia,* trans. Robert Hurley, Mark Seem, and Helen R. Lane (Minneapolis: University of Minnesota Press,

1983), p. 4. For Deleuze and Guattari, the pretense to divide economic relations into independent spheres of production, consumption, and distribution already presupposes structures of capitalism at a particular historical moment that pass themselves off as universal and absolute. But "the real truth of the matter—the glaring, sober truth that resides in delirium—is that there is no such thing as relatively independent spheres or circuits: production is immediately consumption and a recording process (*enregistrement*), without any sort of mediation."

5. The Opera Nazionale del Dopolavoro was primarily for manual laborers and state workers. The best study of the Dopolavoro remains Victoria de Grazia, *The Culture of Consent* (Cambridge: Cambridge University Press, 1981). De Grazia writes: "The establishment of a national agency like the OND even contained a certain risk: that it might become a further source of social division by revealing the very uneven levels of consumption, diverse associational and cultural traditions, and inequality of privileges among its numerous special constituencies.... By using the *Dopolavoro* as an instrument of advertising, and a controlled market outlet, they were able to turn this apparent disadvantage toward the support of the regime's claims to a supraclass identity" (p. 151). "Although in the regime's idealization, the typical *dopolavorista* would have no lack of basic necessities, he would also have no desire for conspicuous consumption. His consumer habits were most commonly described as 'modest.' To encourage further such *restricted* consumption, the OND placed strong emphasis on a hierarchy of suggested expenditures, from the household to the club facilities themselves, balancing these with a range of inducements for the worker to save and contribute towards his social security" (p. 153).

6. Again, the ability to save and its contingent pleasures precludes vast segments of the Italian population during the fascist era. If the savings campaign often addressed women, this could have been a strategy to avoid representing any particular class-based visual, semiotic codes. For the Italian bourgeoisie as a class of savers, and the particular dangers of saving as an "insidious, usurious exploitation of the peasant class," see Antonio Gramsci, *Quaderni del carcere*, ed. Valentino Gerratana (Turin: Einaudi, 1975), vol. 3, p. 2157.

7. The question of a maternal versus a paternal matrix for fascism has been discussed in a variety of sources, and is treated in a most synthetic manner by Alice Yaeger Kaplan, *Reproductions of Banality: Fascism, Literature, and French Intellectual Life* (Minneapolis: University of Minnesota Press, 1986), especially pp. 10–11.

8. Recounted in Dino Biondi, *La fabbrica del duce* (Florence: Vallecchi, 1973), p. 213.

9. And for some critics, *all* advertising necessarily performs this function of creating the illusion of classlessness, so that fascism can be seen as a particularly acute moment in the modernization of Italy's market. For Wolfgang Haug, for example, the lure of commodity-satisfaction is always greater than the force of class consciousness. All capitalists join together to keep the illusion of classlessness alive, and none betrays the pact that binds and maintains them or else they will find themselves instantly and automatically disbarred. See Wolfgang Haug, *Critique of Commodity Aesthetics: Appearance, Sexuality, and Advertising in Capitalist Society*, trans. Robert Bock (Cambridge: Polity Press, 1971), p. 105.

10. Maria Macciocchi makes a highly positive appraisal of this film as a reading of femininity under fascism. See "La donna dal Pappagallo," in a collection of essays edited by Macciocchi, *Le donne e i loro padroni* (Milan: Mondadori, 1978), pp. 92–97.

11. Barbara Spackman discusses this problem in the context of the perceived oxymorons of "fascist ideology" and "fascist philosophy." See *Decadent Genealogies: The Rhetoric of Sickness from Baudelaire to D'Annunzio* (Ithaca, N.Y.: Cornell University Press, 1989), p. 212.

12. For anal narcissism, see Leonard Shengold, *Halo in the Sky: Observations on Anality and Defense* (New Haven: Yale University Press, 1988).

13. Speaking of the paranoiac, Morris Schatzman writes: "What is called paranoia or what could be called paranoidogenicity (the condition of inducing or causing paranoia in

others) may be 'inherited,' not in the genes, but by each generation teaching the next one to fear certain possibilities of mind." Thus Schreber *père* and *fils* are really the same individual, but examined at different stages of the life cycle. See Morris Schatzman, *Soul Murder: Persecution in the Family* (New York: Random House, 1973), p. 145. Also see my comments in chapter 5 on the paranoid despot and the paranoid "everyman."

14. Sidney Mintz, *Sweetness and Power: The Place of Sugar in Modern History* (New York: Viking, 1985).

15. For the futurist pasta debate, see, F. T. Marinetti, *The Futurist Cookbook*, trans. Suzanne Brill (San Francisco: Bedford Arts, 1989).

16. "Esportare," *L'industria dolciaria*, no. 9 (1936): 257–58. For the overturning of this "natural" pretense to "taste," see Pierre Bourdieu, *Distinction: A Social Critique of the Judgement of Taste*, trans. Richard Nice (London and New York: Routledge & Kegan Paul, 1984). For Bourdieu, it is only a working-class mentality (such as that which fascism only pretended to support in its campaigns for grain and the countryside) that equates overeating with well-being. (I say more about this later.)

17. Haug, *Critique of Commodity Aesthetics*, p. 20.

18. Guido Marucco, "Del cacao e del cioccolato," *L'industria dolciaria*, no. 5 (1937): 139.

19. The tennis player depicted in this ad seems to me to correspond to the (fascistized) "body without organs" of Deleuze and Guattari. It does not run like a perfect machine; it gets temporarily stopped up and must be recranked, refueled with a stimulant just long enough so that it can exert itself during a tennis match. Its rigid boundaries seem to stop the flows of desire that are identified in *Anti-Oedipus* with schizophrenia.

20. The slogan is reproduced on the inside front cover of each edition of the industry monthly, *L'industria dolciaria*.

21. "Valorizzazione," *L'industria dolciaria*, no. 2 (1936): 37.

22. For "isotype" in the context of the body, see my remarks in chapter 1.

23. "Valorizzazione," 39.

24. A. Cagliano, "La coltivazione del cacao sull'altopiano etiopico," *L'industria dolciaria*, no. 3 (1936): 71. (Reprinted from 1935 study.)

25. In this sense, my critique of futurist consumption is supported by Baudrillard's critique of Marx's conservatism in his mystification of use value. Daniel Miller, *Material Culture and Mass Consumption* (Oxford: Basil Blackwell, 1987), writes about this critique that "the labor theory of value and the concept of use value are jointly responsible for a conservative attitude to the place of work and utilitarian practices as the 'proper' sites of human self-creation, and a concomitant failure to examine cultural and consumption activities as creative of social relations" (p. 48).

26. Ultimately, as Gramsci noted, the per capita consumption of grain was not important, but rather the fact that in other European countries grain was supplemented by other fundamental foods in greater quantity. The problem is not one of "playing" with the amount of grain, but one of recognizing a fundamental poverty in Italy that is displaced by endless debates on the forms and amount of grain appropriate to an individual diet. For Gramsci's comments, see *Quaderni del carcere*, vol. 1, pp. 191–92.

27. For these anecdotes, see F. T. Marinetti, *The Futurist Cookbook*.

28. Ibid., p. 24.

29. Ibid., p. 25.

30. Ibid., p. 26.

31. Ibid., pp. 26–27.

32. Ibid., p. 29.

33. For a great part of the *ventennio*, tuberculosis preoccupied the regime, and the disease was granted metaphoric significance as a subversive force working to undermine Mussolini's

power. See Domenico Preti, "La lotta antitubercolare nell'Italia fascista," in *Storia d'Italia: Annali: Malattia e medicine,* vol. 7, ed. Franco Della Peruta (Turin: Einaudi, 1984), pp. 955–1021.

34. Sigmund Freud, "The Interpretation of Dreams," *S. E.,* vols. 4 and 5, 1900, pp. 152–53. See also *Wit and Its Relation to the Unconscious,* chapter 2, section 8, and chapter 7, section 2; and Jacques Lacan, *The Seminar of Jacques Lacan: Book 2: The Ego in Freud's Theory and in the Technique of Psychoanalysis,* ed. Jacques-Alain Miller, trans. Sylvia Tomaselli (New York: W. W. Norton, 1988), pp. 146–74.

35. For this, see a typical example of fascist "science" in *Agenda enciclopedica* (Turin: Laboratori Scienza del Popolo, February 1934).

36. Slimness in advertising has been read as a form of female rebellion against the regime's controls, just as anorexia nervosa has been diagnosed as a rebellion against the controls of patriarchy. There is something quite troubling about this formulation, however, in its patness and its failure to recognize the visual disavowal experienced by the victim of anorexia. For a critique of the antipatriarchal model, see my "The Hungry Eye: Anorexia and Anamorphosis," *Stanford Humanities Review,* vol. 1, no. 2 (1991): 7–30. Irene Brin, an astute critic of the fascist age, wrote that girls "all ate fruit salads without oil or sugar. They all weighed themselves, they compared waist sizes, they spoke of how difficult it was to maintain a diet at the family table, they dreamed about leaving for well-known spas where fasting was not only allowed, it was expected." See her *Usi e costumi, 1920–1940* (Palermo: Sellerio, 1981), p. 115. Brin is very good at capturing the sense of being bound and the desire for mobility that characterizes feminine behavior during the fascist period. Here I would put the emphasis not so much on the instinct for self-starvation, as on the entrapment of the domestic sphere. The waistline is the locus, then, for negotiating motion away from, rather than simply a place of pathology. The issue of maternity is approached through a kind of condescending glance at the working classes by the slimmed-down bourgeoisie. As with sugar, the consumption of fats is a *sign* of economic progress, even if a merely *illusory* sign. It is assumed that increased reproductivity of the laborer is tied up with increased consumption of fats, in a reciprocal arrangement. One specialist wrote: "Our country is notoriously poor in fats. . . . It should be noted that the consumption of fats, especially animal fats, is relatively modest and that the progress of the economic condition of the masses will naturally lead to an increase in such consumption, as to the natural increase of the population." See "Il problema dei grassi," *L'industria dolciaria,* no. 6 (1937).

37. Or, as the Americanist Mark Seltzer has recently suggested, motility is the area of supreme anxiety in the machine age, because "the principle of locomotion which in liberal market culture is the sign of agency is in machine culture the sign of automatism. Or rather, since the recalcitrant tensions between the imperatives of market culture and machine culture are central here, what must be considered is how the uncertain status of the principle of locomotion precipitates the melodramas of uncertain agency and also what amounts to an erotics of uncertain agency." See his *Bodies and Machines* (New York: Routledge & Kegan Paul, 1992), p. 18.

38. Elias Canetti, *Crowds and Power* (New York: Continuum, 1981), p. 211.

39. Andrew Hewitt, "Fascist Modernism, Futurism, and Post-modernity," in *Fascism, Aesthetics, and Culture,* ed. Richard J. Golsan (Hanover, N.H.: University Press of New England, 1992), p. 45.

40. Ibid., p. 49.

41. Sigmund Freud, "On Transformation of Instinct as Exemplified in Anal Eroticism," *S.E.,* vol. 17, 1917, p. 130.

42. Quoted in Schatzman, *Soul Murder,* p. 71.

43. Bourdieu, *Distinction,* p. 223. And if this refers primarily to traditionally "male" toys, it is all the more true for traditionally "female" toys with their already restricted mobility. Susan Buck-Morss, in *The Dialectics of Seeing: Walter Benjamin and the Arcades Project* (Cam-

bridge, Mass.: MIT Press, 1989), p. 365, writes: "Ironically, if playing with dolls was originally the way children learned the nurturing behavior of adult social relations, it has become a training ground for learning reified ones. The goal of little girls now is to become a 'doll.' This reversal epitomizes that which Marx considered characteristic of the capitalist-industrial mode of production: Machines that bring the promise of the naturalization of humanity and the humanization of nature result instead in the mechanization of both."

44. Sigmund Freud, "Character and Anal Erotism," *S.E.*, vol. 9, 1908.

45. Ibid., p. 171.

46. For a critique of Freud's writings in this key, see Whitney Davis, "HomoVision: A Reading of Freud's 'Fetishism,'" *Genders,* 15 (Winter 1992): 86–118.

47. Sigmund Freud, "On the Sexual Theories of Children," *S.E.*, vol. 9, 1908, p. 219.

48. In Lacan's French, the drive is described as "turning around" the object—*il s'en fait le tour*—which has a double meaning. Ultimately, we learn that the actual object of the drive is of no importance: the drive both turns around it, and tricks it; it seems to exist projected outside of the body, in a particular structural position with relation to the drive, but almost anything might come there to fill the position and also be duped by the drive (into thinking that it is more important than it really is).

49. Jacques Lacan, *The Four Fundamental Concepts of Psychoanalysis,* ed. Jacques-Alain Miller, trans. Alan Sheridan (New York: W. W. Norton, 1981), p. 196.

50. Reed Benhamou, "From Curiosité to Utilité: The Automaton in Eighteenth-Century France," *Studies in Eighteenth-Century Culture,* 17 (1987): 91–105.

51. Indeed, if the current version of Bibendum can be said to be a threat in any sense, it is through his whiteness. The white homunculus arouses the fear of suffocation, parodied in the popular film *Ghostbusters,* where a huge marshmallow parades through Manhattan, its sticky whiteness provoking a sense of ambiguity about its relative opacity or density.

52. See Giampaolo Gallo, ed., *Sulla bocca di tutti: Buitoni e Perugina, una storia in breve* (Perugia: Electa, 1990), p. 142.

53. Bourdieu, *Distinction,* p. 194.

54. Ibid., p. 199.

55. Henri Bergson, *Du rire* (1900), in English as "On Laughter," in *Comedy,* ed. Wylie Sypher (Garden City, N.Y.: Doubleday, 1956), p. 64. For Bergson's relation with the visual arts, and in particular with cubism and futurism, see Mark Antliff, *Inventing Bergson: Cultural Politics and the Parisian Avant-Garde* (Princeton, N.J.: Princeton University Press, 1993).

56. Bergson, "On Laugher," p. 64.

57. For a possible relation between Bergson and Chaplin, see Flora R. Schreiber, "Bergson and Charlie Chaplin," *French Forum,* 7, no. 2 (1941): 19–20.

58. Bergson, "On Laughter," p. 77.

59. Ibid., p. 79.

60. For the centrality of the category of humanity in Bergson's thought, and the human component in relation to these three terms, see Gilles Deleuze, *Bergsonism,* trans. Hugh Tomlinson and Barbara Habberiam (New York: Zone Books, 1988).

61. Bergson, "On Laughter," p. 92.

62. Ibid., pp. 92–93.

63. Ibid., p. 99.

64. Ibid., p. 97.

65. Jean Baudrillard, *L'échange symbolique et la mort* (Paris: Editions Gallimard, 1976), p. 83.

66. Ibid., p. 84.

67. Ibid., pp. 86–87.

68. "Propaganda," *L'industria dolciaria,* no. 3 (1936): 104.

69. For the relation between literary and artistic *strapaese* and regime goals, see Luisa Mangoni, *L'interventismo della cultura* (Bari: Laterza, 1974).

70. Biondi, *La fabbrica del duce,* p. 154.

71. For an important reading of this film, see Naomi Greene, *Pier Paolo Pasolini: Cinema as Heresy* (Princeton, N.J.: Princeton University Press, 1990), chapter 3, "The End of Ideology." Of course, Pasolini makes an important link between the agrarian devastation and the rebuilding efforts of the Left. For this, also see Palmiro Togliatti, *Lectures on Fascism* (London: Lawrence and Wishart, 1976), "Fascism's Policy in the Countryside," pp. 117–34.

72. Giorgio Candeloro, *Storia dell'Italia moderna: Il fascismo e le sue guerre,* vol. 9 (Milan: Feltrinelli, 1992), p. 124.

73. The hand is also an alibi for what the body may do. It seems somehow ingenuous, but at the same time it cannot dissimulate its place of tremendous privilege within the topology of the body. For the relation of the hand to power, see Elias Canetti, *Crowds and Power,* pp. 218–19. Other important "hands" of poster art include a conscription campaign by Mauzan from 1917, which includes the slogan: "Per la liberazione sottoscrivete!" ("Sign up, for liberation!"), and the image is an enlarged hand, attached to a body outside of the picture plane (literally "off the map"), creeping along what is clearly Italian soil, and dangerously close to a strip of ribbon representing the Piave river, near the Austrian border in the eastern Italian Dolomites. In a propaganda image from the early 1940s, an armor-clad hand crushes the bodies of "rebels and bandits" of the resistance, their miserable bodies flailing, their mouths open in idiotic terror. In the Soviet Union, the only country to experience greater state intervention in industrial production than Italy, the hand also made its appearance. A whole series of hands are raised in a propagandistic poster urging workers to exercise their right to vote. Each hand, when raised, will be counted — at least that is the positive message of the image. Each hand, stiffened, inserts itself into the political process. This image is the equivalent of the topos of the product as the extension of the Roman salute. An image by John Heartfield from 1928 depicts a large, photographed hand with its fingers spread out across the page. The slogan reads: "The hand has five fingers, and with these five he holds back the enemy. Vote for the five list: Communist party (Wählt Liste 5)." A well-known example of American propaganda is the black-gloved, sadistic hand by Carlu, which holds a wrench fixed around the letter "o" in the word "production" in the slogan: "America's Answer, Production." Once again, this hand is utterly disembodied, yet it has a certain corporeality and vigor to it. The list could go on.

74. Discussed in Maria Macciocchi, *La donna nera: Consenso femminile e fascismo* (Milan: Feltrinelli, 1976), pp. 60–61.

75. I owe this imaginary scenario to Mark Seltzer, *Bodies and Machines,* p. 130.

76. I cannot resist here invoking a contemporary version of the hand-without-a-body: the Helping Hand of Hamburger Helper. This hand, complete with a sympathetic smile that all but negates any anxiety it might generate in viewers concerned with the totality of the body image, first made its appearance on television with the advent of the target category "working mother." Primarily motivated by guilt, this target is constantly seeking new ways to prepare instant meals that appear rich and hearty, or, in this case, full of spices that might recall a long-cooking stew. The Helping Hand, which is decidedly masculine in its full-body toque blanche (the male chef intervening for the helpless female who dares to make hamburgers the basis for the evening meal), snaps its fingers and transforms the ordinary into the acceptable, the castrating woman into the maternal caregiver. It pops in and out of the kitchen, always hiding when the rest of the family arrives on the scene. It is the spokeshand for this authorized brand of "cheating" in the kitchen, the secret conscience of the divided female ego. Unlike the hands of 1930s industrial production, then, this hand remains in a fragmentary state not because it represents (over)productivity, but because it has to be able to disappear quickly, in a "snap" with the arrival of the family at the dinner table. The Helping Hand is an animated figure while the woman and her

hamburger are "real" because ultimately, the hand is performing the labor that used to belong to the female in a moment when her labor value was better defined. He goes about his business with a smile because he does not wish to alienate the very target for which he exists, but his status in reality is ambivalent in order to reaffirm the woman's own ambivalence about her position. Moreover, the Helping Hand is soft in the middle, like the Pillsbury Doughboy. He is not a phallic hand because he does not represent a "strong" productivity, and he avoids the male gaze by appearing during "women's television programs" and in a private world of women's magazines. In this sense, he is not a castrated hand, but a true metonymy, a friendly homunculus.

77. "Lavorare in piedi o seduti?" *L'ufficio moderno*, 1930, p. 289. The title serves as an ironic echo of a collection of essays by Leo Longanesi about the culture of fascism. Evoking Mussolini's call to "stand up!," Longanesi's book is titled, *In piedi e seduti* (Milan: Longanesi, 1968).

78. Shengold, *Halo in the Sky*, p. 98.

79. Canetti, *Crowds and Power*, pp. 387–88.

80. Ibid., p. 96.

81. Gramsci, *Quaderni del carcere*, vol. 3, p. 2165.

82. Brin, *Usi e costumi*, p. 178.

83. See Gramsci, *Quaderni del carcere*, vol. 3, pp. 2162–63.

84. Gramsci insists on this point throughout his notebook 22, "Americanism and Fordism," vol. III, pp. 2136–81 of *Quaderni del carcere*.

85. For the specific situation of the *impiegati* under fascism, see Mariuccia Salvati, *Il regime e gli impiegati* (Rome-Bari: Laterza, 1992).

86. "Organizzazione aziendale," *L'ufficio moderno* (February 1939): 51.

87. Canetti, *Crowds and Power*, p. 389.

88. Fortunato Depero, *Fortunato Depero nelle opere e nella vita* (Trent: Legione Trentina, 1940), p. 176.

89. Ibid.

90. See Fortunato Depero, "Il futurismo e la pubblicità," in *Numero unico futurista* (Milan: Campari, 1931).

91. For the house as a protective shell, see Mihaly Csikzentmihalyi and Eugene Rochberg-Halton, *The Meaning of Things: Domestic Symbols and the Self* (Cambridge: Cambridge University Press, 1981), pp. 127–34.

92. I draw support for this reading of Depero the Artisan from Peter Bürger, who speaks of the ultimate failure of the historical avant-gardes to sublate art: "Since now the protest of the historical avant-garde against art as institution is accepted as *art*, the gesture of protest of the neo-avant-garde becomes inauthentic. Having been shown to be irredeemable, the claim to be protest can no longer be maintained. This fact accounts for the arts-and-crafts impression that works of the avant-garde frequently convey." *Theory of the Avant-Garde*, trans. Michael Shaw (Minneapolis: University of Minnesota Press, 1984), p. 53.

93. Or, for a specific example that could well have inspired Depero, see Andrea Pisano, *The Art of Painting*, marble relief, c. 1334 for the Campanile of Florence.

94. Quoted in Renzo De Felice, *Mussolini il fascista*, vol. 2, "L'organizzazione dello stato fascista, 1925–1929" (Turin: Einaudi, 1968), pp. 230–31.

95. From a letter to his finance minister, Volpi, dated August 8, 1926. Quoted in Giorgio Candeloro, *Storia dell'Italia moderna*, pp. 109–10.

96. Canetti, *Crowds and Power*, p. 184.

97. Ibid., p. 185.

98. Ibid., pp. 221–22.

99. Karl Marx, "Grundrisse," in *The Marx-Engels Reader*, 2nd ed., ed. Richard Tucker (New York: W. W. Norton, 1978), p. 226.

100. Ibid., p. 283.

4 / The Body and Its Armors

1. The classic discussion of the female object-position is Laura Mulvey, "Visual Pleasure and Narrative Cinema," *Screen*, 16, no. 3 (Autumn 1975): 6–18. Also see John Berger, *Ways of Seeing* (London: Penguin, 1972). In addition to Mulvey's and Berger's, some other key books on the relation between gender and advertising are Stuart Ewen, *All Consuming Images: The Politics of Style in Contemporary Culture* (New York: Basic Books, 1988), and Erving Goffman, *Gender Advertisements* (New York: Harper & Row, 1976). Both Ewen and Goffman take an anthropological approach to the problem, discussing how images of femininity in advertisement both shape and exploit cultural values. For a more extended bibliography from art history and film studies on the woman as "to-be-looked-at" object, see Abigail Solomon-Godeau, *Photography at the Dock* (Minneapolis: University of Minnesota Press, 1991), n. 4, p. 244.

2. Victoria de Grazia, *How Fascism Ruled Women* (Berkeley: University of California Press, 1992), p. 7.

3. "Che forme," *L'ufficio moderno* (September 1939): 444.

4. See Boccasile's introduction, "Io e le donne," to the collection of his covers *La signorina grandi firme* (Milan: Longanesi, 1981). Boccasile's woman seems to be a sort of visual compromise between the fascist ideal of femininity and what some feminists view as the "female ideal," with its 1920s, "masculinized" profile. Thus, she was able to sell the magazines to an audience of female readers, and still circulate in the male world of exchange as a token of conformity. In a series of comic strips detailing the "adventures of the Signorina Grandi Firme," she moves in the space of only two frames from being alone to being engaged, and in each comic, she uses her beauty (her legs) to hook a man, but there is a sense in which this powerful tool of seduction also borders on the subversive.

5. E. Roggero, *Come si riesce con la pubblicità* (Milan: Hoepli, 1920), p. 77.

6. "Annunci per le donne," *L'ufficio moderno* (June 1931): 376–77.

7. For this polemic, which saw D'Annunzio as emblematic of bourgeois sexuality, see Maria Macciocchi, *La donna nera: Consenso femminile e fascism o* (Milan: Feltrinelli, 1976), pp. 29–30.

8. See "Perchè la donna compera?" *L'ufficio moderno* (January 1932): 56.

9. "L'uomo e la donna," *L'ufficio moderno* (November 1933): 622.

10. Of course, this language echoes not only fascist rhetoric, but also the papal encyclic *Rerum Novarum* drafted in 1891, which stated: "Women ... are by nature made for domestic work, which greatly protects the honesty of the weaker sex, and has a natural correspondence with the education of children and the well-being of the home." For Maria Macciocchi this language has a specific "anti-communist" message, in its suggestion that forcing the woman out of her "natural" position in the home is a result of impoverishment that can only be remedied by capitalist development. See *La donna nera*, pp. 48–49. In this sense, the market as delineated within *L'ufficio moderno* would seem to form part of the line of papal-fascist consensus on the "natural" position of women as aligned with a thriving, capitalist economy.

11. Henri Bergson, "On Laughter," in *Comedy*, ed. Wylie Sypher (Garden City, N.Y.: Doubleday, 1956), p. 85.

12. My use of terms such as "armor" and "chain mail" to describe the protective stances of the (male) body derive from a long and sustained relation with Klaus Theweleit's *Male Fantasies*, vol. 1, trans. Stephen Conway (Minneapolis: University of Minnesota Press, 1987). In particular, volume 2, trans. Erica Carter and Chris Turner (Minneapolis: University of Minnesota Press, 1989), which treats the bodies of soldiers, will resonate throughout this entire chapter. I will not bother to cite every example of how Theweleit sees body armor as a key trope in the psychosexual makeup of his subjects, and rather than repeat his conclusions, in this chapter I will discuss more specifically how certain images of the body work within the marketplace and within a larger economic framework.

13. Michel Foucault, *Discipline and Punish*, trans. Alan Sheridan (New York: Vintage Books, 1977), p. 135.

14. Ibid., p. 137.

15. Elias Canetti is one who laughs at the Italian clothing-without-a-body. In a brief discussion of the peculiar nature of Italian nationalism, he writes: "Fascism attempted what appeared the simplest solution [between old and new Rome], which was to dress up in the genuine antique costume. But this did not really fit; it was much too big and the movements it permitted the body inside it were so violent that every bone was broken." See *Crowds and Power* (New York: Continuum, 1981), p. 177.

16. Ibid., p. 315.

17. Klaus Theweleit, *Male Fantasies*, vol. 1, p. 434. Also see John Dollimore, *Sexual Dissidence* (Oxford: Clarendon Press, 1991), p. 93. As Dollimore points out, the whole line of thinking (which would include Theweleit) that sees the repression of desire as something that might return to haunt fascism, is radically contradicted by Foucault's ideas about legitimation and power, especially in *The History of Sexuality*, trans. Robert Hurley (New York: Vintage, 1990).

18. For another image of the protective raincoat, not displayed as part of any advertising campaign but as a work of "fine art," see Theweleit, *Male Fantasies*, vol. 2, p. 326.

19. Gaston Bachelard writes of water as a sign of the feminine, as Theweleit does. However, he also recognizes a violent, masculinized form of water that pelts the Zarathustra figure, the intrepid marcher in a wind storm. The marcher becomes a flag, a symbol of nationhood and strength: "*Le manteau battu par l'ouragan est ainsi une sorte de drapeau inhérent, le drapeau imprenable du héros du vent.*" See *L'eau et les reves* (Paris: Corti, 1942), p. 218.

20. The museum of umbrellas in Lago Maggiore included a plaque commemorating Mussolini's capture in Dongo. He wore only a raincoat at this time, in spite of a torrential downpour. See Dino Biondi, *La fabbrica del duce* (Florence: Vallecchi, 1973), p. 105.

21. Coll. Bertarelli, busta 44, 1935 propaganda by the Ministry of War.

22. Ministero della Guerra, Comando del Corpo di Stato Maggiore, *Manuale dell'ufficiale istruttore dei corsi premilitari* (Rome: Istituto Poligrafico dello Stato, 1929), pp. 230–35.

23. Ibid., p. 19.

24. Ibid., p. 23.

25. Ibid., p. 237. We see that the problem of military bodies being too closely pressed together forms part of a larger cultural fear about sexuality that still pervades our culture today. In a discussion of the membership of homosexuals in the U.S. military that predated Clinton's "Don't ask, don't tell" policy, the Chairman of the Joint Chiefs of Staff, General Colin Powell, stated that the removal of a ban "would be prejudicial to the good order and discipline." Powell suggested that although homosexuals may make good soldiers, an *open* display of homosexuality would undermine morale. "Field commanders insist that sharing barracks, showers, latrines—especially at sea or in extreme combat conditions—would create serious management problems." See "Clinton to Open Military's Ranks to Homosexuals," *New York Times* (Thursday, November 12, 1992): 1.

26. Theweleit, *Male Fantasies*, vol. 1, pp. 399–402.

27. Ibid., p. 373.

28. For example, the Perugina-Buitoni corporation waged a campaign to promote its chocolates in 1937, and they seemed tacitly to acknowledge not only resistance toward their particular product, but also a "front of indifference" that characterized life under fascism in general. See Giampaolo Gallo, *Sulla bocca di tutti: Buitoni e Perugina, una storia in breve* (Perugia: Electa, 1990), p. 26. For "resistance" and femininity in modernist aesthetics, see Christine Buci-Glucksmann, "Catastrophic Utopia: The Feminine as Allegory of the Modern," in *The Making of the Modern Body*, ed. Catherine Gallagher and Thomas Laqueur (Berkeley: University of California Press, 1987).

29. "Un Esempio: Indanthren," *L'ufficio moderno* (March 1932): 138.

30. For this phenomenon of homosexual encrypting, see Vito Russo, *The Celluloid Closet* (New York: Harper & Row, 1987).

31. During the fascist era, the worker saw the workplace physician as a very hostile entity and he resisted the intrusion on his privacy. Often, the doctor was seen as representing the interests of the factory owners. See Luisa Dodi Osnaghi, "La nocività nelle riviste del lavoro," in *La classe operaia durante il fascismo* (Milan: Feltrinelli, 1981), pp. 232–33.

32. Sigmund Freud, "Psychoanalytic Notes on an Autobiographical Account of a Case of Paranoia," *S.E.*, vol. 12, 1911, p. 63.

33. Ibid., p. 70.

34. Ibid., pp. 78–79. In terms of the military body I have been discussing here, the rays correspond structurally to what Canetti terms the "stings" of command. In the army, the soldier is subjected to stings from a higher-in-command. But in time, like the paranoid son, he takes the place of this officer, inflicting stings (rays) on others. The system never changes, only the place of a particular body within it. See *Crowds and Power*, pp. 315–16. And, like the soldier in *Male Fantasies* who describes his assault as rain, the "stung" soldier bears the mark of his obedience that is transformed into a kind of soul murder. "A man can evade commands by not hearing them; and he can evade them by not carrying them out. The sting . . . only results from the *carrying out* of a command. . . . A command carried out impresses its exact shape on the performer. . . . Their [stings'] persistence is remarkable; nothing sinks so deep into human beings and nothing is so indissoluble. A man can become so completely riddled with them that he has no interest left for anything else and, except for them, can feel nothing" (Canetti, pp. 321–22).

35. See, for example, the analysis offered by Macalpine and Hunter in their introduction to Daniel Paul Schreber, *Memoirs of My Nervous Illness* (Cambridge, Mass.: Harvard University Press, 1988).

36. Ibid., p. 177.

37. Quoted in Morris Schatzman, *Soul Murder* (New York: Random House, 1973), p. 22.

38. Quoted in ibid., p. 32.

39. For the relation between body, spirituality, and the bath, see Alev L. Croutier, *Taking the Waters* (New York: Abbeville Press, 1992).

40. The term "bikini" was not used until the bomb was tested on the island of Bikini Atoll in 1946, but a "modern" version of this swimsuit was well established by the mid-1930s.

41. Giorgio Triani, *Pelle di luna, pelle di sole: Nascita e storia della civiltà balneare, 1700–1946* (Venice: Marsilio, 1988).

42. So, for example, Starace viewed the radio specifically as a means for "introducing the sounds and rhythms of industrial society into the rural world, and of assuring continuous contact between the state and the outlying rural areas," cited in Victoria de Grazia, *The Culture of Consent* (Cambridge: Cambridge University Press, 1981), p. 155. For the radio and advertising, also see Gian Luigi Falabrino, *Effimera e bella* (Turin: Gutenberg 2000, 1990), pp. 151–68.

43. Luigi Dalmonte, "Discorso sulla pubblicità radiofonica," *L'ufficio moderno* (February 1931): 113.

44. For Perugina's sponsorship of radio concerts and their campaign using figurines from a popular broadcast based on the "four" musketeers, see Gallo, *Sulla bocca di tutti*; David Forgacs, *Italian Culture in the Industrial Era, 1880–1980: Cultural Industries, Politics and the Public* (Manchester: Manchester University Press, 1990), p. 67. For the contemporary problematic of sponsorship, see "Duro braccio di ferro sugli sponsor televisi," in *La repubblica* (June 19, 1992): 48.

45. De Grazia, *The Culture of Consent*, pp. 155–56. See also Forgacs, *Italian Culture in the Industrial Era*, p. 64, for a statistical survey of radio programs and subscribers.

46. SIPRA was linked with the Società Idroelettrica Piemonte (SIP), which had a controlling interest in the state radio entity, EIAR, after 1929. Brochure: Coll. Bertarelli, 1931, busta 24 bis.

47. De Grazia, *The Culture of Consent,* p. 155.

48. Forgacs, *Italian Culture in the Industrial Era,* p. 68, quotes a passage from Carlo Levi's *Christ Stopped at Eboli* that seems to exemplify perfectly the kind of cultural ambivalence toward imposed "group listening" within peasant culture. For the scene itself, see *Cristo si è fermato a Eboli* (Turin: Einaudi, 1979), p. 67.

49. Lidia Morelli, "La donna, la casa e la radio," *Radiocorriere,* 8, no. 1 (January 2–9, 1932): 25, quoted in Forgacs, *Italian Culture in the Industrial Era,* p. 64. I would also point to another version of the pull of the radio for the family structure. In a discussion of the relation between theories of fascism and everyday banality, Alice Yaeger Kaplan narrates the centrality of the radio to a home of the period: *Reproductions of Banality: Fascism, Literature, and French Intellectual Life* (Minneapolis: University of Minnesota Press, 1986), pp. 50–51.

50. F. T. Marinetti, *The Futurist Cookbook,* trans. Suzanne Brill (San Francisco: Bedford Arts, 1989), p. 67.

51. For a reading of the liberating somersault within the analytic situation, see Michael Balint, *The Basic Fault* (London: Tavistock, 1968), pp. 127–32. One of Balint's patients, an adult who had been unable to perform the somersault as a child, achieves this gesture in analysis. Balint sees this as an ego-strengthening act, but not as a form of regression or repetition. The jump formed the "new beginning," the analytic *threshold* to regression. It provided a break with the present that allowed the patient to retreat into the basic fault and then, eventually, to arrive at a new way of object relations. For the body-in-flight topos in art, see Clive Hart, *Images of Flight* (Berkeley: University of California Press, 1988).

52. In his *Gender Advertisements,* p. 50, Goffman includes a photographic image of a woman who is suspended in midair, after having made a forward/upward jump. He classes this pose with "body clowning," a form of gender-specific childlike freedom of motility.

53. Bertram Lewin, "The Body as Phallus," *Psychoanalytic Quarterly,* vol. 2 (1933): 24–47, recounts the dream of a female patient who felt herself about to plunge off a cliff into a gaping cavern; to save herself, she becomes a penis. The fear of being swallowed up is related to castration. Rather than delude herself into thinking she *has* a penis, the girl may simply imagine that she *is* one. More importantly, in cases where the entire body becomes a phallus, the mouth is often a significant organ, associated with the urethra. Speech is the equivalent of orgasm, and given that this is a dangerous situation, it makes sense that the man transforms himself into a female phallus in order to be able to speak.

54. In fact, the *salto mortale* is taken by one critic as a metaphor for the release of capital from its embodiment in the commodity. See Wolfgang Haug, *Critique of Commodity Aesthetics,* trans. Robert Bock (Cambridge: Polity Press, 1986), p. 23.

55. Bachelard, *L'eau et les reves,* p. 226. This defiance comes in the context of a (male) initiation rite, a diving into the waters. At first one hears laughter, that of the father. "After the test, which can be very brief, the infantile laughter takes up its franchise, a recurrent courage will come to mask the earlier revolt; the easy victory, the joy of being initiated, the pride of having become, like the father, a being of the water ..." (p. 223). The dive is a way of erasing any previous humiliation; it is a test for the masculine ego, so that in figuring the female body here, our advertisers seem to appeal to the feminine desire for *jouissance,* but under the guise of a beautiful design.

56. For problems in *Beyond the Pleasure Principle* and representation, see Leo Bersani, *The Freudian Body* (New York: Columbia University Press, 1990). For Bersani, one can read a struggle within Freud's work to maintain some legibility to human behavior, but a text such as *Beyond the Pleasure Principle* really points to what many representational texts themselves enact,

namely, the repetition of pain. Also s.; »åÇj˙ö 0CÅfe, *Life and Death in Psychoanalysis,* trans. Jeffrey Mehlman (Baltimore and London: Johns Hopkins University Press, 1976), p. 107.

57. Sigmund Freud, "Beyond the Pleasure Principle," *S.E.*, vol. 18, 1920, p. 36.

58. For a developed version of this critique, see Frigga Haug, *Beyond Female Masochism,* trans. Rodney Livingstone (London and New York: Verso, 1992).

59. See, for example, Ferruccio Antonelli and Alessandro Salvini, *Psicologia dello sport* (Rome: Lombardo, 1978), pp. 252–54.

60. Incidentally, it is difficult for me to conceive of this sort of model of the masculine sport-nucleus without thinking of Reich's suppressed "little man," which he associated with one of the primary causes of fascist consent. An attempt to "understand" fascism through a consideration of different ego models is certainly relevant to the considerations I am making here, but it is also a complex issue that I prefer not to tackle head-on for reasons of space. I refer the reader to Theweleit's writing on the subject.

61. Felice Fabrizio, *Sport e fascismo: La politica sportiva del regime, 1924–1936* (Rimini: Guaraldi, 1978), p. 113.

62. Rosella Isidori Frasca, *. . . e il duce le volle sportive* (Bologna: Patron editore, 1983), p. 58. The phrase "to resolve the problem of life" is part of everyday speech in Italian, and its irony emerges forcefully in Pier Paolo Pasolini's documentary *Comizi d'amore* (*Love Meetings,* 1964). The director poses the question of sexuality in precisely these terms, and the respondents almost all automatically understand "resolution" to mean "marriage," unaware, of course, of the unstated equivalency they make between "marriage" and "the resolution of life," that is, "death."

63. Reproduced in Frasca, *. . . e il duce,* p. 71.

64. M. Tapparelli, "Psicologia pubblicitaria," *L'ufficio moderno* (January 1930): 42.

65. For the diving body as exemplary of personal liberty in modernist aesthetics, one might refer to the fifth *Duino Elegy* of Rilke. The elegy of the tumblers is often cited in studies of moderism. In 1915 Rilke had spent some time in the home of Hertha Koenig, the owner of Picasso's *Les saltimbanques* of 1905. In Rilke's poem, tumbling is a figure for human existence (the acrobats physically form the letter "D" of *Dastehn*). On the brink of losing balance, the young boy represents a stage of incompetence:

> Wo, o wo ist der Ort, — ich trag ihn im Herzen —,
> wo sie noch lange nicht konnten, noch von einander
> abfieln, wie sich bespringende, nicht recht
> paarige Tiere —

But at the end of the poem, Rilke introduces a pair of lovers, who, in the afterlife, are projected into a possible moment of redemption, where they finally learn to perform showy, daring acts upon the heart's trapeze (*ihre kühnen / hohen figuren des Herzschwungs*). They could have a tremendous effect on their audience of dead, and they are "finally, truthfully smiling" (*endlich wahrhaft lächelnde*). Remaining still, they have both died and yet defied death.

66. Sigmund Freud, "New Introductory Lectures," *S.E.*, vol. 22, 1933, p. 80.

67. This is one of the most important aspects of their work in *Anti-Oedipus* and *A Thousand Plateaus*. For an account of molarization versus molecularization, see Brian Massumi, *A User's Guide to Capitalism and Schizophrenia: Deviations from Deleuze and Guattari* (Cambridge, Mass.: MIT Press, 1992): "Molarization is another word for 'fascism.' Fascism is a manic attack by the body politic against itself, in the interests of its own salvation. More precisely, it is an attack by the 'whole' of society, its image of unity or plane of transcendence, against its 'parts,' its bodies or plane of immanence. It is desire turned against itself" (p. 116). The job of the fascist, if we like, is to maintain order and to "become the same." Massumi summarizes Deleuze and Guattari as suggesting that democratic regimes allow more

choice for the subject, as long as that subject lives within the bounds of "good or common sense" under a form of "minidespotism." To the degree that I am sympathetic with this way of thinking, I see the diving bodies as molar bodies that stay within the bounds, and do not break out into a frenzied vortex of "becoming other."

5 / The Body Disappears: Negation, Toxicity, Annihilation

1. For the differences between "negation" and "disavowal" see Jean Laplanche and J.-B. Pontalis, *The Language of Psychoanalysis,* trans. Donald Nicholson-Smith (New York and London: W. W. Norton, 1973); also Gilles Deleuze, "Coldness and Cruelty," introduction to *Masochism* (New York: Zone Books, 1991).

2. The notion of "raw material" assumes tremendous importance for this discussion, since, as I have repeatedly suggested, the Italian body and its images are inextricably linked to the specter of productive autarchy. Furthermore, rayon is one of the few products that satisfies the regime's desire for absolute self-containment. Any product that relies on imported materials, even if they are vastly transformed in the processes of production, still bears a tainted aura.

3. For Lacan's use of this term and its relation to his "Imaginary," see *Écrits,* trans. Alan Sheridan (New York: W. W. Norton, 1977). A recent book, Drew Leder, *The Absent Body* (Chicago: University of Chicago Press, 1990), provides a more developed model of the phenomenology of perceptual states of the body, focusing on interoceptive and exteroceptive categories.

4. Quoted in Susan Buck-Morss, *The Dialectics of Seeing: Walter Benjamin and the Arcades Project* (Cambridge, Mass.: MIT Press, 1989), pp. 37–38.

5. Ibid., p. 279.

6. While the large-scale department store, the *grand magasin,* had coexisted with the smaller, closed space of the boutique since the mid–nineteenth century in France, in Italy the "open market" form of the all-in-one, multitiered shopping palace was still quite novel. The difference between these two spaces primarily concerns the moral obligation to buy that is encoded in the boutique and that still permeates many of the luxury shops in Italy today. For the "open" department store in the formation of the French bourgeoisie, see Phillipe Perrot, *Les dessus et les dessous de la bourgeoisie* (Paris: Fayard, 1981), p. 113.

7. Spencer R. Weart, *Nuclear Fear* (Cambridge, Mass.: Harvard University Press, 1988). This book has been a great inspiration for much of the work that appears in this chapter.

8. F. T. Marinetti, *The Futurist Cookbook,* trans. Suzanne Brill (San Francisco: Bedford Arts, 1989), p. 40.

9. For the historical and philosophical importance of the X ray as penetrating the "secret regions" of the viscera, see Leder, *The Absent Body,* pp. 44–45.

10. Giulia Poli, *Gioventù del littorio in vacanza* (Florence: A. Rossini, 1940), p. 25.

11. A. Cagliano, "Gli animali dannosi all'industria dolciaria e la loro distruzione," *L'industria dolciaria,* no. 3 (1937): 80.

12. For the Indanthren headquarters as a form of advertising, see *L'ufficio moderno* (January 1931): 47.

13. Daniel Paul Schreber, *Memoirs of My Nervous Illness,* trans. and ed. Ida Macalpine and Richard A. Hunter (Cambridge, Mass.: Harvard University Press, 1988), p. xi.

14. Ibid., p. 17.

15. Ibid., p. 98.

16. Weart, *Nuclear Fear,* pp. 21–24.

17. Schreber, *Memoirs,* p. 88.

18. Ibid., pp. 137–38.

19. Ibid., p. 177.

20. Elias Canetti, *Crowds and Power* (New York: Continuum, 1981), p. 441.

21. Ibid., p. 461.

22. Ignoring the shortcomings of Lanital, Marinetti accepted a commission for a praise-poem by the Sniaviscosa company. In 1937 he published a brochure with his poem of milk-wear ("Il poema del vestito di latte") superimposing words-in-freedom onto a visual text composed of photomontages. The poem follows a narrative trajectory from the battlefields of Africa (the failed locus of utopic fascist sheep and raw materials) to Italy. Drained and thirsty from his struggle, the futurist calls for a restorative drink of milk. This "sweet liquid" is interchangeable with Italy itself: the lactating motherland, but also the "milky altar of the Patria [fatherland]." Moving from a victory celebration in the Colosseum, the hero commands an industrial battle of productivity that also is clearly a battle of parturition: "The man commands: Milk, divide yourself! / Having abandoned all of its butter, milk, feeling / skinny, falls into a desperate state of powder / uncertain if it should declare itself to be straw-colored or greenish." The process that Marinetti goes on to describe in futurist terms is one of spinning the milk into a thickened coagulant that may then be woven into cloth. Without human intervention, the Sniaviscosa bobbins turn maniacally. The spinning machine, in Marinetti's poem, is termed the "MaternalTextile" ("*Tessutomaterno*"). Finally, the futurist calls on all consumers to exalt the "milk of armored tanks, milk of war, militarized milk." In the spinning process glorified here, the factory is both male and female, paternal and maternal, warrior and life-giver. A year later, however, a technophobia intimately connected with misogyny will surface in the ambivalent poem of "Torre Viscosa" to be discussed later.

23. See Giorgio Candeloro, *Storia dell'Italia moderna: Il fascismo e le sue guerre,* vol. 9 (Milan: Feltrinelli, 1992), p. 434.

24. "Opinioni sulle fibre tessili" (Florence: Sansoni, 1937), p. 7. This brochure was part of a series of "opinions on" various issues of importance to the regime.

25. Fascist economics, like other conservative ideologies, tries to locate scarcity in the failure of nature to provide abundant resources. From the Left, however, scarcity "may be regarded from another viewpoint as stemming from an allocation of abundant resources in a wasteful, unjust, and irrational manner.... The threat of scarcity is a premanent feature of our present society, no matter how vast the supply of available goods, because the escalation of material demands only plunges individuals more deeply into the ambiguous ensemble of satisfactions and dissatisfactions." See William Leiss, *The Limits to Satisfaction* (Toronto: University of Toronto Press, 1976), p. 29.

26. Franco Fornari, *Psicanalisi della situazione atomica* (Milan: Rizzoli, 1970), essentially sustains this thesis.

27. See the introduction to *Cloth and Human Experience,* ed. Annette B. Weiner and Jane Schneider (Washington, D.C.: Smithsonian Institution Press, 1989). For the specific cultural links between embroidery and femininity, see Rozwitha Parker, *The Subversive Stitch* (London: Women's Press, 1984).

28. Jane Schneider, "Rumpelstiltskin's Bargain: Folklore and the Merchant Capitalist Intensification of Linen Manufacture in Early Modern Europe," in *Cloth and Human Experience,* p. 207.

29. Pergentino Cipriani, "Il prezzo di costo nell'industria tessile," *L'ufficio moderno* (March 1931): 147.

30. For dehydration measures, see Enrico Vigliani, "Bevande per i lavoratori delle industrie tessili," pamphlet. *La medicina del lavoro,* vol. 45, no. 5 (May 1954).

31. Between 1931 and 1937, the percentage of females in the artificial fiber industry declined from 69 percent of the workforce to 45 percent. See Victoria de Grazia, *How Fascism Ruled Women* (Berkeley: University of California Press, 1992), p. 185.

32. G. Lazzeri, ed., *Vedere: Le fibre tessili artificiali* (Milan, 1941), p. 12. The autarchic problem was not utterly resolved by rayon because Italy was forced to use trees imported from Scandinavian countries since its own forest industry was poorly developed. This problem was only resolved in 1938 with the construction of the Torviscosa to produce cellulose.

33. Marie Curie, *Pierre Curie,* trans. Charlotte Kellogg and Vernon Kellogg (New York: Macmillan, 1923), p. 101.

34. For a history of these measures, see de Grazia, *How Fascism Ruled Women,* pp. 166–200.

35. See F. T. Marinetti, "Il poema di Torre Viscosa" (Milan: Officina Grafiche Esperia, 1938). As Cinzia Blum has pointed out, the publication of this poem also coincides with the regime's official denunciation of "modern" and "degenerate" art, which includes futurism. Although Marinetti accepted his commission from the Torre Viscosa, he may also be expressing anti-Mussolini sentiments at this moment.

36. *Vita femminile,* no. 10 (November 1, 1938): 47.

37. See, for example, a propaganda brochure for Ital Rayon, Coll. Bertarelli, busta 7 bis, 1933, which makes this "learned" philological connection explicit for consumers. It is clear that the coiners of the term, seeking a convenient brand name for artificial silk, seized upon the French meaning of "rayon" in the sense of a "ray of light(ness)." The term makes an early appearance in a column in the London industry weekly, *Draper's Record.* "City Echoes" (June 14, 1924): 685: " 'Glos' having been killed by ridicule, the National Retail Dry Goods Association of America has made another effort to produce a suitably distinctive name for artificial silk. This time their choice has fallen on 'rayon' which, from a phonetic point of view, certainly sounds happier. Yet I cannot agree that it is particularly appropriate to the article itself." It is of course ironic that Italy stuck with the French spelling throughout its autarchic campaign, whose thrust was implicitly against the Parisian fashion industry. The contradictory semantic power of a French word—there had been so many in the Italian language, but they had all been replaced with sometimes awkward equivalent coinages during the thirties—representing the great economic hope of the nation should not be overlooked.

38. For this form of female knowledge, see *Manuale di economia domestica* (Rome: Editori Novissima, 1935), published by the Fasci Femminili.

39. Ibid., p. 47.

40. Ibid.

41. The term "vampiresque" is reported in Irene Brin, *Usi e costumi, 1920–1940* (Palermo: Sellerio, 1981), p. 103.

42. Ibid., pp. 204–5.

43. For this ad, see Gian Luigi Falabrino, *Effimera e bella* (Turin: Gutenberg 2000, 1990), p. 146.

44. See Brin, *Usi e costumi,* p. 80.

45. Ibid., p. 45. "Not just the simple pleasure of smoking, but a very special culture of brands, attitudes, manias, and even illnesses, animated smokers, male and female, with a particular intensity. Around 1920 the discussions about whether women of 'good principles' should smoke in public culminated, and then quickly ended.... Soon every prohibition fell.... The divas of the cinema were often hospitalized in order to be denicotinized. Colored smoke was tried, without success. Finally, everyone lined up at the tobacco stores." Also see Richard Klein, *Cigarettes Are Sublime* (Durham, N.C.: Duke University Press, 1993).

46. See Ross Chambers, "Le poète fumeur," *Australian Journal of French Studies,* vol. 16, no. 2 (January–April 1979): 138–51.

47. For mesmerization and hypnosis in Italy, see Clara Gallini, *La somnambula meravigliosa: Magnetismo e ipnotismo nell'Ottocento italiano* (Milan: Feltrinelli, 1983).

48. Weart, *Nuclear Fear,* p. 45.

49. Gallini, *La somnambula*, p. 67.

50. Ibid., p. 65.

51. For the rationalized sales strategies of the company, see "L'organizzazione al Calzificio Santagostino," *L'ufficio moderno* (January 1933): 67.

52. For the "problem" of the brand, see G. Sapelli, "La razionalizzazione della vendita: Alle origini del marketing e della pubblicità in Italia," *Quaderni di sociologia*, 27, 2-3-4 (1978): 134–51.

53. Jacques Lacan, *The Four Fundamental Concepts of Psychoanalysis*, trans. Alan Sheridan (New York: W. W. Norton, 1973), p. 116.

54. For the problem of the maintenance of attention, see Maria Luisa Falorni, "Studi sull'attenzione negli anormali psichici," *Rivista di psicologia*, 35, no. 6 (1939): 335–75.

55. For a developed discussion of fetishism in this context, see Marcia Ian, *Remembering the Phallic Mother* (Ithaca, N.Y.: Cornell University Press, 1991).

56. See Fornari, *Psicanalisi della situazione atomica*.

57. Dario de Martis, "Note sui deliri di negazione," *Rivista sperimentale di freniatria*, 91 (1967): 1119–43.

58. Victor Tausk, "On the Origin of the 'Influencing Machine' in Schizophrenia," *Psychoanalytic Quarterly*, vol. 2 (1933): 519–56.

59. Joan Copjek, "The Anxiety of the Influencing Machine," *October*, vol. 23 (1982): 55.

60. Tausk, "On the Origin of the 'Influencing Machine,'" 556.

61. De Martis, "Note," 1137.

62. Kenneth Dean and Brian Massumi, *First and Last Emperors: The Absolute State and the Body of the Despot* (New York: Autonomedia, 1992), pp. 80–81.

63. See Eric Schmitt, "Somali War Casualties May Be 10,000, U.S. Says," *New York Times* (December 8, 1993): A4.

Index

Karen Pinkus teaches in the Department of French and Italian at Northwestern University. She has recently completed a book titled *Picturing Silence: Emblem, Language, Counter-Reformation Materiality* forthcoming from the University of Michigan Press series The Body, in Theory. She has also written on a variety of topics in cultural studies, including anorexia nervosa, visual theory, and psychoanalysis. For the University of Minnesota Press, she translated Giorgio Agamben, *Language and Death: The Place of Negativity* (1991), and Renato Barilli, *A Course on Aesthetics* (1993).